D1605476

Contemporary Biographies in Hospitality & Tourism

Contemporary Biographies in Hospitality & Tourism

SALEM PRESS
A Division of EBSCO Information Services, Inc.
Ipswich, Massachusetts

GREY HOUSE PUBLISHING

∞ The paper used in these volumes conforms to the American National Standard for Permanence of Paper for Printed Library Materials, Z39.48-1992 (R1997).

Library of Congress Cataloging-in-Publication Data

Contemporary biographies in hospitality & tourism. -- [First edition].

   pages : illustrations ; cm. -- (Contemporary biographies in--)

Edition statement supplied by publisher.

Companion to book titled Careers in hospitality & tourism.

Part of a series that is supplemental to the Salem Press series: Careers in--

Contents extracted from the monthly magazine: Current biography.

Includes bibliographical references and index.

ISBN: 978-1-61925-481-7

1. Hospitality industry--Biography. 2. Tourism--Biography. 3. Biography. I. Companion to (work) Careers in hospitality & tourism. II. Title: Contemporary biographies in hospitality and tourism III. Title: Subseries of Careers in-- IV. Title: Extracted from (work) Current biography.

TX910.3 .C668 2014

647.94092/2

Contents

Publisher's Note

Contemporary Biographies in Hospitality & Tourism is a collection of twenty-eight biographical sketches of "living leaders" in the fields of hospitality and tourism. All of these articles come from the pages of *Current Biography*, the monthly magazine renowned for its unfailing accuracy, insightful selection, and the wide scope of influence of its subjects. These up-to-date profiles draw from a variety of sources and are an invaluable resource for researchers, teachers, students, and librarians. Students will gain a better understanding of the educational development and career pathways of the contemporary hospitality and tourism specialist to better prepare themselves for a career in these industries.

The geographical scope of *Contemporary Biographies in Hospitality & Tourism* is broad; selections span the Eastern and Western Hemispheres, covering numerous major geographical and cultural regions. All of the figures profiled are still working at one or more of their specialties, including the restaurant, casino, food, travel and hotel businesses.

Articles in *Contemporary Biographies in Hospitality & Tourism* range in length from 1,000 to 4,000 words and follow a standard format. All articles begin with ready-reference listings that include birth details and concise identifications. The article then generally divides into several parts, including Early Life and Education, and Life's Work, a core section that provides straightforward accounts of the periods in which the profiled subjects made their most significant contributions to the hospitality and tourism industries. Often, a final section, Significance, provides an overview of the person's place in history and their contemporary importance. Essays are supplemented by Selected Readings, which provide starting points for further research.

As with other Salem Press biographical reference works, these articles combine breadth of coverage with a format that offers users quick access to the particular information needed. Articles are arranged alphabetically by last name. An appendix consisting of ten historical biographies culled from the Salem Press *Great Lives* series, introduces readers to professionals in hospitality and tourism of historical significance integral to those whose work and research revolutionized these industries.

The book ends with a general Bibliography that offers a comprehensive list of works for students seeking out more information on a particular individual, plus a separate bibliography of Selected Works that highlight the significant published works of the professionals profiled. A Profession Index, listing subjects by profession is also included.

The editors of Salem Press wish to extend their appreciation to all those involved in the development and production of this work; without their expert contribution, projects of this nature would not be possible. A list of contributors appears at the beginning of this volume.

Contributor's List

Anderson, Carolyn

Broadus, Matt

Buller, Jeffrey L.

Cole, Forrest

Cullen, Christopher

Davis, Anita Price

Duda, Karen E.

Dvorak, William

Eniclerico, Ronald

Exum, Kaitlen J.

Feller, Thomas R.

Fitzgerald, Terence J

Hartig, Seth

Kim, David J.

Kiper, Dmitry

Malinowski, Nicholas W.

Moldawer, David

Muteba, Bertha

Orens, Geoff

Polley, Michael

Ramm, David

Rich, Mari

Sipiera, Paul P.

Tarullo, Hope

Webb, Shawncey

Contemporary Biographies in Hospitality & Tourism

Adrià, Ferran

Spanish chef, culinary innovator, restaurateur

Born: 1962, L'Hospitalet de Llobregat, Spain

With his renowned restaurant El Bulli, on the Costa Brava, the Spanish chef Ferran Adrià "changed haute cuisine more than any other chef of the past 20 years," according to a writer for the *Economist* (March 15, 2014), who characterized Adrià as not only a brilliant chef but an "exhaustive note-taker, risk-taker and master of introspection, obsessed with assessing every recipe he created." Many commentators, and those fortunate enough to have dined at El Bulli, would agree but extend that time frame. Yet Adrià by his own account was indifferent to food while growing up and appears to have stumbled into his career after dropping out of school. The only culinary training he received was on the job, both before and after he took over, at age 24, as the top chef at El Bulli. (The name, which means "the bulldog," is usually given as elBulli in the company's own publications.) Adrià 's food is often written about as if it were the result of not just an advanced culinary education but a scientific one as well. Eager to name a trend, writers have generally described the products of El Bulli, which Adrià co-owned with his longtime business partner, Juli Soler, as an expression of the food science called molecular gastronomy, dubbing Adrià 's food "molecular cuisine" (a term Adrià dislikes). Although he embraces and promotes culinary science, Adrià insists that it came second at El Bulli. "We have never ascribed any scientific origin to our creations, which have come about from a purely culinary quest: observation and curiosity have been part and parcel of our activity, in my case for almost a quarter of a century," he wrote in *The Story of elBulli,* which he made available on the restaurant's website. "Naturally," he added, "if a chef wants to label his work as molecular cuisine, he is perfectly at liberty to do so. But in the name of that liberty, I claim to be merely a cook; and everything we do at elBulli as cooking."

The most influential of Adrià's inventions so far are hot gelatins, culinary foams—frothed distillations of such foods as asparagus or foie gras—and their even more rarified descendants, almost textureless substances he calls "airs," which take a single ingredient, such as celery, and reduce it to little more than a bubble. To supplement these, servers at El Bulli sometimes sprayed an aerosol over the table to evoke a particular setting or memory. The idea in all cases was to produce a singular experience of taste and smell—with a dash of theater, even irony. "My philosophy," Adrià told Phyllis Richman of *Gourmet* (October 1999), "is to make a carrot something more than a carrot." Reporters or critics visiting El Bulli often describe themselves as initially skeptical about the value of such gimmicky-sounding, willfully provocative food—only to be won over by the actual dining experience. Corinna Hardgrave, writing for the *Irish Times* (June 10, 2006) after the British trade journal *Restaurant* named El Bulli the best restaurant in the world for 2006, asked: "Is El Bulli the world's best restaurant? Is it worth the wait? Is it worth the journey? The answers have to be yes. Because, despite how it sounds, El Bulli is not at all pretentious. Yes, it pushes culinary boundaries to extraordinary degrees, but it never loses sight of the fundamental elements of taste." In *Vanity Fair* (October 2010), Jay McInerney confessed that he had wondered beforehand if the meal he would eat at El Bulli "would be too intellectual to be genuinely enjoyable," but in fact, he wrote, "it was a hedonistic revel, a feast more than a mind game, Dionysus and Apollo wrestling on the plate, the senses ultimately triumphing over the brain."

Open only six months a year, from April through September, El Bulli offered one meal a day, consisting of roughly 25 courses, to about 8,000 diners annually—a tiny fraction of the roughly one million people who, according to a 2010 estimate, attempted to reserve a seat each year. (Some commentators set the figure at more than two million.) Reservations were obtained by lottery; "Getting a reservation at El Bulli," Jeffrey Steingarten noted in the December 2004 issue of *Vogue,* "is three times as hard as getting into Harvard and ten times more difficult than getting into Yale or Princeton." Having received, in 1997, the highest rating (three stars), from the *Guide Michelin,* which has long been considered an international benchmark of culinary quality, El Bulli has also been lauded by the world's top chefs. In the 1990s Joël Robuchon, considered one of the best chefs of the twentieth century, pronounced Adrià his heir and the "best cook on the planet," as Arthur Lubow related in an influential article in the *New York Times Magazine* (August 10, 2003). One Spanish chef described Adrià to Lubow as "stratospheric, a Martian," while another, Juan Mari Arzak, told Lubow that Adrià was the "most imaginative cook in all history."

In January 2010 Ferran Adrià and Juli Soler stunned the culinary world with the announcement that El Bulli would close in 2012 for a "two-year period of reflection" and would "reopen in a new format." As Lisa Abend reported in *Time* magazine (Feb. 18, 2010), Adrià said that El Bulli would "change from a restaurant to a nonprofit foundation, operating as a think tank where talented young chefs will explore new directions in gastronomy. … Discussions led by prominent chefs and leaders in art and design will complement their research." "Each year," Abend explained, the foundation would "release a book and video that catalog its discoveries, and a team will disseminate those ideas at chefs' conferences and culinary schools. The fellows will also help Adrià compile an encyclopedia of contemporary cuisine." Adrià and Soler planned to retain the famed kitchen and the comfortable dining room but add an audiovisual facility and a library. Adrià's announcement led numerous commentators to assess his accomplishments to date. Abend wrote that beyond "any one dish or technique, he has changed the way people think about food. Chefs around the world have adopted not only his dazzling concoctions but his ethos—to bring science, art and cooking into closer collaboration; to use food not only to please and satiate but also to amaze and provoke; and above all, to constantly reinvent." For his part, Adrià explained his decision to close El Bulli: "Part of my job is to see into the future, and I could see that our old model is finished," he said, according to Abend. "It's time to figure out what comes next."

Education and Early Career

The older of the two sons of Ginés Adrià, a housepainter, and Josefa Acosta, Ferran Adrià Acosta was born on May 14, 1962, in a city adjoining Barcelona called L'Hospitalet de Llobregat. Sources offer somewhat contradictory impressions of how important food was in Adrià's family when he was young. His official biography on the website for El Bulli described a "marked interest in everything related to food in his home," while Anna Murphy, in a profile for the London *Sunday Telegraph* (July 20, 2003), wrote that Adrià's parents were "unusually lackadaisical in the kitchen." Murphy quoted Adrià as saying that his parents "never did any special cooking. It was very mundane." By all accounts, Adrià's own tastes as a child and young man were certainly straightforward. "All I ate were French fries and pasta," he told Elaine Sciolino of the *New York Times* (July 28, 2004). "I was a horrible child." Looking back, Adrià has argued that this indifference has served him in the long run. "If my parents had told me, 'You have to do it like this and this,'" he told Murphy, "well, then I would have been influenced by them and I might not have examined things so much." As it was, Adrià explained to Michael Paterniti of *Esquire* (July 1, 2001), "I came as a virgin to the kitchen."

> **"We have never ascribed any scientific origin to our creations, which have come about from a purely culinary quest: observation and curiosity have been part and parcel of our activity."**

By 1980 Adrià had abandoned his studies at Barcelona's Institut Politecnic Verge de la Merce, a secondary school preparing students for business careers, intending to spend time on the beaches of the famed Mediterranean island Ibiza. To earn money for his trip he washed dishes in the restaurant of the Hotel Playafels in the resort town of Castelldefels, not far from Barcelona. After the hotel's chef exposed him to Spanish haute cuisine using the influential nineteenth-century manual *El Practicón* by Ángel Muro, Adrià went on to Ibiza, where for four months in 1981 he held a position with a club on the Cala Leña beach. Brief stints at a series of Barcelona restaurants followed, but this early professional experience ended when he had to report for his obligatory term of military service (a requirement Spain abandoned at the end of 2001). Stationed with the navy in the southern Spanish port city of Cartagena, Adrià worked in the kitchen of a high-ranking officer alongside another budding chef, Fermí Puig, who introduced Adrià to nouvelle cuisine—the lighter, more imaginative, and somewhat more internationally minded style of food then fashionable in elite restaurants around the world.

Encouraged by Puig, Adrià joined him in devoting their month-long break in August 1983 to cooking at one of Spain's most revered outposts of nouvelle cuisine, El Bulli, located on the Costa Brava near the small town of Roses (Catalan; in Spanish, Rosas). (The restaurant is said to have gotten its name because the original owners kept bulldogs as pets.) In *The Story of elBulli*, Adrià described his first month at El Bulli as "highly intense" and "a real immersion in the world of haute cuisine, since it was the first time I had heard of all the trappings of this world: the critics, the running of a restaurant, gourmet guides, and so on." Enjoying the work and evidently making a positive impression on Juli Soler, who had been the restaurant's manager since 1981, Adrià was asked to return the following March, once he had finished his military service and the restaurant, then open ten months a year, had reopened for the 1984 season.

Fewer than seven months after Adrià returned, Soler divided the position of chef de cuisine, the top spot in the kitchen, between Adrià and a coworker, Christian Lutaud. At the beginning of the next season, in mid-March 1985, Adrià's brother, Albert, then only 15, quit school and joined the staff, becoming the restaurant's pastry chef in 1987, the same year Ferran Adrià was made the sole chef de cuisine. Though he had risen quickly through the ranks, Adrià remained inexperienced when compared with the chefs running other top-flight restaurants on the continent, and as part of his education he spent part of 1985 interning in the restaurants associated with two practitioners of nouvelle cuisine, Georges Blanc and Jacques Pic.

Throughout these early years, he and Lutaud, along with one of the restaurant's then-owners, also developed their knowledge of contemporary cooking by traveling to France for meals at some of the country's best restaurants. Carles Abellán, an El Bulli cook during Adrià's first years there, told Thomas Matthews of *Wine Spectator* (December 15, 2004), "It was never easy. I remember weeks in winter when we didn't have a single customer." But, Abellán continued, "Ferran was preoccupied, an evil genius. Ferran—at 22!—told me he didn't want a girlfriend, because she would only get in the way. He didn't have a house or a car. He had an objective. He was always looking ahead. At first, he was looking to France. Later, he found himself."

A key turning point for Adrià came on a trip to southern France in 1987, at a presentation by the chef Jacques Maximin. Asked by an audience member to define creativity, Maximin answered, according to the *Story of elBulli*: "Creativity means not copying." Adrià embraced Maximin's idea wholeheartedly. While still employing many of the same principles as nouvelle cuisine, he began putting aside recipes that were clearly outgrowths of French tradition, instead taking up more characteristically Spanish dishes, which he then revised or refined with the addition of more rarified ingredients, such as caviar, lobster, and truffles. Although the project did not turn the restaurant around immediately, it did contribute to El Bulli regaining, in 1990, its second Michelin star, which had been taken away in the mid-1980s.

Later Career

Soon after Soler and Adrià bought the restaurant, they embarked on a series of renovations, altering the landscaping around the building and updating and dramatically expanding the kitchen until it was as large as the dining area and, by all accounts, a considerably more impressive space. The restaurant's reputation was also being upgraded during these years. In 1992 Joël Robuchon visited El Bulli and, after a meal composed of such dishes as sautéed veal marrow with caviar, accompanied by puréed cauliflower, began trumpeting the restaurant and advising Adrià on how to develop his cuisine. That same year Adrià won the Spanish Academy of Gastronomy's award for best chef de cuisine. At the same time, he was recording some of his recipes and beginning to set down his ideas about food in preparation for his first book, *El Bulli: El sabor del Mediterraneo* (which translates as "El Bulli: The Taste of the Mediterranean"), published in 1993.

While *El sabor del Mediterraneo* had essentially put forward Spanish cuisine varied along French lines, Adrià soon began more actively seeking out techniques that could put El Bulli's food outside any established tradition—other than the broad one of artistic innovation and evolution. In *The Story of El Bulli*, the name given to this new approach is "technique-concept cuisine," and Adrià's dedication to creating a truly original type of cooking was evidenced by the creation, in 1994, of a "development squad" that would take charge of creating new dishes without first thinking of how they would work in the restaurant itself. In the two years previous Adrià had already begun mixing components traditionally associated with sweets into savory foods, as in the case of a potato flavored with vanilla, and vice versa, creating, for example, a mousse made with corn or an avocado sorbet.

In spring 1994 Adrià finally perfected a process he had been working on, sometimes with comically disastrous results, for roughly four years: creating highly flavorful savory foams that would convey a single clear flavor, with just air and a gelling agent to give them shape and structure. "Foam grew out of the idea of mousse," Adrià told Virginia Gerst of the *Chicago Tribune* (March 13, 2006). "I was looking for a way to maintain 100 percent of the integrity of the product, with pure taste and no fat or heavy cream. Then I thought of the foam that forms when you put an orange in a juicer at high speed." First experimenting with a bicycle pump (which he used to inject air into a tomato), Adrià eventually settled on a device used for making whipped cream. By mixing the liquefied form of an ingredient with a thickener and injecting that with nitrous oxide, he was able to create an extremely light but solid substance that offered diners a revelatory insight into foods that had come to seem banal. Seized upon by the gourmet world, foams swiftly became a point of controversy—with some chefs doubting whether they could be called food at all—but also of imitation. As the 1990s progressed, foams appeared with increasing frequency on menus around the world, and today, although still found only in a certain type of elite restaurant, they have become a standard part of the repertoire. As Adrià told Thomas Matthews in 2004, "Ten years ago the foams were a scandal. Now they're routine."

Bolstered by Adrià's growing reputation as a genuinely innovative chef, El Bulli began to receive the kind of critical praise enjoyed by only a handful of restaurants in the world. In 1995 it received almost perfect scores from the Spanish guide *Lo mejor de la gastronomía* and the highly influential French series Gault Millau. The next year Robuchon designated Adrià his heir and called him the world's best chef. (In 2003 Robuchon revised his compliment slightly, telling Arthur Lubow, "Ferran is the best cook in the world for technique.") Then, in 1997, the *Guide Michelin* awarded El Bulli a third star: the three-star designation was shared at that time by only about two dozen other restaurants in the world. The honor, according to the *Story of elBulli,* "could not but overwhelm us with pride. Without any doubt this marked one of the major milestones for the understanding of our story, and changed the gastronomic world's outlook and recognition of our cuisine." Indeed, the French-based *Guide Michelin* had, to some degree, helped reinforce the perception that that country's chefs have a stranglehold on the highest levels of cuisine, and Adrià seized on fact that El Bulli and two other Spanish restaurants had achieved three stars to announce what he saw as Spain's new importance to the world of fine food. "French cooking is over," he had declared, according to Phyllis Richman. Adrià later elaborated to Lubow: "It is a movement in Spain. It is not only me. In a culture with a very strong traditional gastronomy, there is a cuisine for the first time with new techniques and concepts. It is a new nouvelle cuisine." In his text Lubow agreed, arguing that Adrià and a group of new Spanish chefs, many of whom worked at one time at El Bulli, bring an "idealism" to cooking that is "so sadly missing in France." "Besieged with soaring costs and smothering regulations," Lubow added, "French cooks think more imaginatively about brand extension than about recipe invention. They cling to the past, to a tradition of nouvelle cuisine that is becoming as hoary as [the nineteenth-century French chef Auguste] Escoffier. In Spain … young chefs still touchingly believe they can change the world."

The same year that El Bulli received its third star, Adrià and the other culinary leaders at El Bulli, including Albert and the chef Oriol Castro, opened a workshop that, located in Barcelona and separate from the restaurant proper, would work exclusively on developing other examples of technique-concept cuisine. In 2000 the workshop, called elBullitaller in the company's literature (*taller* is Spanish for "workshop"), moved into permanent quarters and took on a full-time, year-round staff, with Adrià joining them during the restaurant's off-season. In the years after the workshop was first formed, it helped lay the groundwork for some of Adrià's other famous innovations, including the "airs" first served in 2002 and the many variations the restaurant served, from summer 1998, on hot gelatin—almost a contradiction in terms, since gelatins had traditionally been thought of as needing to be at room temperature or cooler in order to set.

Adrià has always been surprisingly open about his discoveries. He regularly taught classes and invited journalists and other chefs to join him in the workshop, and every year the ranks of the restaurant's cooking staff were swollen by interns who come from all over to train, often working for room and board alone. As the brother of one such cook told Paterniti, "In 20, 30, 40 years, they're going to say Ferran Adrià was the best that ever was, and it's going to be an honor for my brother to say he chopped his vegetables."

Adrià also disseminated information about his discoveries by publishing an unprecedented amount of material about El Bulli's cuisine. In addition to releasing, in 1997, *Los secretos de El Bulli* ("The Secrets of El Bulli"), Adrià embarked, in 2000, on an ambitious project of cataloging the thousands of dishes made in El Bulli's kitchen from the time he joined the staff, in 1983. The end result was, first, a series of three books (divided into the years 1983 to 1993, 1994 to 1997, and 1998 to 2002) that exhaustively named, numbered, photographed, and explained years of cuisine; the books were then supplemented by detailed recipes on CD-ROMs. (Published over three years in Spain beginning in 2002, the books became available in the United States in 2005.) In subsequent years, the catalog was supplemented by two further volumes (one on 2003 to 2004 and another on 2005). In March 2014 the art publisher Phaidon published *elBulli 2005–2011,* a seven-volume "catalogue raisonné," in the publisher's description. The first six volumes comprise the catalogs from 2005 to 2010-2011; the seventh, *Evolutionary Analysis,* covers El Bulli's history and discusses Adrià's creative process. Some 700 recipes are included. To Adrià the effort was part of establishing a clear historical record analogous to the type used by art historians. Without such a record, he told Lubow, "It's as if one were talking of art and they say, 'Picasso, what year was that painting?' and you say, 'I don't know.' If we want to talk seriously of creativity, it is necessary that all cooks make a catalog for people a hundred years from now." Some of his other publications include *Cocinar en casa* (roughly, "Home Cooking"), a 2003 collaboration with the Spanish grocery chain Coprabo that contains recipes using ordinary ingredients from the supermarket, and *Chefs contra el hambre* (2003; published in the United States in 2006 as *Chefs against Hunger*), a fund-raising effort for an international relief organization.

Adrià and Soler significantly expanded the company's reach by branching out into a range of related businesses, including work with major food conglomerates to develop new products, such as flavored oils, or to refine existing ones. In 1995 they opened a catering wing of El Bulli in Barcelona, and the following year they began consulting with a group opening a new high-end restaurant in Barcelona's Olympic Port. In 1998 the El Bulli company undertook another consulting project, this time with the Hacienda Benazuza in the town of Sanlúcar la Mayor, helping to shape the hotel's restaurants; the establishment is now designated an "elBulli Hotel," according to the company's website. In 2004 the first of what was intended to be a chain of relatively low-cost restaurants, called Fast Good, opened in Madrid. A direct competitor of such fast-food chains as McDonald's and Burger King, Fast Good was later run by NH Hoteles. One reason Adrià undertook such a variety of work was, as he frankly stated, "to buy my creative freedom," as Elaine Sciolino of the *New York Times* (July 28, 2004) quoted him as saying with respect to Fast Good: to help support El Bulli, which, he insisted, made very little money, in part because the price was roughly half to a third what other three-star restaurants typically cost. "I could charge a thousand euros for the meal and still book every seat," he told Matthews. "But that's not the character of El Bulli." Despite its fame the restaurant did not make a profit, according to Adrià, except in 1998–2000.

Adrià was named by *Time* magazine to its list of the world's 100 most influential people in 2004. In 2002 and then from 2006 through 2009, *Restaurant* magazine declared El Bulli to be the best restaurant in the world. Adrià, however, evidently began to feel that the demands of the restaurant were stifling his creativity. In the view of Jay McInerney, "The pressure of customers, the spectacular disparity between the supply of seats and the number of customers who want them, seems to have reached some kind of tipping point" for

Adrià, who told McInerney, speaking of the foundation, "It will not be a restaurant. No Michelin, no customers, no pressure. Every year will be different."

Adrià closed El Bulli on July 30, 2011. He turned to business schools for suggestions for realizing his vision for the El Bulli Foundation, and in May 2013, as reported by PRI International (May 10, 2013), at a breakfast event at the IESE business school in Barcelona, he announced that the El Bulli Foundation would fund a food lab where cooks would keep on inventing and then publish their findings, on a webpage called Bullipedia. El Bulli itself would be reopened as an interactive museum, visitor's center and source of inspiration. "What we want to endure is El Bulli's concept of innovation," he said. "The spirit of the place, of all the people who passed through our doors." In October 2012, however, the resourceful and charismatic Juli Soler, whom McInerney called "Adrià's business brain," resigned as co-director of El Bulli Foundation, owing to medical problems.

In 2004 Adrià helped establish an organization devoted to food and science called the Alicia Foundation. Beginning in 2010 Adrià collaborated with Harvard University on it famed Science and Cooking lecture series pairing "world-class" chefs and Harvard researchers, which was developed by the Harvard School of Engineering and Applied Sciences (SEAS) and the Alícia Foundation. The Harvard web page devoted to the course explains that it "uses food and cooking to explicate fundamental principles in applied physics and engineering." Adrià also collaborated with the MITMedia lab on elBulli1846, a visual record of every dish Adrià created at El Bulli and one of the three primary initiatives of the El Bulli foundation. In 2005, the Camilo José Cela University in Madrid created an endowed professorship named the Ferran Adrià Chair for the Study of Food Culture and Science.

In 2006 Adrià cooperated in the making of the DVD *Decoding Ferran Adrià.* Hosted by the chef and television personality Anthony Bourdain, the DVD traces the creation of an El Bulli meal from workshop to table. A German documentary, *Cooking in Progress* (2011), followed the restaurant's 2008–2009 season. In addition to his El Bulli catalogs, Adrià had been involved in educational and art activities before the restaurant closed; afterward, in advance of the opening of his foundation, he helped develop *Innovation in the Science of Food,* an exhibit mounted at the Museum of Science in Boston that opened in February 2014. Around the same time, the exhibit "Ferran Adrià: Notes on Creativity" opened at the Drawing Center in Manhattan, the first stop on a two-year tour of museums in Europe and the United States. "Notes on Creativity" presented, as Roberta Smith reported in the *New York Times* (February 13, 2014), "drawings, notes, notebooks, diagrams, pictograms and prototypes by Mr. Adrià and his various collaborators, among them the chefs Albert Adrià (his brother) and Oriol Castro, the graphic designer Marta Méndez Blaya and the industrial designer Luki Huber." Smith drew analogies to the work of Joseph Beuys, Joan Snyder, and Cy Twombly, and she noted the "archival instinct that has compelled Mr. Adrià, post-El Bulli, to establish the Bullipedia, which will document all of Western cooking."

In about 2004 Adrià, who speaks Castilian, Catalan, and French, married his longtime girlfriend, Isabel, who for many years was an administrator at the Barcelona Aquarium, where El Bulli's catering division and the workshop first came into being. The two shuttle between Roses and Barcelona and reportedly live with great simplicity in both locations.

Further Reading:

Economist Mar. 15, 2014

El Bulli website

Esquire p116+ July 1, 2001

New York Times F p1 Sep. 15, 1999, Jul. 28, 2004, Apr. 16, 2013

C27 Feb. 14, 2014

New York Times Magazine p38+ Aug. 10, 2003

PRI International May 10, 2013

[London] Telegraph Aug. 2, 2012

Time magazine Jan. 26, 2010, Feb. 18, 2010, Aug. 1, 2011

Vanity Fair Oct. 2010

Wine Spectator p36+ Dec. 15, 2004

Selected Books:

El Bulli: El sabor del Mediterraneo, 1993

Los secretos de El Bulli, 1997

Cocinar en casa, 2003

Chefs contra el hambre, 2003

The Family Meal, 2011

elBulli 2005–2011, 7 vols., 2014

Barnes, Brenda

Business executive

Born: 1953, Chicago, Illinois, United States

Brenda Barnes was the president and CEO of the Sara Lee Corp., a worldwide manufacturer and marketer of foods and beverages, household products, and apparel. Taking the reins of the company in 2005, Barnes faced the difficult task of reinvigorating the sluggish sales of Sara Lee's older products in the food business, while competing for market share with items named for grocery retailers, which provided a lower-priced alternative to traditional brand-name foods. Barnes began her career at PepsiCo, where she held a number of high-ranking positions and was the heir apparent to the CEO. She stunned observers in the business world in 1997, when, after 22 years at the company, she resigned her post as head of Pepsi-Cola's North American division to spend more time with her family, a move that engendered a significant amount of comment and controversy. "I was the poster child," she related, "for having quit my job."

Seven years later she joined Sara Lee, where, as CEO, she oversaw the company's ambitious efforts to streamline its diversified businesses, with sales of its subsidiaries totaling $8.2 billion. She also centralized Sara Lee's operations, concentrating more of its North American businesses in the Chicago area. "I am a marketing person by discipline. I'm also an operating person by discipline," she told Delroy Alexander for the *Chicago Tribune* (February 11, 2005), "and I think the transformation of those two [is] what is embedded in this transformation of Sara Lee." In 2005 *Forbes* magazine ranked Barnes eighth on its list of the world's most powerful women, one step ahead of the talk-show legend Oprah Winfrey, and the *Wall Street Journal* named her one of its 50 Women to Watch.

Barnes's career took an unexpected—and tragic—turn when she suffered a massive, life-threatening stroke in 2010. She was placed into a medically induced coma for a week and thankfully survived, but not without damage. It also ended her tenure at Sarah Lee.

Education and Early Career

The third of seven daughters, Barnes was born Brenda Czajka on November 11, 1953 in Chicago and grew up in nearby River Grove, Illinois. Barnes has credited her mother, a homemaker, and her father, a factory worker, with being very influential figures in her life, telling Alexander that her parents gave her "a strong work ethic." Following high school graduation, Barnes--whom her fellow students voted most likely to succeed--enrolled at Augustana College, a liberal-arts and science institution in Rock Island, Illinois. According to John Gogonas, Barnes's childhood neighbor and fellow student at Augustana, she maintained a single-minded focus on her studies. "She didn't join a sorority, didn't do cheerleading. She didn't get into that part of college," he told John Schmeltzer for the *Chicago Tribune* (October 28, 2005). In 1975, after graduating from Augustana with a degree in business and economics, Barnes worked for a year as a waitress and a postal clerk before becoming a business manager at Wilson Sporting Goods, which was then a subsidiary of PepsiCo, Inc. Barnes was undeterred by the company's policy against hiring women in its team-sports division owing to their perceived lack of knowledge regarding such items as baseball gloves and footballs. "I knew there were certain people who were uncomfortable dealing with me as a woman . . . but I went about doing my job. I probably wasn't terribly sensitive to those things," she told Shelley Donald Coolidge for the *Christian Science Monitor* (October 8, 1997). Barnes was promoted to head of sales at the company. Meanwhile, she completed night classes at Loyola University, in Chicago, where she received her MBA in 1978.

"I've always looked at my life as a book, with each experience as a new chapter. This chapter is certainly not one of my favorites, but it is one of many."

In 1981 Barnes joined Frito-Lay, another PepsiCo subsidiary, serving as a brand manager before becoming vice president in charge of marketing for the Lay's, Ruffles, and O'Grady's brands of potato chips. She moved in 1984 to the company's beverage division, Pepsi-Cola. After being named the group vice president of marketing at Pepsi USA, she relocated to the company's headquarters, in Purchase, New York. In 1988 she made the decision to switch from marketing to sales and was appointed vice president of on-premise sales for the eastern region, based in Somers, New York. Two promotions at the senior-vice-president level followed.

In January 1992 Barnes accepted the position of president of Pepsi-Cola South. With that appointment Barnes reached a milestone in her career, becoming the highest-ranking female executive at the Pepsi-Cola division of PepsiCo. As president Barnes was in charge of Pepsi-Cola's manufacturing, sales, and distribution operations for the southern region, which covered 13 states. In 1993 Barnes was named chief operating officer for PepsiCo South. At the time PepsiCo was undergoing a reorganization, switching from 24 separate domestic areas of operation to one national business unit, consisting of 16 nationwide business and 100 separate market units in charge of front-line sales and marketing. That move, for which Barnes was one of the key planners, was meant to "put decision-making as close to the customer as possible," as she explained to Katherine Hauck for *Prepared Foods* magazine (August 1993). Barnes led the company's market units for the southern and western regions, which also involved managing the operations of company-owned and franchise-business units. (Franchise-business units are authorized to sell or distribute a company's goods or services in a particular region.) Barnes's regions were largely responsible for the company's 22 percent increase in first-quarter profits during fiscal year 1993. In 1994 Barnes was promoted to chief operating officer (COO) of the North American arm of Pepsi-Cola, also based in Somers; in April 1996 she became the president and chief executive officer of Pepsi-Cola, which was then a $3 billion business. Up until that time, the company had sold its beverages to licensed bottling companies, which then sold and distributed the products in designated regions of North America. As CEO, Barnes oversaw the acquiring of bottling operations, resulting in a tripling of sales. Discussing her successful management of the Pepsi-Cola division, Barnes told Katherine Hauck, "I just had someone tell me they thought I was tough, but that I always treated them with dignity and respect. I set the bar high, but make sure people have what they need to jump over it."

In September 1997 Barnes shocked the business world when she resigned from her $2 million-per-year position as president and chief executive officer of Pepsi-Cola North America, after 22 years with PepsiCo. Although it had been widely speculated in the media that Barnes would succeed the chairman and CEO of PepsiCo, Roger A. Enrico, following his retirement in 2001, she cited a desire to devote more time to her husband, Randall C. Barnes, a retired PepsiCo executive, and their three young children. (As quoted by Delroy Alexander, Barnes told a TV talk-show host that she didn't want to miss "another of my kids' birthdays.") "I hope people can look at my decision not as 'women can't do it' but 'for twenty-two years Brenda gave her all and did a lot of great things.' I don't think there's any man who doesn't have the same struggle. . . . You have to make your choices. Maybe I burned [the candle] at both ends for too long," she told Nikhil Deogun for the *Wall Street Journal*, as quoted in the Fort Lauderdale, Florida, *Sun-Sentinel* (September 25, 1997). Barnes did not completely disappear from the business world: From November 1999 to March 2000, she served as the interim president and chief operating officer of the Starwood Hotels and Resorts in White Plains, New York, whose luxury-hotel chains include the Sheraton, the Westin, the Luxury Collection, St. Regis, W, and Four Points by Sheraton. In 2002 she also became an adjunct professor at Northwestern University's Kellogg Graduate School of Management, in Evanston, Illinois, and at North Central College, in Naperville, Illinois.

Later Career

In July 2004 Barnes accepted an offer from the Chicago-based Sara Lee Corp. to become the company's president and chief operating officer, replacing then-chairman and chief executive officer C. Steven McMillan, who had not hired a president and COO since he had vacated those posts in 2000. With her oldest child preparing for college and her two younger children in the eighth and tenth grades, respectively, Barnes felt ready to return to the corporate business world, following a seven-year hiatus. "Being away from the day-to-day was very helpful. I feel recharged," she told Michael Arndt for *Business Week Online* (May 17, 2004). Barnes was placed in charge of global marketing and sales and was expected to call upon her consumer-brand experience at PepsiCo to help implement Sara Lee's new brand-segmentation strategy. (That long-term strategy involved investing marketing, research and development, and management resources in the company's projected consumer brands while limiting the investment in its low-growth brands.) She was viewed in the media as the eventual successor to McMillan, who had overseen an unsuccessful four-year plan to restructure the company by consolidating acquisitions and streamlining the company's decentralized business operations.

Under McMillan, Sara Lee had downsized its portfolio of 200 diverse brands, which ranged from Wonderbra and Kiwi shoe polish to Endust furniture polish, Ball Park hot dogs, and Chock full o'Nuts Coffee, by selling off its unrelated product lines--including its Coach leather-goods business, Champion athletic wear, and the PYA/Monarch food-service unit--and investing the savings in the marketing of its core businesses: food and beverages, underwear/intimate apparel, and household products. (Sara Lee had only one billion-dollar product line, its Hanes line of underwear and socks.) McMillan's strategy to jumpstart the company's profits also involved the acquisition of brands or product lines that were not only closer to Sara Lee's core businesses, but appeared to have the potential for higher-than-average growth. However, his $2.6 billion acquisition of Earthgrains, America's second-largest fresh-bread manufacturer, in 2002, drew criticism from investors, who accused him of overpayment, and managed a return of less than $100 million in operating profits in 2003. Between 1998 and 2001 the price of the company's stock also plummeted, to $22.50 per share, a decrease of nearly 30 percent. During the same period sales grew by only 1.7 percent, to $17.7 billion, and operating earnings increased by only 5.6 percent, to $1.2 billion, according to Julie Forster, writing for *Business Week* (September 10, 2001, online). The Sara Lee Corp. also experienced a drop in sales in its apparel division.

Following five years of substandard sales and growth-investment returns, Barnes was named to succeed McMillan in the position of CEO in February 2005. McMillan remained in the role of chairman until October of that year. As part of her five-year plan, Barnes restructured the organization into three lines of business: North American retail, which targeted bakery, packaged-meat, and coffee businesses on the continent; North American Foodservice, encompassing restaurants and other food-service businesses; and Sara Lee International, which focused on brands outside North America. She also moved the company's North American headquarters from downtown Chicago to Downers Grove, a Chicago suburb, concentrating its domestic businesses there.

In February 2005 Barnes announced the company's intention to convert its remaining apparel business, Sara Lee Branded Apparel/Americas Asia, into an independent, publicly traded company; that process was completed in September 2006. In October 2005 Sara Lee's $300 million U.S. retail coffee business, including Chock full o'Nuts, Hills Bros., and Chase & Sanborn, was sold to the Italian-based company Segafredo Zanetti Group. The following month the company sold its European apparel business and it completed the sale of its European nuts and snacks businesses. The Sara Lee Corp. also completed the sale of its $450 million direct-selling business in Latin America and Asia (encompassing cosmetics, skin-care products, fragrances, toiletries, and clothing). .

In fiscal year 2005 the Sara Lee Corp. reported revenues of $19.3 billion, an increase of only 1 percent from the previous year, and a net income of $719 million, a decrease of 43.5 percent from 2004. The company experienced a fourth-quarter net loss of $148 million, which was the result of an increase in commodity costs, millions of dollars in reorganization expenses, and a 5.2 percent decrease in sales revenue, for a total of $4.75 billion. Sara Lee showed no great financial improvement during the first quarter of fiscal year 2006. Despite the company's poor showing, Barnes remained optimistic. "While we exceeded our forecasted earnings per share target, we still are not satisfied with our business performance. However, our ongoing transformation initiatives are building the momentum needed to drive improvement," Barnes said, as quoted in the company's November 3, 2005 press release.

Barnes and her husband, Randall C. Barnes, divorced after nearly thirty years of marriage. She has two grown sons and a daughter, Erin, who was instrumental in her post-stroke rehabilitation. Barnes has been quite open about her physical devastation as well as her tenacity and determination to rebuild a normal life. "I've always looked at my life as a book, with each experience as a new chapter," she has commented. "This chapter is certainly not one of my favorites, but it is one of many." Although sidelined from the world of business, she has not—by any stretch—been sidelined from life.

Further Reading:

Augustana magazine, May 30, 2012
Chicago Tribune C p1 Feb. 11, 2005
Lifestyles p3 Oct. 14, 2007
Christian Science Monitor p1 Oct. 8, 1997
Directors & Boards p49 June 22, 1998
Prepared Foods p35 Aug. 1993
Sara Lee Corp. Web site

Bastianich, Joseph

Restaurateur, winemaker

Born: 1968, Queens, New York City

In a manner contrasting with that of his more widely known business partner, the boisterous celebrity chef and television personality Mario Batali, Joseph Bastianich, without much fanfare, has become one of the most successful restaurateurs in the country. Described by Julia Sexton in *Westchester* magazine (July 2008) as "a force of restaurant-world nature," he has founded nearly two dozen restaurants across the country.e Bastianich opened his first, Becco, in 1993, in partnership with his mother, the award-winning chef, cookbook author, and public-television host Lidia Bastianich. Becco, located in New York City's theater district, quickly became known for its innovative prix-fixe wine list and traditional pasta dishes. In 1998 Bastianich teamed up with Batali to found Babbo, which was named the best new restaurant in America by the James Beard Foundation and was widely credited with revitalizing Italian cuisine in New York City. "Among the restaurants that make my stomach do a special jig, Babbo ranks near the top," the esteemed restaurant critic Frank Bruni wrote in his three-star review for the *New York Times* (June 9, 2004). (According to the newspaper's rating system, three stars indicates an "excellent" restaurant, while the rare four-star establishment is considered "extraordinary." Bruni withheld a fourth star from Babbo because of the hard-rock music blaring from its sound system and the "slightly ragtag quality" of its ambience.) Bastianich and Batali have since coounded other establishments, including Lupa, Esca, Otto, Casa Mono, and Del Posto, in New York City; Osteria Mozza and Pizzeria Mozza, in Los Angeles and Singapore; B&B Ristorante, Enoteca Otto Pizzeria, and Carnevino, in Las Vegas; and Tarry Lodge, in Port Chester, New York.

Bastianich, who has been heralded for his extensive knowledge of wine, is also the owner of three wineries in Italy. "Wine has been the driving force in my life--it's how I met my wife, how I've gotten work, how I've maintained a physical and emotional connection to my heritage and my family," he wrote on his Web site. "[My mother] taught me that all of her values were somehow captured in the spirit and essence of wine. She really drove it home--from the vineyard to the bottle, the wine we drink has a rich history, it is part of a deep-rooted tradition, and often it travels the whole world to get to our table. It reaches across all levels of society. It was a happy metaphor."

Among Bastianich's ventures is Eataly, a massive Italian food and wine marketplace that opened in New York City's Flatiron District in 2010. For those not living in New York or one of the other cities to which Bastianich's empire has spread, he is perhaps best known as a judge on the televised cooking competition *MasterChef*, which debuted on the Fox network in 2010.

Education and Early Career

Joseph Bastianich was born on September 17, 1968 in the New York City borough of Queens. His parents, Felice Bastianich and the former Lidia Matticchio, had both come to New York in the late 1950s from Istria, which was described by David Savona for *Cigar Aficionado* (February 2007) as "a part of northeastern Italy lost to the cartographers who reworked the maps of Europe after the Second World War." Savona explained: "Istria became part of Yugoslavia, and many of the region's ethnic Italians found themselves in the strange, unwelcome world of Tito's communist Yugoslavia." After fleeing to the U.S., Felice and Lidia met and married. They raised Joe and his younger sister, Tanya, in Bayside, Queens. In the early 1970s they opened Buonavia, an Italian restaurant, on Queens Boulevard, in the nearby neighborhood of Forest Hills. On his Web site, Bastianich described Buonavia as a "typical . . . red-sauce joint, with velvet wallpaper and fake paintings of Venice." The family later opened a second restaurant, Villa Seconda. Bastianich began working with his parents at an early age, washing dishes, hosing down the sidewalk in front of the restaurants, and accompanying his father to wholesale-meat markets. "I learned the business the old-fashioned way. Full immersion. That's the Harvard MBA in restaurants. You learn from the ground up," he wrote.

The family visited Italy regularly, and those trips heightened Bastianich's passion for Italian food, wine, and culture. He became determined to follow in his parents' footsteps, a plan his mother and father did not encourage. Bastianich told Richard Bienstock for *Guitar Aficionado* (December 2008), "Their ideof success was to be something like an accountant or a dentist." (Bastianich was interviewed for that magazine because of his large collection of vintage guitars.)

In 1981 Bastianich's parents sold both of their Queens restaurants and launched their first Manhattan-based venture, Felidia. The restaurant, located not far from the U.N. building, in an expensive East Side neighborhood, quickly earned acclaim around the city. Lidia, who still runs Felidia, subsequently became a best-selling cookbook author and has hosted public-television cooking shows since the late 1990s. (Bastianich's parents divorced in 1997, at which point his father left the family business.) Bastianich worked at Felidia throughout his teens before enrolling at Boston College.

After graduating in 1989 with a degree in political science and philosophy, Bastianich began to work on Wall Street as a corporate bond trader. He remained there for only a short time before returning to his family's restaurant business. As he explained to Amy Zuber in *Nation's Restaurant News* (January 25, 1999), "The [Wall Street] work was interesting and rewarding, but at the same time it didn't offer the satisfaction that I got growing up in the restaurant environment. Working in the financial world, I felt a void without the interaction of making people happy through food and hospitality. So one day I just up and left."

After leaving Wall Street, Bastianich—at his mother's urging-- spent a year in Italy. He wrote on his Web site: "I was a cellar rat, grape picker, waiter, cook, private driver--you name it. I met and worked with the people who embodied the very essence of Italian food and wine culture." The experience solidified his decision to become a restaurateur. He told Zuber, "At that point I realized that I had a natural affinity and love for wine and food and the culture of the Italian table as it relates to products and hospitality. But I didn't abandon the experience of Wall Street and how money is made in the world. I thought that ultimately if I could marry the two in some reasonable way, it could be the greatest fulfillment."

In 1991 Lidia lent Bastianich half of the $80,000 he needed to lease a brownstone on a then-unfashionable stretch of West Forty-sixth Street in Manhattan. He opened Becco, his first restaurant, in one part of the building and lived in another part. The 140-seat restaurant offered pasta served tableside and a prix-fixe wine list containing more than 100 selections, each costing $15 per bottle. Bastianich explained to Zuber,

"What I found from my experience is that people would read wine lists from right to left and first find a price parameter before selecting a bottle. My goal was to take the price point out of the wine-making decision and therefore allow the customer to be able to freely choose wines that really pair with what they are eating." The idea for the wine list was considered groundbreaking, and it quickly won Becco a large following.

With the success of Becco, Bastianich was able to launch his second venture, Frico Bar, which opened in 1995. The 75-seat restaurant, located a few blocks from Becco, specialized in cuisine from the Friulian region of northwest Italy. In a review for the *New York Times* (January 5, 1996), Eric Asimov, who assessed inexpensive restaurants for the paper, wrote: "Becco, [Bastianich's] first restaurant, is a solid value with its offbeat prix fixe menu. Frico is an even better bargain. The name Frico refers to the house specialty, a torte from the Friulian region . . . , made of grilled Montasio, a cow's milk cheese, with stuffings like sausage, mushrooms and potatoes and onions. As a diet food, the frico . . . is a disaster. But it's delicious, rich and filling enough to be a small meal with a salad or plate of grilled vegetables. It's also typical of the casual delights of Frico Bar, where meals can range from informal soups and panini, or sandwiches, to small pizzas to complete meals."

"It comes down to a very simple concept.... We buy things, we fix them up, and we sell them for a profit.... We're not full of ourselves. We can't afford to be."

In 1998 Bastianich teamed up with Mario Batali--then an up-and-coming chef and the founder of the acclaimed Italian restaurant Po--to open Babbo, an Italian restaurant in New York City's Greenwich Village. Bastianich told Richard Bienstock, "Babbo was about creating the restaurant of our dreams. We wanted to take what's good and right about the Italian table and transform it into a user-friendly format." Featuring a wide array of dishes made with offal, such as tripe alla parmigiana and beef-cheek ravioli, and an all-Italian wine list of more than 1,200 selections, Babbo opened to rave reviews and instantly became one of the most popular restaurants in New York City. It has been awarded three stars by the *New York Times* twice--first by Ruth Reichl in 1998 and then by Frank Bruni in 2004--and is one of the few Italian establishments in the city ever to garner that rating. Bruni wrote in his review, "Some restaurants revel in exquisite subtleties, while others simply go for the gut. Babbo, blessedly, hangs with the latter crowd." Babbo was named the best new restaurant of the year at the James Beard Awards ceremony in 1999, and it has since been credited with redefining Italian cuisine in New York City. Bastianich told Erica Duecy in *Nation's Restaurant News* (May 22, 2006) that Babbo had also "become the definitive place for Italian wines in America. It has kind of led the revolution of Italy both in the bottle and on the table." In 2006, a year in which Babbo brought in $8 million in revenue, it became one of the few Italian restaurants in the city to receive a star in the prestigious *Michelin Guide.*

Bastianich, who was concurrently helping his mother open restaurants in other cities, teamed with Batali again in 1999 to open Lupa Osteria Romana on Irving Place, a tony street in the Gramercy Park section of Manhattan. The following year they opened Esca (*bait* in Italian), a 70-seat restaurant in Midtown Manhattan that specializes in *crudo*, Italian-style raw fish. In 2003 the two opened both Otto Enoteca Pizzeria, a gourmet pizza parlor near Washington Square Park, and Casa Mono, a 35-seat taverna on Irving Place. Casa Mono, which marked their embrace of Spanish cuisine, received a two-star rating from the *New York Times* and was the highest-rated Spanish restaurant in the 2006 and 2007 editions of the *Zagat Guide*. It has also won acclaim for its wine list, which includes nearly 600 Spanish wines and has been honored with awards from *Wine Enthusiast* and *Wine Spectator* magazines. Next door to Casa Mono, Bastianich and Batali later opened Bar Jambon, which serves the flavorful appetizers and snacks known as tapas.

In early 2004 Bastianich became a partner in the Spotted Pig, a highly popular gastropub in Greenwich Village. He made a foray into French cuisine in 2005 with Bistro du Vent, but the restaurant, which was co-owned by Batali and David Pasternack, the chef at Esca, failed to take off and closed after 15 months. In a posting for the culinary Web site *SlashFood.com* (April 26, 2006), Nicole Weston wrote, "[The bistro] received reviews ranging from 'not bad' to 'deeply satisfying' and Frank Bruni gave it two stars, so the food isn't what is causing the [closure]." Quoting a *New York Post* piece, she theorized, "Its downfall was probably helped by the scandal that occurred last year, in which 'four employees--including a chef--were caught on [security] videotape in a steamy after-hours sex romp' in the restaurant. Though the employees were subsequently fired, it's not the sort of thing that necessarily enhances a restaurant's reputation." In late 2005 Bastianich, his mother, and Batali teamed up to open Del Posto (*of the place* in Italian), a 24,000-square-foot, 180-seat restaurant in Manhattan's Chelsea section. According to David Savona, "Del Posto boasts one of the most opulent dining rooms in Manhattan, a grandiose main space with balconies overlooking the dining floor and a wide staircase in the middle. Marble and black mahogany are virtually everywhere." Awarding the restaurant three stars, Frank Bruni wrote for the*New York Times* (March 1, 2006), "Much has been said about the marble, mahogany and millions of dollars poured into Del Posto, but the risk that Mario Batali and Joseph Bastianich have taken with this grand Italian restaurant is best measured in the gutsy way they have defied what their fans expect. They have crumpled up page after page of the script that made their previous ventures so beloved and written a new libretto, emphasizing refined notes over rustic ones, sacrificing hip on the altar of elegant." Bruni continued, "Teaming for the first time with Mr. Bastianich's mother, Lidia, whose restaurant Felidia is a more relevant point of reference, the two men have challenged New Yorkers to accept Italian cuisine presented with fastidious rituals and opulent trappings usually reserved for French fare. . . ." Bruni's successor, Sam Sifton, awarded Del Posto four stars in 2010, making it the highest-rated Italian restaurant in the city in over three decades. Sifton wrote for the *New York Times* (September 29, 2010), "Del Posto's is a pleasure that lasts, offering memories of flavors that may return later in a dream." In 2007 Del Posto earned two stars in the *Michelin Guide,* making it the only Italian restaurant in New York City to earn more than one star.

In November 2006 Bastianich, Batali, and the chef Nancy Silverton opened Pizzeria Mozza in Los Angeles, and the following year the trio added a free-standing mozzarella bar, Osteria Mozza, to the upscale pizzeria; the two-part venture was nominated by the James Beard Foundation in 2007 as the best new restaurant. Also that year Bastianich and Batali opened B&B Ristorante and Enoteca Otto Pizzeria at the Venetian Hotel in Las Vegas. In a review of B&B for the travel section of the *Los Angeles Times* (July 25, 2007), S. Irene Virbila wrote, "In a city where ersatz is celebrated, in a hotel and casino where gondoliers float revelers down 'canals' filled with chlorine-puffing water, Batali and Bastianich have installed a restaurant that exudes Italian soul."

In 2008 Bastianich and Batali opened their first steakhouse, Carnevino, at the Palazzo Hotel in Las Vegas. In the fall of that year, the two launched their first suburban venture, Tarry Lodge, in Port Chester, New York. Colman Andrews, writing for *Gourmet* magazine (October 13, 2008), pointed out that Bastianich and

Batali were among "a few prominent New York chefs and restaurateurs [who] have been looking toward the northeastern suburbs lately."

In 2010 Bastianich joined his mother, Batali, and other partners to open the first U.S. branch of Eataly. (The original is in Torino, Italy.) The 50,000-square-foot marketplace, which includes an espresso bar, a cheese store, a wine shop, and a cooking school, among other amenities, caused considerable buzz even before it opened and has continued to be a source of excitement for the city's food enthusiasts. "Upon walking into Eataly," Jaya Saxena wrote in the *Gothamist* (August 25, 2010), "you might actually think you were in Italy. Besides the produce, nearly everything is imported, and the 50,000 sq. ft. bi-level space is filled with rows upon rows of dried pasta, nougat, olive oils and anchovies piled 12 feet high. You're welcomed with a smart espresso bar as the space opens into seven 'restaurants,' 14 food stations and a full 'piazza' with a raw bar, fresh-cut prosciutto and marble-top tables." Sam Sifton wrote in the *New York Times* (October 19, 2010), "It is giant and amazing, on its face, a circus maximus."

In addition to his restaurant ventures, Bastianich owns an upscale wine shop, Italian Wine Merchants, in New York, and he now owns three wineries in Italy. He has emerged in recent years as a leading expert on Italian wines, co-authoring *Vino Italiano: The Regional Wines of Italy* (2002) and a companion volume,

Vino Italiano Buying Guide (2004), with the food and wine writer David Lynch, who has worked at Babbo. (The buying guide has been revised and updated.) Bastianich's third book, *Grandi Vini: An Opinionated Tour of Italy's 89 Finest Wines*, was published in 2010. That year he became a judge on the U.S. version of the televised cooking competition *MasterChef*, hosted by the celebrity chef Gordon Ramsay. As if refusing to be pigeonholed, Bastianich authored a 2012 memoir, *Restaurant Man*, in which he lays out his uncomplicated, yet powerful, credo: *It comes down to a very simple concept.... We buy things, we fix them up, and we sell them for a profit. That's been our mantra since we started. We're not full of ourselves. We can't afford to be.*

Bastianich lives in Greenwich, Connecticut, with his wife, Deanna, and their three children: Olivia, Miles, sand Ethan. He is an avid guitar player and amateur opera singer. After being diagnosed with sleep apnea caused by being overweight, he dropped 45 pounds and began running seriously. His "evolution from bon vivant to endurance athlete," wrote Jason Gay in the *Wall Street Journal* (December 9, 2011), "is something of a New York food world legend by now.... The transformation made Bastianich a kind of improbable fitness inspiration.".

Joe Bastianich prefers to remain in the background of his food and wine empire. As he explained to Edward Lewine in the *New York Times* (September 23, 2010): "I am Lidia's son and Mario's partner and Gordon Ramsay's judge, and I am good with that."

Further Reading:

Cigar Aficionado Feb. 2007

Food & Wine July 2004

Gothamist Aug. 25, 2010

Gourmet Oct. 13, 2008

Guitar Aficionado Dec. 2008 *Los Angeles Times* July 25, 2007, July 27, 2010

Nation's Restaurant News p14 Jan. 25, 1999, May 22, 2006

New York Times F p1+ Dec. 7, 2005, D p1+ Sep. 29, 2010, Jan. 5, 1996, June 9, 2004, Mar. 1, 2006, Oct. 27, 2008, Sep. 23, 2010, Oct. 19, 2010

Wall Street Journal Dec. 9, 2011
Westchester July 2008

Selected Books:

Vino Italiano: The Regional Wines of Italy
(with David Lynch)(Clarkson Potter, 2002)
Vino Italiano Buying Guide (with David Lynch) (Clarkson Potter, 2004)
Grandi Vini: An Opinionated Tour of Italy's 89 Finest Wines, (Clarkson Potter, 2010)
Restaurant Man (Viking, 2012)

Cointreau, André

Business executive, culinary entrepreneur

Born: c. 1948, Cognac, France

When André J. Cointreau, a scion of two major liquor empire families, purchased France's most famous cooking school, Le Cordon Bleu, in 1984, he set out to teach French culinary techniques to an increasingly international audience. Capitalizing on Le Cordon Bleu's reputation for producing the world's finest chefs, Cointreau embarked on an expansion program to create new worldwide branches of the French school, where students could earn the coveted Grande Diplôme de Cordon Bleu. Since then, according to Le Cordon Bleu's website, it has "evolved from a Parisian cooking school to an international network of culinary arts and hospitality institutes." "We are beginning to be a huge company, but we are still a family business," Cointreau told Michael Prentice of the *Ottawa Citizen* (April 26, 2001). Currently there are more than 40 Cordon Bleu schools in some 20 countries the world over.

Enjoying skillfully prepared meals, Cointreau believes, is an essential part of enjoying life; he told Hwang You-mee for the *Korea Herald* (December 2, 2003), "We promote the art of living. We want to share the values of life regardless of different languages and culture."

In an article for the *New York Times* (June 24, 1998) evaluating the relative strengths and weaknesses of Le Cordon Bleu and the Culinary Institute of America—the French model versus the American model of training chefs—Amanda Hesser outlined the program at Le Cordon Bleu. "Students," she wrote, "are first taught the fundamentals, from technique to palate education. The second semester focuses on French regional cooking, and the third refines skills and lets students unleash their creativity on classic dishes. But they never learn how to run a restaurant." Hesser went on to quote André Cointreau: ''We are only dealing with hands-on culinary training at the highest level,'' he said, and Hesser added that "Many prefer this to learning how to fold napkins and calculate costs." Le Cordon Bleu "sniffs at trends and ignores fads," she continued. "The student will come out with a thorough understanding of a cuisine. Not just any cuisine, but one whose techniques form the base of most Western cooking."

Le Cordon Bleu continues to emphasize "achieving excellence through constant practice and refinement," as is stated at its website. Yet it has evolved considerably since 1998; its offerings have been expanded to "focus on the demands of a growing international hospitality industry" and now include Bachelor's and Master's degrees in business. It can hardly be denied that Le Cordon Bleu "is considered to be the guardian of French culinary technique," but today, in Cointreau's words, "Le Cordon Bleu emphasizes the appreciation of French technique at the service of world cuisine."

Education and Early Career

André J. Cointreau was born in about 1948, the second of seven children born to Max and Genevieve Renaud Cointreau, of the Cointreau orange liqueur and Rémy Martin cognac empires, respectively. He was born and raised on his family's estate in Cognac, France. When he was 11, the family moved to Paris. His paternal grandmother was Scottish. "We lived in two worlds," Cointreau told Scott Kraft of the *Los Angeles Times* (July 25, 1995). "The British approach and the French approach are absolutely irreconcilable. There is a very strong, genuine and civilized British way. And there is a very strong, genuine and civilized French way. But there's no middle ground." Cointreau had a series of British nannies and speaks English fluently—with a plummy English accent.

The two sides of Cointreau's family had grown quite wealthy due to the lasting success of each of their signature products—Cointreau orange liqueur was invented in 1849, and Rémy Martin was established in 1724—but Cointreau was determined to establish a fortune all his own. "On the one hand, the family name opened doors," he told Kraft. "You're not in the anonymous crowd when you're a Cointreau. But, on the other, you probably have to prove yourself more if you want to play the game."

Cointreau attended the prestigious business-management school Hautes Études Commerciales (HEC) in Liège, France, where he took a business degree in 1972, and in Paris, where he earned a political science degree in 1974. He then worked for various companies, including the health conglomerate Unilever and American Express. In 1977 he became commercial director of his own family's Groupe Cointreau, later serving as chairman and managing director of the company Pagès and secretary-general of Cognacs Frapin. He was involved in the holding company created to govern the family-owned assets of Rémy Martin and Cointreau, later renamed Rémy Cointreau. He left the liqueur business in 1989, however, owing to a protracted family feud over inheritance claims. (More than 30 lawsuits were filed between the two sides of the family during the 1980s.) Of the dispute, Cointreau told Jonathan Dawson of the *London Evening Standard* (December 14, 1994), "It was all very unpleasant but let us just say it was a necessary time of re-assessment. The co-presidency lies with my two cousins who are very talented, and everything is in excellent hands."

Instead Cointreau began concentrating completely on L'Ecole de Cuisine et de Pâtisserie Le Cordon Bleu, familiarly known as Le Cordon Bleu, which he had bought from its longtime owner, Élizabeth Brassart, a family friend. "I asked myself, 'Do you want to lay back and enjoy, or risk problems and failure but also reward?'" he explained to Scott Kraft. "I chose the risk."

Le Cordon Bleu ("The Blue Ribbon") had been founded in 1895 by a French journalist named Marthe Distel, publisher of a magazine called *La Cuisinière Cordon Bleu,* so that renowned chefs could provide recipes and lessons for her readers. (Its name was derived from France's noble tradition: in the sixteenth century, members of the highest order of knights wore a blue ribbon; later, cooks' aprons were often decorated with a blue ribbon or sash.) While servants to wealthy families made up much of the student base shortly after its inception, by mid-century the school's clientele had expanded to include students—many from far-distant countries, including the United States and Japan—eager to pursue a career in cooking. One of the more celebrated students was Julia Child, who graduated in 1951. Child (who later commented, "The truth is that Mme. Brassart and I got on each other's nerves") went on to co-author the classic and phenomenally popular cookbook *Mastering the Art of French Cooking* (1961), among other books, and host the acclaimed public-television show *The French Chef,* through which many Americans became familiar with Le Cordon Bleu's name.

In 1988, to accommodate an ever-increasing enrollment, Cointreau moved Le Cordon Bleu from its cramped quarters in Paris's fashionable Champ de Mars district to a larger, more modern building on the rue Léon Delhomme. (The new location was opened by the French minister of economy and finance, in an inauguration ceremony attended by 24 ambassadors from various countries.) Cointreau began greatly expanding the school's course offerings. He offered week-long classes for professional cooks interested in learning more about a specific topic, and he catered, as well, to avid home cooks not interested in a culinary career. At Le Cordon Bleu visitors could, for a fee, witness a demonstration of French cuisine or partake in a hands-on, four-day crash cooking course. Cointreau also introduced English translation in Le Cordon Bleu's non-diploma classes. The changes proved quite successful: between the time Cointreau purchased Le Cordon Bleu and May 1990, enrollment at the Paris school more than tripled.

Later Career

In June 1988 Cointreau had acquired a cooking school in Ottawa, Canada. Eleanor Orser had founded the school in 1980 after graduating from Le Cordon Bleu, and Cointreau appointed her his new branch's director. In May 1990 Cointreau purchased the financially ailing London-based Cordon Bleu Cookery School Ltd. for about $1 million. The London school had been founded in 1933 by Rosemary Hume, a Cordon Bleu graduate, but, despite the similarity in their names, there had never been an official affiliation between the two institutions. "Le Cordon Bleu has established a long tradition of excellence in culinary training, and this marriage allows us to use the trademark which reflects that tradition worldwide," Cointreau announced in a Cordon Bleu press release (May 29, 1990). "With the London acquisition, our group can defend and protect that trademark in the U.K. and Commonwealth countries." Cointreau renovated the school, updated its program, and reopened it as Le Cordon Bleu London in June 1991.

Cointreau, an admitted Anglophile, was also focusing on making Le Cordon Bleu more accessible to an English-speaking audience. In 1991 the school produced a recipe book in English, *Le Cordon Bleu at Home,* which was sold with a series of videos of Le Cordon Bleu chefs preparing food. (Chef Patrick Martin, head of the Tokyo branch, toured America to promote the book.) In 1992 Le Cordon Bleu and the London newspaper the *Independent* announced their first annual Cook Competition, inviting cooks to send in recipes to a panel of expert judges, including Cointreau. The winner was awarded a three-day trip to Paris and free meals at several high-profile restaurants, a meal at a London restaurant, and a copy of *Le Cordon Bleu at Home.*

Le Cordon Bleu's international expansion continued. In October 1990 Cointreau announced that he would be opening a school in Tokyo, Japan, through a joint venture with Japan's Seibu Department Stores Ltd. (Seibu pulled out in 1993, leaving ownership completely to Le Cordon Bleu.) The school's curriculum had already proved to be popular with Japanese students; by the time of the acquisition, 20 percent of Le Cordon Bleu's students were Japanese. In June 1992 Cointreau opened a Cordon Bleu branch in Adelaide, Australia, in the city's Regency Hotel School.

In July 1993 Cointreau acquired Pierre Deux, a chain store marketing French interior decoration and furniture in the United States and Japan; Cointreau became the chief executive officer of its parent company, Arts de Provence de France. Pierre Deux began selling Le Cordon Bleu products, such as vinegar, cookies, and cookbooks. Over the next several years, Le Cordon Bleu awarded its seal of approval to a growing range of both kitchen accessory and food lines. The pairing was lucrative: between 1993 and 1994, revenues at Le Cordon Bleu grew by 30 percent, and sales at the eight Pierre Deux stores rose 40 percent.

When the International Association of Culinary Professionals held its annual meeting in Paris, in November 1995, Le Cordon Bleu hosted the opening reception. At that meeting, Cointreau surprised conference attendees by proclaiming that Australia was moving to the forefront of the world's gastronomic scene. Three months later he announced the imminent opening of a Le Cordon Bleu branch in Sydney, Australia, at the Ryde Technical and Further Education (TAFE) college. "Australia is the place where the cuisine of 21st century is developing," he told Cherry Ripe for the *Weekend Australian* (March 23, 1996). "Australia is at the crossroads of Europe and Asia, just as France is at the crossroads of north and south Europe. It benefits from a vast variety of very good quality ingredients from many different cuisines, [all] available for fusion, with its cultural capital Sydney ready to make a synthesis as Paris did." In March 1998 Cointreau announced that Le Cordon Bleu's second Australian branch, in Adelaide, was developing an international restaurant management course—Le Cordon Bleu's first; classes began in early 1999. The Adelaide school soon proved so successful that in October 2000 Cointreau signed an agreement to build an international hotel-management school in Adelaide, for an estimated cost of $15 million. Several of the Le Cordon Bleu affiliates began to offer restaurant-management curricula, based on the Adelaide program.

"It's not the brand that makes the school so revered. It's really the success of the students that makes us known across the world."

In November 1998 Cointreau announced a partnership with the United States Career Education Corporation (CEC) to offer a Cordon Bleu-approved curriculum at five of the CEC's culinary schools: in Pasadena, California; Portland, Oregon; Pittsburgh, Pennsylvania; Scottsdale, Arizona; and Mendota Heights, Minnesota. Later that November, he announced that Le Cordon Bleu was expanding into Brazil as well, through a joint venture with the Universidade de Brasilia. In December 1998 he announced the imminent opening of yet another branch, in Mexico, through a joint venture with the Universidad Anahuac, in Mexico City.

By January 2000 the Ottawa school was so successful that Cointreau purchased a larger building, which was opened in April 2001; attached to the school was Signatures, Le Cordon Bleu's first restaurant in North America. (In June 2004 Signatures was ranked the best restaurant in Ottawa by the editors of the popular guide *Where to Eat in Canada*.)

In the mid-1990s Le Cordon Bleu cultivated a partnership with Silversea, a fledgling cruise line. Silversea chefs attended classes at the school and received help developing their menus, and several of Le Cordon Bleu's master chefs were sent to prepare food and conduct seminars on select cruises. Cointreau's five-year partnership with Silversea ended in October 2000, when he signed an exclusive partnership with Radisson Seven Seas Cruises (later Regent Seven Seas Cruises) to provide similar services. Regent's 110-seat Signatures restaurants are directed by Cordon Bleu chefs, and the line also offers (at an extra cost) Le Cordon Bleu cooking cruises offering three onboard workshops, a special chef's dinner, and a market visit in port. In recent years David Bilsland, a former Cordon Bleu London instructor, has conducted "Relais & Châteax L'École des Chefs" on Silversea cruises, geared to the cruise destinations.

On the occasion of inducting Cointreau into its Hall of Fame in 2005, the International Food and Beverage Forum credited him with "pioneering Le Cordon Bleu's recent resurgence as the top-ranking culinary academy in the world, as well as its place as the custodian of French culinary tradition," adding that he had "brought a new dynamic style to what was once a classical Parisian cooking school. … André Cointreau has shared the spirit, the passion and the appreciation of the French 'art culinaire' with governments, universities, culinary organizations and the hospitality industry, throughout the world."

Cointreau helped create the Fondation Science & Culture Alimentaire (Science and Food Culture Foundation) within the Académie des Sciences, and in 2004, with Reims University, he launched an annual intensive two-week multidisciplinary gastronomy program called the Hautes Etudes du Goût de la Gastronomie et des Arts de la Table, during which students spend a week at Le Cordon Bleu and a week at Reims University. In January 2008, at the launch of the Fondation Alliance française, Cointreau was named a Chevalier of l'Ordre National de la Légion d'Honneur "for his contributions and accomplishments as President/CEO of Le Cordon Bleu and for his unique educational concept." He is a member of the board of directors of the Alliance française Paris and a founding member of the Fondation Alliance française.

Writing for the Adelaide *Advertiser* (June 3, 2009), Samala Harris asserted that under Cointreau's leadership, "Le Cordon Bleu grew from the classic culinary branding of its tradition to this advanced global empire wherein food is just a facet of a sophisticated educational empire." While Cointreau certainly brought entrepreneurial acumen to the evolution of Le Cordon Bleu, he remained committed to the idea that using the highest-quality ingredients was the foundation of gastronomical excellence. "Name on your menus where things come from. Glorify your ingredients," Cointreau told Harris. Moreover, despite his focused branding efforts, Cointreau credited Le Cordon Bleu's reputation and success to its students: "It's not the brand that makes the school so revered. It's really the success of the students that makes us known across the world."

André Cointreau is married to Hedwige Cointreau de Bouteville, who served as president of Pierre Deux. By 2011 the company had 23 boutiques in the United States. Its products were highly regarded, but despite, or because of, its high prices, the company had struggled. In 2002 Pierre Deux filed for Chapter 11 bankruptcy reorganization in New York. It emerged from Chapter 11, but in June 2011 it filed for Chapter 7 bankruptcy in New Jersey, where Arts des Provinces de France was headquartered. Nevertheless, Pierre Deux fabrics, perhaps its signature product, remain available through the trade distributor Kravet, with which Pierre Deux had a licensing agreement of several years' standing before its collapse. Carole Sloan, writing for *Home Textiles Today* (August 8, 2005) quoted Heather Ryan, the head of sales and marketing for Pierre Deux, commenting on Hedwige Cointreau de Bouteville's role in Pierre Deux's fabric line: "'The fabrics produced by Kravet are interpreted by them from designs, colors and styles of French country looks suggested by Mme. Hedwige Cointreau de Bouteville, president and creative director.'" Cointreau de Bouteville remains involved in some of André Cointreau's other business interests.

The couple owned houses in London, Paris, New York, and Angers, France. They spent most of their time at their London residence, a four-story mansion in the city's Knightsbridge neighborhood. There they raised their four children: Charles, Rodolphe, Isaure, and Aliénor.

Regarding his career, Cointreau told Jonathan Dawson, "I am very lucky, I am working with food and wine, probably the most wonderful things anyone could wish to work with."

Further Reading:

[Adelaide] *Advertiser* Jun 3, 2009

Canberra Times A p11 Nov. 8, 2000

(Tokyo) *Daily Yomiuri* [now the Japan News] p9 Dec. 6, 1994

Furniture Today, Jul. 8, 2011

Home Textiles Today, Aug. 8, 2005

International Food & Beverage Forum website

Korea Herald Dec. 2, 2003

Le Cordon Bleu website

Los Angeles Times World p1 July 25, 1995

Malaysia Tatler Dec 13, 2013

Reference for Business website

Weekend Australian p37 Mar. 21, 1998

Cora, Cat

Chef, restaurateur, television personality

Born: 1967, Jackson, Mississippi, United States

Cat Cora began to appear on the popular Food Network show *Iron Chef America* in 2005. She won fame as the first female Iron Chef, competing alongside such high-profile males as Bobby Flay, Mario Batali, and Masaharu Morimoto. Each installment of the show pits one of the Iron Chefs against a culinary newcomer in a contest to create five dishes that must be based on a "secret" ingredient, which is unveiled at the start of the show. The dishes are then judged by a panel of experts for taste, visual appeal, and creativity. "Cora has not only stood the heat [on *Iron Chef America*], she's turned it up, bottled it and repurposed it for several sizzling careers," Chris Mann wrote for *WellBella* magazine (May 2011). In addition to her work on television—which came to include other Food Network projects and a culinary-themed reality show on Bravo—Cora has coauthored cookbooks, opened restaurants, and served in an advisory role as executive chef for *Bon Appetit* magazine .

Cora founded the philanthropic organization Chefs for Humanity, which provides nutrition education and humanitarian food aid around the world. Referring to the distinctive toques often donned by professional chefs, the group's motto is, "The good guys still wear white hats."

Education and Early Career

One of the three children of Spiro and Virginia Cora, Catherine Cora was born on April 3, 1967, in Jackson, Mississippi, where her family was part of a small, close-knit Greek community. (Some sources mistakenly give the year of her birth as 1968 and the date as January 1.) Her father, a high-school history teacher, was born in the Mississippi Delta shortly after his parents emigrated from Skopelos, a Greek island. In her book *Cat Cora's Kitchen: Favorite Meals for Family and Friends* (2004), Cora wrote that he possessed "the warmth and fun-loving appetite of a Greek and the humor and charm of a Southern gentleman." She told Mann, "For me, food was really all about our family. Being Greek and also being from the South, I had all of these very rich cultures all around me. We were eating great Greek food and then great Southern food. So it was really rewarding learning about these different cuisines. But also just being around the cultures together—they're such strong food cultures— … it made a huge impact on me." Cora wrote in *Favorite Meals* that her father was a natural cook. "In my earliest memories of my dad cooking, he's sitting by the fire, checking the smoke occasionally and happily reading a book. No matter how hectic my surroundings [now], if I want to lower my blood pressure by ten points, I just envision my father smoking a brisket."

Cora's mother, Virginia, is a nurse. (She had originally wanted to become a veterinarian, but her father, an army physician, told her that that was not a suitable career for a woman.) Currently, she teaches at the School of Nursing of the University of Mississippi Medical Center. When Cora was in junior high school, her mother returned to school and earned a D.S.N. (doctor of science in nursing) degree. Cora's maternal grandmother, Alma, who was an accomplished cook, moved into the family home to help care for Cora and her two brothers.

Cora told Kara Kimbrough for GetFitMississippi.com, "Ever since I was little I was involved in some way with food. I loved to host tea parties and bake cookies or roll grape leaves for church events. Most of my childhood memories growing up in Jackson center around food, family gatherings and all the warmth and excitement that comes with gathering around the dinner table." Cora recalled in an article she wrote for *O, The Oprah Magazine* (September 2011), "When I was growing up … there was always that time between 5 and 6 in the evening when my two brothers and I would storm the house, famished from school and sports and wanting to eat *right now*. My mom would be at the stove, and the smell of browning onions or searing chicken would only make us hungrier. My grandmother, who lived with us, came up with the idea of turning that restless interlude into family happy hour. … She'd put out Kalamata olives and nuts, along with Feta cheese or sharp Cheddar and crackers. Then she and my mom would pour themselves a glass of wine, my dad would pop open a beer, and we kids would get juice or milk in grown-up glasses. We'd all sit together in the kitchen and talk about what had happened at school or work that day. The ritual allowed my mom a few extra minutes to finish cooking dinner. And it taught me that happy hour doesn't have to involve prowling around bars and drinking 100-proof rum—it can be just as fun to gather as a family."

Cora's godfather, Peter "Taki" Costas, too, was a major influence on her. "Taki owned several restaurants in Jackson," Cora wrote in *Favorite Meals*. "The fanciest was the Continental, an old-style restaurant with big leather booths that you sank into when you sat down. The continental was my favorite place in the world to eat because Taki would come out to the dining room, take me by the hand into the kitchen, and lift me up onto the counter where I'd sit talking to the cooks. I remember them asking me, 'What do you want to eat; we'll cook you anything you like.' When you're five years old, sitting in an enormous kitchen with three people asking what they can cook for you, of course you develop a fondness for restaurant kitchens."

"When I was about 13, I really became interested in cooking, and Peter Costas taught me how to make roast chicken," she recalled to Kimbrough. "I invited my godparents over and prepared dinner for them." Virginia Cora confirmed for Kimbrough, "It was a delicious chicken dinner served with root vegetables that were cooked to perfection. We knew right then that she was going to be a great cook." By the time she was 15, Cora had drawn up a business plan for the restaurant she dreamed of opening one day.

Rather than diving into a culinary career immediately after high school, Cora attended the University of Southern Mississippi, in Hattiesburg, where she studied exercise physiology and biology. She graduated with honors in 1990. "College taught me to be articulate, helped me be well read and shaped me as a businesswoman. Studying wellness plays into my platform today, which is healthy cooking," she told Suzanne Riss for *Working Mother* magazine (August/September 2010). Intrigued by the idea of continuing her education at a formal culinary school, Cora attended a book signing in Natchez by the legendary chef Julia Child. Determined to speak to Child, she lingered at the end of the line until the other autograph seekers had gone. "She spent 45 minutes with me," Cora recalled to Riss. "We discussed where I'd go to culinary school, and she suggested the Culinary [Institute] of America. I applied the next day."

The Culinary Institute of America, often referred to as the CIA, is a renowned institution with campuses in Hyde Park, New York; St. Helena, California; San Antonio, Texas; and Singapore. Widely characterized as the "Harvard of cooking schools," it boasts alumni from recent decades including such luminaries as Anthony Bourdain, Rocco DiSpirito, and Todd English. "Women were just starting to go [to the CIA], so there were only about six of us in a class of 60," Cora told Riss. "There were still some old-school professors who gave us trouble. ... I was told I should be barefoot and pregnant in the kitchen, things like that. If you let yourself feel inspired rather than discouraged when you hear comments like that, it can be a very powerful motivator. Instead of making me insecure or shrink against a challenge, it made me step up even more."

Cora excelled at the CIA, and upon completing her studies in Hyde Park, she found work at the New York City restaurant Arcadia, run by the chef Anne Rosenzweig, with whom she had apprenticed as a student. "At Arcadia," the food critic Ruth Reichl wrote for the *New York Times* (April 22, 1994, on-line), "the food does not allow itself to be ignored. This is a place where a Caesar salad is made with peppery arugula instead of wimpy romaine lettuce and the croutons are made of buttery brioche instead of plain old bread. ... What [really] sets Ms. Rosenzweig apart from many chefs is the elegance with which she puts her plates together. She is not satisfied to serve a piece of fish with a random vegetable and a starch, but offers a careful composition, each element complementing the others." Cora also worked under the chef Larry Forgione at the Beekman 1776 Tavern, in Rhinebeck, New York. Forgione was already a legend in the food world. Matt DeLucia wrote for *Restaurant Insider* (January 1, 2008), "Since the mid-1980's, Larry Forgione's name has rarely been mentioned in the press without 'The Godfather of American Cuisine' tacked onto the end of it."

Cora subsequently traveled to Europe, where she completed apprenticeships under George Blanc and Roger Vergé, both Michelin three-star chefs. (Under the Michelin system, a chef may earn one to three stars; a three-star ranking, which is very rarely awarded, indicates that a chef is creating exceptional cuisine that is worth a special journey for diners.) After she returned to the United States, Cora became a sous chef (second in command) at the now-closed Old Chatham Shepherding Company Inn, working under chef Melissa Kelly, whom she had originally met at the Beekman.

Cora next moved to California and began working at the Bistro Don Giovanni, long considered one of the finest restaurants in Napa Valley. She served as the chef de cuisine (the chef in charge of running the kitchen). She also began writing a food column, "Cooking from the Hip," for a local newspaper, the *Contra Costa Times*. (The column later provided the title for Cora's second cookbook, published in 2007.)

Later Career

In 1999 Cora made her television debut, as one of a rotating roster of co-hosts on the Food Network show *Melting Pot*, which explored various ethnic cuisines. The Food Network, which was launched in 1993, was not yet the ratings powerhouse that it is today, but it was attracting loyal viewers with its mix of instructional cooking programs, food-related travel shows, and culinary competitions. Cora quickly proved to be a network favorite, and she went on to appear on such shows as *Kitchen Accomplished* and *Celebrity Cooking Showdown*. When she cooked a dinner in April 2002 at the James Beard House, at the invitation of the James Beard Foundation (whose self-described mission is "to celebrate, nurture, and preserve America's diverse culinary heritage and future"), the network aired a special documentary, *Cat's in the Kitchen*, about the event.

In 1993 a televised culinary competition called *Ryori no Tetsujin* ("Ironmen of Cooking") premiered in Japan. Broadcast on the Fuji Television Network, the campy show included an elaborate backstory involving a wealthy gourmand known as Chairman Kaga, who retains a team of "Iron Chefs." For his own entertainment he has built a "kitchen stadium," to which he invites cooks from all over the world to compete with his team. In each installment a challenger and a chosen Iron Chef must each prepare a multi-course meal, prominently featuring a secret ingredient that has just been revealed to them. One journalist described the show by asking readers to imagine that Julia Child had joined the World Wrestling Federation and moved to Asia. (The wrestling comparison was apt: on occasion the *Ryori no Tetsujin* chefs were injured during the filming. Once, for example, Masaharu Morimoto was bitten by a monkfish, and Hiroyuki Sakai was bitten by a squid.)

"For me, food was really all about our family."

Ryori no Tetsujin attracted a passionate cult following in Japan, and in 1999 the Food Network began airing Japanese episodes dubbed in English. In 2004 the network presented an English-language miniseries called *Iron Chef America: Battle of the Masters*, in which American chefs, including Bobby Flay and Mario Batali, were pitted against Sakai and Morimoto. The premise of the miniseries was that Chairman Kaga had dispatched his nephew, played by the martial artist Mark Dacascos, to build a kitchen stadium in the United States. The miniseries proved to be popular, and the Food Network began broadcasting *Iron Chef America* the following year as a regular series. (*Iron Chef America* is not to be confused with *Iron Chef USA*, an ill-fated series starring William Shatner that aired for just two episodes on UPN in 2001.) "The faces have changed, but the mythology remains the same," William Grimes wrote for the *New York Times* (January 14, 2005). Stephen Kroopnick, the executive producer of the series, told Grimes, "The goal was to preserve what the die-hards love, and also to make it exciting for people just coming to it. You don't have to know Episode 121, Battle Octopus."

Cora made her debut as the first-ever female Iron Chef in late 2005, in a match against Alex Lee, the executive chef at the exclusive New York City restaurant Daniel. The secret ingredient was potato, and Cora triumphed over Lee in the competition by one point. Since then Cora has faced such challengers as Kerry Simon, Sam Choy, Michael Psilakis, Elizabeth Falkner, and Paul Miranda. To date she has won the majority of her matches on the show, which is taped in the Chelsea section of New York City.

In May 2012 Cora expanded her television presence with Bravo's *Around the World in 80 Plates,* a chefs' competition and "culinary race" reality show she co-hosted with Curtis Stone. For the Food Network, in spring 2014, she was a chef-mentor representing the South on *America's Best Cook,* a six-episode series hosted by Ted Allen of *Chopped* fame.

Cora owns several restaurants: Cat Cora's 'Que (CCQ), in Costa Mesa, California, which she opened in 2008 in partnership with Macy's, and which features barbeque from around the world; Kouzzina by Cat, a Mediterranean-themed establishment at Disney World, in Orlando, Florida, which opened in 2009; and the Cat Cora's Kitchen restaurants, the first of which was launched in 2011 at the San Francisco International Airport as a "sophisticated dining option for airport travelers," according to Cora's website. Additional Cat Cora's Kitchen restaurants were subsequently opened at the Houston and Salt Lake City airports, and Cora planned to expand to other airports as well. Associated with the Salt Lake City Cora Cat's Kitchen is Cora Cat's Gourmet Market, which offers healthful takeout options. In 2013, in partnership with Resorts World Sentosa, she opened Ocean Restaurant by Cat Cora in the S.E.A. Aquarium on Sentosa Island, Singapore. Cora's restaurants serve her own wines, bottled under the label Coranation.)

In September 2010 Cora again partnered with Disney, this time on *Muppets Kitchen,* a series of "webisodes" at Disney Online. "Co-hosted" by Cora and an Italian Muppet named Angelo, the series promoted constructive family time together through the "joy of cooking." An accompanying series of webisodes called *HastyTasty Cooking Tips with Cat Cora and the Muppets* provided Cora's commentary on how to motivate children to cook as well as step-by-step cooking demonstrations.

All three of Cora's cookbooks were co-authored by Ann Krueger Spivack. In addition to *Cat Cora's Kitchen*, they are *Cooking from the Hip: Fast, Easy, Phenomenal Meals* (2007), which offers recipes that can be prepared quickly, and *Fresh Takes on Favorite Dishes: Cat Cora's Classics with a Twist* (2010), which contains simpler, more healthful versions of such dishes as nachos, stroganoff, and fried calamari. Of her sophomore effort, a reviewer for *Publishers Weekly* (January 15, 2007) wrote, "Cora … aims to translate the fast, flashy style of that high-pressure [*Iron Chef America*] kitchen into recipes that home cooks who have similar time constraints but comparatively modest gadgets and pantries can enjoy. The results are generally pleasing and more accessible than many of the concoctions presented on TV by battling chefs." In 2012 Cora released an iPad app, Cat Cora's Kitchen, with video tutorials and a scheduling feature assisting cooks at various skill levels to "plan, prepare and serve individual dishes or complete menus from her repertoire with absolute confidence." Cora has also written a children's book, *A Suitcase Surprise for Mommy* (2011), aimed at youngsters (like her own) whose parents' jobs require them to travel a lot.

In 2005 Cora founded Chefs for Humanity, modeled on the organization Doctors Without Borders. Its aim, according to the Chefs for Humanity website, is to provide "nutrition education, hunger relief, and emergency and humanitarian aid to reduce hunger across the world." Additionally, Cora serves as a spokesperson for UNICEF. In 2010 she accepted an invitation from the White House to prepare a meal in honor of Greek Independence Day, and in that year she also participated in First Lady Michelle Obama's Chefs Move to Schools campaign offering schools nutritional guidance and education.

Cora is a member of the Macy's Culinary Council, a group of chefs who endorse the store's culinary and houseware products, and since 2006 she has served as *Bon Appetit*'s executive chef, advising the editorial staff and representing the magazine at various media events. Cora also lent her name to a line of cookware and a line of gourmet products, including olive oils, prepared cooking sauces, and packaged olives. Profits from Cat Cora by Starfrit cookware and *Cat Cora's Kitchen by Gaea support Chefs for Humanity.*

Openly gay, Cora has been married to her partner, Jennifer Johnson Cora, a former nanny, since 2001. "I remember as a child of 4 or 5 having crushes on babysitters," Cora told Suzanne Riss. "Of course, a little girl can have crushes, and that doesn't mean she's gay. I didn't know what it meant. But it's who I was, just like when you have brown hair or blue eyes." She continued, "All through high school and college I dated boys, but by then I knew I was gay. I had a girlfriend in high school while I was dating a guy. I couldn't tell anybody. My first love. My first kiss. And I couldn't tell my mom. It was a lonely place. I came out to my parents when I was 19. … I was tired of hiding my pain or my happiness. … My parents had always told us that it was okay to be different, that they'd always love us. They were open-minded. But it was hard for them. That was in the '80s at the height of the AIDS epidemic. Then they talked to people. They [eventually] accepted it."

Together, Cat and Jennifer Cora—employing the same sperm donor and in-vitro fertilization—have four sons, ranging in age from seven to two: Zoran, Caje, Thatcher, and Nash. The family live in Santa Barbara, California.

Further Reading:

Advocate p24 Dec. 18, 2007

New York Times Apr. 22, 1994, Jan. 14, 2005, Feb. 11, 2007

O, The Oprah Magazine Jul. 2011, Sep. 2011

Parenting Magazine Feb. 24, 2012

Publishers Weekly Jan. 15, 2007

Shape Magazine May 9, 2012

WellBella p22 May 2011

Working Mother p50 Aug./Sep. 2010

Selected Books:

Cora, Cat, and Ann Krueger Spivack: *Cat Cora's Kitchen: Favorite Meals for Family and Friends*, 2004

--*Cooking from the Hip: Fast, Easy, Phenomenal Meals*, 2007

--*Fresh Takes on Favorite Dishes: Cat Cora's Classics with a Twist*, 2010.

Cora, Cat, *A Suitcase Surprise for Mommy*, illustrated by Joy Allen, 2011

Donald, Arnold

Business executive

Born: 1954, New Orleans, Louisiana, United States

"I've never focused on a title; I've never focused on trying to please a boss; and I've never focused on trying to network with certain people," Arnold W. Donald told Ronald E. Childs for *Black Enterprise* (May 2003). "What I did was to focus on 'What's the result? How am I maximizing my return to shareholders over the life of the firm?' Simply stated, I've always looked for jobs and opportunities, which gave me experiences that trained me well for that task." That approach seems to have worked well for Donald, who emerged from humble origins to become a top executive at Monsanto, a founder of the tabletop sweetener Merisant, a chief executive in the nonprofit sector, and president and chief executive officer of Carnival Corporation, the world's largest cruise operator, with ten individual cruise lines, including Holland America, Princess, Cunard, and Seabourn.

Donald has made a point of supporting causes in which he believes, in the hope that he may help other African Americans to fulfill their ambitions, in part through his own example. While acknowledging the relatively low number of blacks in high-level corporate positions, he said to Beverly Schuch on the CNN television show *Business Unusual* (December 28, 2000), "I think the opportunities are certainly there—case in point, myself—for African Americans, and other minorities to ascend to CEO-type positions." Donald served for two years at the helm of the Executive Leadership Council, a professional network and leadership forum for African American executives. He told Chris King of the *St. Louis American* (June 27, 2013), "I look across corporate America, and one thing that influenced me to take this role [at Carnival] is the relative lack of African-American participation in the leadership of Fortune 500 companies. Hopefully, in taking on this role and joining the ranks of, unfortunately, very few others I will help make it possible for others to follow at other corporations."

Andrew Bursky, a Connecticut-based businessman and a college friend of Donald's, said about him in a conversation with Thomas Lee of the *St. Louis Post-Dispatch* (January 13, 2002), "He is a general who leads from the front. He's not the big bureaucratic type. He gets the best out of everybody." Another businessman, Leonard Guarraia, told Lee about Donald, "He is an honest person. You may not like what he has to say, but he will say it. … But he really does care about people."

Education and Early Career

Arnold W. Donald was born on December 17, 1954, in New Orleans, Louisiana, to Hilda and Warren Donald. Neither of his parents had graduated from high school. Donald grew up in the city's poor, rough Desire neighborhood, living with four older siblings and, over time, some 27 foster children in a house built by his father, a carpenter. "We were poor, but I was blessed with a loving and nurturing family," he told Cassandra

Hayes for *Black Enterprise* (September 30, 1997). "My parents did whatever they could to make life good for us." Thanks to his family's support, "I really believed that I could do whatever I wanted," Donald said to Nancy Rotenier for *Forbes* (May 22, 1995). Donald learned how to read, write, and do basic math under the tutelage of his sister Yvonne before he even entered kindergarten. Donald attended the black Catholic boys' school St. Augustine, in New Orleans, which had a reputation for producing excellent athletes as well as high achievers in academics. He characterized St. Augustine for Patricia R. Olsen of the *New York Times* (June 24, 2007) as "phenomenal and very rigorous. We won national debate and math contests and were No. 1 in most sports in our division. Three times a day, the principal would announce on the intercom: 'Prepare yourselves. You are going to run the world.'" Donald also took summer courses at prep schools in Exeter, New Hampshire, and Andover, Massachusetts, and he benefited from the informal mentoring of successful St. Augustine alumni. Donald was a driven student, as a St. Augustine faculty member, Edwin Hampton, who led the marching band in which Donald was saxophone line captain, told Allen Powell II for the New Orleans *Times-Picayune* (August 10, 2001). "He was just No. 1, a gentleman and scholar," Hampton said. "He learned his craft, and always strived for perfection." By his junior year of high school, Donald had decided on his career, as he told Cassandra Hayes: "I wanted to be a general manager at a science-based company whose products would make a difference in the world."

In order to work in the realms of both science and business, Donald felt that he would need to study economics and mechanical engineering and earn an M.B.A. degree. As a graduating senior in 1972, Donald turned down offers to attend Yale University, Stanford University, and West Point in favor of Carleton College, a small liberal-arts school in Northfield, Minnesota. He graduated in 1976 with a B.A. degree in economics, then earned a second bachelor's degree, a B.S. in engineering, from Washington University in St. Louis, Missouri. On his graduation, in 1977, Donald took a job in industrial chemical sales with the Monsanto Company, a St. Louis-based maker of agricultural products such as pesticides, animal-food supplements, and lawn and garden products. Meanwhile, he also attended the University of Chicago, where, in 1980, he received his master's degree in business administration with a concentration in finance and international business. "My strategy was always to maximize the probabilities," he explained to Cassandra Hayes. "Although I had no desire to work in finance, I thought that knowing it would be important to general management, so I immersed myself in it."

At Monsanto Donald was quickly pegged as a rising star and promoted successively to the posts of senior market analyst, U.S. product director of Roundup herbicide, vice president of the residential-products division, and vice president and general manager of the crop-protection products division. In the latter position he was one of the more vocal advocates for the development of crops enhanced through the use of biotechnology. Talking with Laurie Kretchmar for *Fortune* (September 9, 1991), Donald revealed his guiding principle for maintaining what he called a "high-performance organization": "Have three people do five jobs but pay them like four." Donald was noted not only for his managerial skills but for his success in promoting Roundup, a weed killer that, with Donald's help, became the best-selling herbicide in the world.

In 1988 Donald was named lawn and garden director for the company's industrial and residential business unit, and in four years in that position, he brought about a fivefold increase in retail revenues. He became Monsanto's group vice president of North America in 1993 and president of the company's agricultural sector in 1995. In the latter capacity he was responsible for the department that, through the sale of crop, industrial, and turf agricultural products throughout the United States, Canada, and Latin America, accounted for half of Monsanto's operating profits. As president of the agricultural sector, Donald worked closely with the

Environmental Protection Agency and the U.S. Department of Agriculture to ensure that all Monsanto products would adhere to guidelines set to protect the environment. The National Agri-Marketing Association named Donald Agri-Marketer of the Year for 1997, the same year that *Black Enterprise* singled him out as its Corporate Executive of the Year. In 1998 he became senior vice president of the company and president of its Consumer and Nutrition Sector, responsible for worldwide growth and technology initiatives.

Later Career

When the Monsanto decided to sell its ownership of more than 20 brands of what the industry calls "low-calorie, high-intensity" sweeteners, including Equal and its European counterpart, Canderel, Donald concluded that it would be a wise business decision to assemble a group of investors and buy the sweetener division. Urged by Andrew Bursky, a friend from his engineering-school days at Washington University, Donald successfully pitched the idea to investors such as the private-equity firm Pegasus Capital Advisors (with which Bursky was associated); MSD Capital LP, an investment fund affiliated with Michael Dell, chairman of Dell Computer Corp.; and the Brener International Group. In 2000 Donald left Monsanto, and he and his fellow investors created the privately held Merisant Company, which bought the tabletop sweeteners from Monsanto for $570 million. "I was really happy at Monsanto," he told Thomas Lee. "Even when I chose to do this, I was really enjoying my Monsanto experience. But I have to tell you, as wonderful as that was, it pales in comparison to this."

Donald became chairman and CEO of the newly formed company, which counted among its executives six former Monsanto employees. One of them, Karl Sestak, Merisant's vice president of communications, told a writer for the *St. Louis Commerce Magazine* (April 1, 2002), "People love to work with Arnold." Kevin Eichner, former CEO and president of the GenAmerica Financial Corporation (now a subsidiary of Met Life), described Donald for the same article as "very bright, very gracious. He has an accommodating style. He's the type of person who is an excellent leader … that smart combination of strength and empathy that I think resonates with many people."

By acquiring Equal, Canderel, and other sugar substitutes, which accounted for over a third of the global market share of tabletop sweeteners, Donald immediately became head of a $400 million business. "All of us are excited about our shift from a company division to a stand-alone business," Donald announced to Joe Ruklick for the *Chicago Defender* (March 21, 2000). "The company is the undisputed leader in the tabletop sweetener market, and there are huge opportunities in foreign countries." In order to increase sales of Equal, Merisant's best-known product in the United States, Donald wanted to both strengthen its hold in the tabletop market as a sweetener for coffee and tea and to promote its uses in baking. "Equal should be a household staple," he told Thomas Lee. "People who don't even use ketchup have ketchup in their homes. Why? For friends who come to visit, for guests. It's a staple." In 2002 *Fortune* magazine identified Donald as one of the 50 most powerful black executives in America. In 2003, however, Donald resigned as CEO of Merisant while retaining his post as chairman, turning over many of his previous duties to Etienne Veber, the former chief operating officer of the company.

One of the first actions Donald took as head of Merisant was to announce the formation of the Equal Foundation, a nonprofit organization dedicated to combating diabetes, which Donald described to the *Los Angeles Sentinel* (June 13, 2001) as a "health threat of enormous proportions in the African American community." He added, "The rate of increase in diabetes cases among African American adults is at an all time high—and more than one-third of those afflicted with the disease don't even know they have it." Initially through United Way fund-raising leadership roles while at Monsanto, Donald had long been an active supporter of the Juvenile Diabetes Research Foundation (JDRF). A few years after leaving Merisant, he held a national fund-raiser for JDRF at his home attended by JDRF's president and CEO, Peter Van Etten. Unbeknownst to Donald, Van Etten was about to announce his retirement, and he recommended Donald to the JDRF as his successor. When the position was offered, Donald—after considering the demands raised by heading a nonprofit, at which his chief allegiance would be to donors, as opposed to heading a for-profit, at which his goal would be maximizing profit for shareholders—accepted. He served as president and CEO of JDRF from January 2006 to February 2008, when he resigned owing to "family matters." Two years later he took up the same roles for the Executive Leadership Council, where he remained from November 2010 until June 2012.

"Have three people do five jobs but pay them like four."

When Donald became president and chief executive officer of the cruise and vacation company Carnival Corporation in July 2013, the company was facing dire challenges. In January 2012 its Costa Concordia, carrying 4,252 passengers, had sunk off the coast of Italy, causing 32 deaths. Then, in February, the Costa Allegra caught fire in the Indian Ocean and was left drifting without power for three days. A year later, in February 2013, the Costa Triumph experienced a similar fire in the Gulf of Mexico and drifted for four days without power before it could be towed to port. These catastrophes had a cumulative effect on the cruise industry as a whole, and particularly on Carnival. Chairman and CEO Micky Arison, the son of the company's founder, stepped down as CEO while remaining as chairman, and Donald—who had been a member of the company's board for some 12 years—was brought in to retrieve the company's fortunes. A cruise aficionado, although without experience in the industry, Donald he was well aware that he was considered an unconventional choice for the position. "When someone says I have no cruise experience, I guess I could be funny and just say: I've cruised a lot," Donald told the Associated Press in June 2014. "The reality is, business is business."

After taking over in July 2013, Christopher Palmeri and Carol Massar wrote for Bloomberg, Donald began "implementing changes that include a $700 million investment in shipboard fire prevention and back-up power systems, a new marketing campaign and an effort to get Carnival's 10 cruise lines to collaborate and become more efficient." Palmeri and Massar noted that "Carnival was already deep into a public-relations makeover when Donald ascended to CEO," with a new "vacation guarantee" and the "Moments that Matter" ad campaign featuring customers' home movies. Donald undertook a five-year evaluation of all of Carnival's cruise lines, brought the lines' management together, and sought previously untapped economies of scale. In particular he made a concentrated effort to repair frayed relations with cruise booking agents, which had suffered as the result of an automated online booking service Carnival offered. Carnival's share price rose modestly, but the discounts offered to entice customers hurt the bottom line. Carnival expected a full recovery to take until 2015.

Donald married his wife, Hazel, when both were sophomores at Carleton College; they had met on the school's campus when each was a visiting high-school student. The couple have three children, Radiah, Alicia, and Stephen Zachary. The Donalds live in Town and Country, Missouri. Donald credits affirmative action with providing him with many opportunities when he was a young man; he and his wife, who are ardent supporters of educational causes, created the Donald Scholars Program, which provides scholarships for two students per year from St. Augustine or Xavier University Preparatory School to attend the Donalds' alma mater, Carleton. They also were the founders and original sponsors of a summer program through which 50 African American high-school juniors spend a week at Carleton, expense-free, and they have served as co-chairs of the Charmaine Chapman Society, which recognizes African Americans who give $1,000 or more to the annual United Way campaign in St. Louis. Donald recalled for the Carleton College Web site (March 1, 2001) that when he and his wife attended the university, they were two of but a few black students. Some of their white classmates "would ask to touch our hair. … They hadn't had any exposure to African Americans and it was honest curiosity on their part. The campus was inviting and warm, but there was still a lot of [racial] separation." Through their donations to and other support of the college, Donald and his wife sought to diversify the student body in the hopes of adding to the quality of the educational experience for all students at Carleton.

Interviews with Donald appeared in the film *The Director's Dilemmas* (2005), which was co-developed by professors at Washington University, in St. Louis, Missouri, in conjunction with a St. Louis law firm. The film, created mainly for teaching purposes, examines questions of ethics that face the heads of major corporations, by interspersing a story about the dilemmas of a fictional company with insights from actual CEOs.

Donald sits on the boards of numerous institutions, including Bank of America, BJC HealthCare, Crown Holdings, Laclede Group, and Oil-Dri Corporation, and Washington University. He is a trustee of Carleton College, Dillard University, and Washington University in St, Louis and is a member of the Dean's Council for Harvard University's Kennedy School of Government. Donald has supported and served as a board member for many of St. Louis's educational and cultural institutions, including the United Way of Greater St. Louis; the St. Louis Art Museum; the Missouri Botanical Garden; the Opera Theatre of St. Louis; the St. Louis Science Center, and the St. Louis Regional Commerce and Growth Association. He was appointed to serve on the President's Export Council for international trade in November 1998 and reappointed in 2003. Donald has also won a number of awards, among them the Washington University Distinguished Alumni Award (1998), the Eagle Award from the National Eagle Leadership Institute (1999), and the Black Engineers President's Award (2000).

Further Reading:

Associated Press, Jun. 5, 2014

Black Enterprise p107 Sep. 30, 1997

Bloomberg News Nov. 25, 2013

Chicago Defender Mar. 21, 2000

Diabetes Close Up November 2006

Ebony Apr. 2006

Los Angeles Sentinel p10 June 13, 2001

merisant.com

New York Times Jun. 24, 2007, Feb. 28, 2008

St. Louis American Jun. 27, 2013

St. Louis Commerce Magazine Apr. 1, 2002

St. Louis (Missouri) *Post-Dispatch* E p1 Jan. 13, 2002

Ghermezian, Eskander

Canadian real-estate and retail developer

Born: 1939 or 1940, Tehran, Iran

Eskander Ghermezian heads a North American real-estate and retail empire. After his late father, Jacob, made the family a fortune by trading and selling Persian rugs upon immigrating to Canada from Iran, Eskander and his three younger brothers took over business operations in the 1970s and multiplied the family's wealth by astutely investing in property in the western Canadian province of Alberta. In 1981 the future linchpin of the family's wealth was unveiled: the West Edmonton Mall, a sprawling complex that promised to be Western Canada's largest mall for decades to come. Over the course of several expansion efforts, the mall became the largest in the entire world, a spectacle and a tourist attraction that not only drew Canadian shoppers and landmark seekers, but also those from the United States willing to drive hundreds of miles to see what Eskander and his brothers dubbed "the eighth wonder of the world."

The Ghermezians' first major venture in the United States was Minnesota's Mall of America, the largest mall in the nation and a tourist attraction in its own right. Jacob Ghermezian had been born into a Jewish family in 1902 in Azerbaijan, a region bordering present-day Russia and Iran; when he was in his late 30s, he moved with his wife, Nenehjan (later anglicized to Miriam), to Tehran, Iran, to start a carpet-export business. (Carpet trading had been a family vocation since the mid-18th-century). He soon became successful enough to establish foreign offices in France and Italy. Eskander (his name is often spelled *Eskandar*) Ghermezian was born in 1939 or 1940 (sources differ); within the span of five years, Miriam gave birth to three more sons--Nader, Raphael, and Bahman. The home in Tehran became a gathering place for Allied military brass during World War II. (The Ghermezians have claimed that the Tehran Conference--a 1943 meeting between Franklin Roosevelt, Winston Churchill, and Josef Stalin regarding the formation of a united force against the Nazis--occurred at their house.)

Growing up in Tehran was lively for the siblings. The five-story building in which they resided was home to their extended family of 65. The four brothers have credited their memory of the bazaars of Tehran, in which a bevy of merchants offered a wide range of wares to wandering shoppers, as the inspiration for the malls they would develop in their adulthoods.

Jacob had soon attained such prestige that he served in the postwar government under Muhammad Reza Pahlavi, the last Shah of Iran. Yet the patriarch eventually sent his children to the West. In 1959 Eskander, Nader, and Raphael enrolled in a business program at Montreal's McGill University. The brothers quickly opened a Persian rug shop in that city. Jacob, Miriam, and Bahman, the youngest brother, joined them in Montreal in 1963. Jacob had incorporated the Montreal rug-importing business under the name Ghermezian Brothers in 1962, and by 1964 the enterprise had grown to 16 stores, many in the United States. Using their now-considerable wealth, Jacob's sons invested in land, purchasing thousands of acres in Edmonton, the capital of Alberta, shortly after oil was found in the region. The entire clan moved from Montreal to Edmonton during the mid-1960s, and by the end of the decade, they owned 15,000 acres of Edmonton land. The family founded Ghermez Developments Limited in 1967, and during the next several years they continued to buy land, reselling some of it for a profit and building offices and apartment buildings on other parcels. In 1973 they changed the name of the firm to Triple Five Corporation Limited. Jacob soon relinquished control of Triple Five to Eskander, and each of the brothers carved out his own specialty in the family empire: Eskander handled the finance and construction of projects, Raphael focused on legal matters, Nader became the spokesman and primary intermediary with local governments, and Bahman concentrated on real estate and operations.

Although the family had become the largest private landholder in Edmonton, they received little media attention. The brothers' business practices first caught the public eye in May 1974, when a city alderman accused Raphael of offering him a $40,000 bribe. A lengthy inquiry followed, but the brothers were cleared of any wrongdoing. Many, however, have credited the accusation and the ensuing controversy for the family's reclusiveness over the next several decades. Still, their reluctance to be in the spotlight did not prevent them from aggressively pursuing several lucrative projects. During 1979 and 1980, the Ghermezians sold seven parcels of land to the local government for a total of $22 million, making a tremendous profit--three of the seven properties had been purchased for a total of $199,000 and were sold for a total of $5.6 million. Even though Alberta's economy was floundering in the early 1980s, Triple Five continued to thrive and expand. While the brothers had bought much of their land for prices ranging from $100 to $200 an acre in the 1960s, by the early 1980s much of their land was worth about $40,000 an acre.

In 1974 the brothers had announced ambitious plans to build a massive shopping complex. The West Edmonton Mall was finally completed in 1981; encompassing 1.2 million square feet and containing 225 stores, it was Western Canada's largest shopping center. It produced $113 million in revenues its first year. The brothers decided to double the mall's size shortly after its initial construction, but instead of merely including more stores, the Ghermezians--inspired by a landscaper's suggestion that they include a carousel in the addition--decided to construct an entire amusement park. Eskander was particularly excited by the amusement park idea, and, during a research trip to a Kansas City theme park, he convinced his brothers to agree to the purchase of several state-of-the-art rides. The brothers placed the new rides in a 50,000-square-foot corner of the mall. The expansion also included a National Hockey League-sized skating rink, saltwater aquariums, and aviaries. This second phase was completed in September 1983; the mall now encompassed about 2.8 million square feet and included more than 400 stores.

For the third phase of the mall, begun shortly after the second phase was completed, the Ghermezians envisioned a tourist attraction that would draw world travelers to their doors. They decided to construct an enormous artificial lake, complete with sharks; a replica of one of Christopher Columbus's ships, the *Santa Maria* (three-quarters the size of the original); and submarines visitors could ride. Also included in the third phase were an indoor roller coaster, movie theaters, video-game arcades, car showrooms, and an 18-hole miniature golf course. With the completion of the third phase, the mall now included 836 stores and encompassed five million square feet: it won places in the 1986 *Guinness Book of World Records* for being the world's largest shopping center and for having the world's largest parking lot (which provided spaces for 30,000 cars).

By November 1985 the mall was drawing a weekend crowd exceeding 400,000 visitors, nearly half from outside Alberta. In 1986 two more additions, both Eskander's ideas, were added: the World Waterpark, complete with a wave pool, and the Fantasyland Hotel, whose theme rooms were inspired by Las Vegas's Caesars Palace hotel. In response to detractors who accused the mall of drawing customers away from other Edmonton businesses, the Ghermezians countered that the people they drew to the city also patronized other businesses and that the mall raised significant tax revenue for Edmonton. (Sales in 1985 exceeded $560 million.) Still, by 1985 the company had gained a negative reputation by aggressively lobbying the Edmonton city council for tax and rezoning concessions. Even though the mall gained additional negative publicity in June 1986--when one of its roller coasters jumped off the rails, killing three people and causing the ride to be temporarily shut down--by October 1986 more than 100,000 people, about 40 percent of whom came from the United States, walked through its doors every day.

By the mid-1980s the Ghermezians controlled a real-estate empire of about $1.5 billion in assets, and by late 1986 Triple Five held about $4.3 billion in assets, making it one of Canada's biggest firms. Aside from the West Edmonton Mall, the brothers owned several high-rise apartment buildings, six hotels, and a popular Edmonton nightclub. Looking to expand into other markets, in July 1985 the Ghermezians secured a deal to build a megamall, dubbed the Mall of America, in Bloomington, Minnesota, a suburb of the twin cities of Minneapolis and Saint Paul. However, the new project was hindered by cash-flow problems, when a Triple Five effort to convert the West Edmonton Mall's short-term financing to long-term loans failed in late 1986. The Ghermezians began to sell off some of Triple Five's assets, including holdings in a retail and office complex and a large apartment development project.

The Ghermezians soon agreed to halve the size of the Mall of America as they had originally envisioned it, and they negotiated a 22.5 percent stake in its ownership. While they assisted in the development of the project, the Ghermezians remained largely silent partners. The lead developer was Melvin Simon and Associates, run by Melvin Simon and his brother Herb, who also controlled a 22.5 percent stake. The majority stake in the Mall of America—55 percent—was owned by the Teachers Insurance and Annuity Association of America (now known as TIAA-CREF), a pension fund. The Mall of America, which cost about $700 million to build, opened in 1992.

Financial difficulties and failed negotiations with local authorities led the Ghermezians to shelve other expansion efforts, including malls in Niagara Falls and Toronto and other large development projects in West Germany and England. Despite the earlier setbacks, in 1989 Citibank Canada announced that it had sold $350 million worth of mortgage bonds for Triple Five property (a mortgage is a loan using real estate as collateral) to several large Ontario institutions. The $350 million was divided into two large loans, of $300 and $50 million, both of which collected significantly lower interest rates than Triple Five was currently paying. Citibank also arranged a $100 million long-term loan for Triple Five. The agreement was perceived as a vote of confidence on the part of the Ontario financial community on the sustainability of the Ghermezians' business interests. The loans, however, did not prevent cash-flow problems from continuing to sour relations between the Ghermezians and Alberta officials, who remained frustrated with the Ghermezians for failing to pay taxes on time and grew increasingly impatient with the brothers' demands for tax concessions.

The first of the Citibank loans (the $300 million mortgage) was due in 1994, five years after it was issued. When the Ghermezians defaulted on the loan, the West Edmonton Mall was in danger of being taken over by creditors, led by the Toronto-based Gentra Canada Investments. By September 1994 the West Edmonton Mall was nearly $500 million in debt. Vacancies at the mall had increased, and management had sold many of the animals formerly kept at the mall to zoos. Yet, the Ghermezians announced on November 7, 1994 that they were now able to secure the refinancing, had repaid their creditors in full, and remained owners of the mall and all its property through the new WEM Holdings Incorporated. They did not announce how they had accomplished the refinancing.

Despite their newfound relative financial security, the Ghermezians remained largely unsuccessful in their efforts to expand outside of Edmonton. In September 1995 they began to lobby for the construction of a megamall in Silver Spring, Maryland, a suburb of Washington, D.C., but in the face of local opposition (largely resulting from concerns over the traffic congestion the mall could conceivably bring the city) the project failed. Redirecting their focus to Edmonton, in 1997 the Ghermezians repurchased Edmonton's Plaza Hotel, which they had built and sold in 1991, and embarked on a fourth phase to expand the West Edmonton Mall by adding a 10-story hotel, another cinema complex, an IMAX screen, and a large zoo. (Following the completion of phase three, the mall housed a total of 2,000 exotic birds and 400 mammals scattered throughout the premises, and the complex retained a zoo accreditation, even though the dwellings and treatment of the animals had been grounds for concern from environmental organizations.)

In August 1998 the Alberta Treasury Branches (ATB) bank announced that they had uncovered several illicit aspects to the November 1994 West Edmonton Mall bailout. Officials at the bank revealed that the ATB had granted the Ghermezians and the mall a $420 million loan ($65 million interest-free for 30 years, and a $353 million loan through Toronto Dominion Bank) and had given the family the rights to manage the mall for 99 years, beginning in 2000; there had been no rational reason why an earlier offering, which awarded management of the mall to the creditors led by Gentra, had not been accepted instead. At the time of the 1998 announcement, the ATB was mired in other accusations of bribery and illicit lending practices, mostly through its previous management. Officials of the ATB accused their former acting superintendent, Elmer Leahy, of accepting bribes totaling about $250,000 from the Ghermezians, and requested that Canadian courts negate the 1994 deal. In response to the suit, the Ghermezians, denying the bribery allegations, filed a counter-suit against the ATB. They claimed that Gentra, whose headquarters were not in Alberta, had been squeezed out of the deal not by Leahy alone, but by the Alberta government, which had exerted undue pressure on the ATB to keep the mall under local management.

The following year the Ghermezians took the role of plaintiff in a court case, when they filed a suit against the Simon brothers, codevelopers of the Mall of America, for secretly negotiating the acquisition of a 27.5 percent stake from TIAA-CREF, which gave the Simons a controlling portion of the mall. The Ghermezians claimed they had been denied a chance to make the purchase themselves and sued for the option to buy the stake for the same price. (They also accused the Simons of physically threatening members of Triple Five's staff.)

The Ghermezians have earned a reputation as masters of litigation, and they proved their mettle in both the ATB and the Simon lawsuits. The ATB suit was settled out of court in December 2002, and, despite media clamor, the settlement was kept confidential; the Ghermezians remained owners of the mall. In September 2003 the Ghermezians attained a managing and controlling stake in the Mall of America, when a Minnesota judge ordered the Simons to sell 27.5 percent of the mall to Triple Five for $81.4 million; the management of the mall was officially transferred in August 2004.

By October 2004 the West Edmonton Mall covered the area of 48 city blocks, and contained seven theme parks, more than 800 stores, more than 110 restaurants, 26 movie theaters, and an IMAX screen. It drew more than 20 million visitors a year.

The family has purchased substantial real estate in the Las Vegas area and have focused much of their efforts on developing upscale shopping venues. Aside from their malls and property investments, the Ghermezians also own holdings in technology, finance, and venture-capital interests. They are also known for their philanthropic contributions to local Edmonton and Canadian causes.

At the behest of Miriam, the family matriarch, the Ghermezians began practicing Orthodox Judaism in 1981. Though they work for 12 to 16 hours a day, six days a week, the brothers rest on the Jewish Sabbath. Miriam is said to have chosen all four of her sons' wives. The couples each have at least six children, giving Miriam more than 30 grandchildren. Jacob Ghermezian died on January 3, 2000 at age 97.

Eskander and his wife, Deborah, married in about 1970. Two of their sons, David, born in about 1972, and Don, born in about 1973, have recently become more involved in the business decisions of the Ghermezian empire. (For the past several years Eskander has made occasional references to his possible retirement.) Both have earned business degrees; David has assisted in the development of the family's holdings in Nevada and Arizona, and Don helps manage the West Edmonton Mall.

The Ghermezians are all fervent Edmonton Oilers hockey fans. Although Eskander and his brothers are fluent in English, they often interrupt their business negotiations to converse among themselves in Farsi or French.

There is not extensive information on Eskander—or the Ghermezians as a whole. "The family is secretive," Jeff German and Steve Kanigher reported in the *Las Vegas Sun* (May 15, 2006), "which is why very little is known about them….During rare interviews, they have declined to answer personal questions and almost never agree to be photographed."

Further Reading:

Calgary Sun p22 Aug. 27, 1998, with photo

Canadian Business p68 Sep. 1994

Edmonton Journal A p14 Jan. 7, 2000, with photo, D p6 Nov. 4, 2001, with photo, F p1 Sep. 20, 2002

Las Vegas Sun (May 15, 2006)

Maclean's p34 Apr. 15, 1985, p14 Dec. 22, 1986, with photo, p36 Oct. 4, 2004

New York Times C p1 Sep. 12, 2003

Ottawa Citizen H p4 Dec. 21, 2002

(Minneapolis) *Star Tribune* A p1 Aug. 9, 1992, D p1 Apr. 9, 2000, A p11 Aug. 6, 2002 *Washington Post* A p1 Nov. 25, 1985, K p7 Aug. 10

Ho, Stanley

Business executive and gambling mogul

Born: 1921, Hong Kong

A former Portuguese colony composed of two small islands and a small piece of land barely touching mainland China, Macao—now a Chinese special administrative region with a population of some 560,000— attracts 30 million tourists each year. Most of these visitors come to Macao for one reason: to gamble. In order to do so, they almost inevitably do business with ventures launched by Stanley Ho, whose gambling empire made him one of the wealthiest people in Asia. Ho held exclusive gambling rights in the territory for 40 years, through 2002, and he expanded his empire in Macao to include most of the region's transportation, hotel, and restaurant accommodations as well. His gambling operations proved so successful that Macao was labeled the "Las Vegas of Asia." (The earnings of the gambling industry in Macao surpassed those of Las Vegas in 2006 and now far outstrip them; in 2013 Macao's gambling take was seven times that of Las Vegas.) Ho's holdings were extensive enough that by the mid-1990s, taxes collected on his gambling operations by the Macanese government amounted to about 50 percent of the territory's revenue.

Although competing casinos entered Macao in 2003, Ho's grip on Macao's gambling industry remained secure. His flagship hotel and casino, the Hotel Lisboa, opened in 1970, continued to be a prime Macao destination. It is still a property of the privately held holding company Ho founded, Sociedade de Turismo e Diversões de Macau ("Macao Tourism and Amusement Company," or STDM). Ho's gambling interests also included a horse-racing track, run by the Macau Jockey Club, and the Canidrome, a dog-racing venue. In 1972 Ho formed Shun Tak Holdings, through which he made substantial investments in transportation and real estate that neatly complemented his casino interests. Shun Tak was listed on the Hong Kong Stock Exchange from 1973.

According to its website, STDM's publicly traded subsidiary Sociedade de Jogos de Macau (SJM) currently operates 18 casinos in Macao as well as the Grand Lisboa Hotel, adjacent to the Hotal Lisboa. SJM also has a 51 percent stake in the Sofitel Macau at Ponte 16, and in February 2014 it broke ground on its most ambitious project yet, the Lisboa Palace, on Cotai, now considered Macao's premier location. STDM itself is controlled by a holding company, Lanceford, originally founded by Ho with himself as the sole owner, with just two shares. In 2011 a maneuver for control of Lanceford precipitated the succession struggle over Ho's fortune.

In 2011, according to *Forbes,* Ho's personal wealth was about US$3.1 billion, and he was the thirteenth-richest person in Hong Kong. In 2012, however, his name was absent from the *Forbes* list. In 2011, in a closely watched and controversial transition, Ho's business interests were divided among his three surviving wives and his many children. Ho had four "wives": Clementina Leitão, whom he married in 1942; Lucina Laam King-ying, whom he legally married in Hong Kong, in 1962; Ina Chan Un-chan, who became Ho's third "wife" in 1985; and Angela Leong On-kei, whom he met in 1988. (Hong Kong made multiple marriages illegal in 1972 but honored those that existed before that.) Whatever the legalities of his marriages, Ho viewed all of them as equal. He expressed a desire to apportion his wealth equally among his four families, which grew to include 17 children, 11 daughters and six sons (the eldest of whom died in an automobile accident in 1981). After considerable dissension and the filing and then withdrawal by Ho of a lawsuit seeking an injunction against his second and third wives and five of his children (as well as his longtime banker), Ho in March 2011 declared himself satisfied that his wishes had been accomplished.

On the 2014 *Forbes* list of Hong Kong's Richest people, two of Stanley Ho's children from his second marriage, Pansy Ho and Lawrence Ho, were ranked ninth and twelfth, respectively; Pansy Ho's net worth was set at $6.8 billion and Lawrence Ho's at $3.4 billion. Angela Leong, a Macau legislator, was ranked nineteenth richest, at $2.86 billion. Ina Chan appeared among the top 50.

Education and Early Career

Stanley Ho Hung-sun was born into a prestigious family in Hong Kong on November 25, 1921. His mother was Portuguese, and his father, Ho Sai-Kwong, came from Hong Kong's Hotung family, famous for its relationship with foreign merchants based in Hong Kong. Ho Fook, Stanley's grandfather, had worked as a comprador—a Chinese middleman in business affairs—for the British trading house Jardine Matheson & Company. Ho Sai-Kwong worked as a comprador for the Sassons, a Baghdadi Jewish family that manufactured and traded goods in East Asia; Sassons was one of the larger firms in Hong Kong. The Hos had a comfortable middle-class lifestyle during the 1920s and early 1930s, but Ho Sai-Kwong lost all of his money in the stock market in 1934 as a result of a series of unsuccessful stock trades. Disgraced and broke, he fled to Saigon, Vietnam, leaving his wife and their 13 children, including 13-year-old Stanley, destitute. Because of their misfortune, Ho's family was shunned even by relatives. "People would turn their face on me when they saw me on the street," Ho recalled to Tony Wong of the *Toronto Star* (February 11, 1990). "I learned to be truly humble." Despite his poverty Ho excelled academically, and his achievements entitled him to scholarships for high school and, later, Hong Kong University, where he studied science. His schooling was interrupted, however, by World War II. Japanese forces marched into Hong Kong in 1941; during the siege, Ho volunteered to be a telephone operator in the air raid warden's office. After eight days of battle, Hong Kong soldiers surrendered to the Japanese. Finding his way aboard a junket boat, Ho left Hong Kong for Macao, where he had an uncle. Macao, leased by China to Portugal for almost 400 years, shared Portugal's neutral status and was safe from Japanese attacks.

After working briefly for his uncle, Ho landed a secretarial job in a large trading firm, and he quickly rose through its ranks. One of his early triumphs at the firm was negotiating exclusive rights for trade between Macao and Japanese-occupied Hong Kong. Machinery, surplus parts, and boats were given to the Japanese in return for food—badly needed to feed a growing population of war refugees. One year after he started, Ho became a partner in the company, and was given a one-million-pataca bonus. (The pataca is the Macanese currency, currently pegged to the Hong Kong dollar; according to one of Ho's Web sites, the average Macanese resident at the time of his raise made 35 patacas a month). One of his responsibilities as a partner was accompanying the firm's ships carrying goods between Macao and other Japanese-occupied territories; these trips were dangerous and often subject to pirate attacks. Using his newfound wealth, Ho established his own companies trading gold, toys, and textiles, and he also bought and developed real estate in Hong Kong after the war.

In 1961 the Portuguese-appointed Macanese government decided to auction off exclusive gambling rights for the territory. The government suspected that the previous holders of the monopoly, the Fus, were cheating them out of tax income. Ho and a consortium of business partners—including the Hong Kong property and construction tycoon Henry Fok, Ho's brother-in-law Teddy Yip, and the famous gambler Yip Hon—successfully bid for the rights for their company, Sociedade de Turismo e Diversões de Macao, to operate Macao's gambling enterprises. STDM won the rights in part because it pledged to upgrade Macao's infrastructure and transportation system. The promise was lucrative for STDM: the company built high-speed ferries to shuttle gamblers between Macao and Hong Kong and opened high-quality hotels and restaurants, increasing foreign interest in visiting the region. The Casino Estoril, the first of Ho's casinos, opened in 1962. Ho added new professional touches to his casinos by dressing his croupiers in uniform and introducing such games as blackjack and baccarat, which joined Chinese games of chance. In 1970 STDM opened the Hotel Lisboa, with a 24-hour casino; in 1972 Ho formed Shun Tak Holdings Limited. In 1982 Ho bought out the portion of STDM owned by Yip Hon, one of the original partners in the company, for about $350 million.

Later Career

Because STDM is a privately owned company, it does not reveal yearly profits to the press. Many observers, however, have estimated its yearly profits based on the taxes it supplies to the Macanese government, which levies gambling operations a specific percentage (now 35 percent but with additional levies that can bring the total to 40 percent) of their yearly revenue. According to such estimates, STDM's gambling revenues increased by some 40 percent over 1985–1988, and from 1988 to 1990, revenues more than doubled. Shun Tak's yearly profits, available to the public, nearly tripled between 1986 and 1987. The leap in profits between 1986 and 1987 was caused largely by the increasing amount of traffic between Hong Kong and Macao. That increase was due in part to eased travel restrictions between Hong Kong and Macao; legislation had passed allowing Hong Kong residents to show only their Hong Kong identity card, not their passport, to travel to Macao.

Stanley Ho brought air travel to Macao. From the late 1970s he had pushed for the construction of an airport in the territory, and in 1989 STDM, in an alliance with the Macao government and a Chinese company, began to build one. Macao International Airport was completed in December 1995. Air Macao, of which Ho owned a major part, made the first flight. (In early 2011 STDM owned 33 percent of the airport and 14 percent of Air Macao, which in 2006 launched Air Macao Express, a low-cost carrier.) Ho also made large investments in another airline, Air Hongkong. Ho founded Hong Kong Express Airways Limited, incorporated in March 2004, and in 2006 sold a 45 percent stake in the carrier to the HNA Group, the parent company of Hainan Airlines, which in 2013 converted Hong Kong Express to a low-cost carrier. Shun Tak Holdings in June 2013 acquired a one-third share in Jetstar Hong Kong, a joint venture of Australia's Qantas Airways and Shanghai-based China Eastern Airlines Corporation currently seeking a license to operate out of Hong Kong's phenomenally busy airport. Shun Tak's involvement was thought to fulfill the regulatory requirement that applicants be incorporated in Hong Kong and have a principal place of business in the territory.

Ho was widely suspected of having ties to criminal gangs, most notably to Chinese criminal societies called Triads, but he long denied connections to these groups. Ho was exonerated from ties to organized crime in a 1992 U.S. Senate Committee Hearing investigating the Triads, although the hearing linked several of Ho's associates, including his former partner Yip Hon, to known criminal organizations. Concerns regarding Ho's possible criminal connections increased in the mid-1990s, when crime became a problem in Macao. Several reporters traced the origin of the increase in crime to Ho's opening of VIP rooms to "high rollers," beginning in the mid-1980s: "high rollers" were defined by their ability to spend, and some of the guests had criminal connections. Claiming that no violence ever occurred in the casinos themselves, Ho denied any connection between crime and the VIP rooms, instead pointing to the crackdown on the Triads by Hong Kong police (in anticipation of the city's handover to China in 1997) and similar police enforcement in Taiwan as the cause for an exodus of the area's criminal element to Macao. Ho claimed that criminal gangs, having fled to the tiny quarters of Macao, were waging war against each other; he also blamed the violence on the leniency of the Portuguese court system, which, unlike China's, did not impose the death penalty on Triad members. The crime wave, which resulted in the deaths of several government and foreign officials, threatened the financial stability of Macao. "People say that Macao is becoming a little dangerous," Ho told a reporter for the *Financial Times* (February 15, 1997). "And this naturally will affect business." While the years before had shown significant growth, revenues for Ho's operations fell between 1995 and 1996. Shun Tak was further weakened by the Asian financial crisis of the late 1990s.

In the midst of Macao's troubles with crime, the territory's administration was transferred from Portugal to China in 1999. In 1974 Macao had been declared a Chinese territory, but the government was still Portuguese; 13 years later, the Chinese and Portuguese governments agreed to return the island to Chinese administration in 1999, agreeing on December 20, 1999, as the date of transfer. As early as 1987, the Chinese government announced that gambling would continue to be legal in Macao, but that citizens from the mainland, where gaming was forbidden, would not be allowed to gamble there. Hong Kong citizens, however, could legally patronize Ho's establishments. (In 2009, however, 90 percent of visitors to Macao were from Hong Kong and mainland China.) Despite media speculation that the Chinese government might try to curb his gambling business, Ho displayed little worry about the transition. "It will be the same pattern like in Hong Kong but it will be even smoother … there will be no confrontation up to the end because we have no democrats and this question of human rights will not come out," he told Greg Torode for Hong Kong's *South China Morning Post* (March 14, 1998).

The handover, which relinquished one of the last colonies of Europe's imperial era, indeed occurred without incident. One of the positive results of the transition, at least for Ho's business interests, was the serious action taken by Chinese authorities against crime in Macao; the Chinese government decided to dispatch an army unit to Macao, partially to manage the crime problem. One prominent triad gang leader was arrested and given a long prison sentence; another leader and two of his associates were executed in mainland China after being convicted of criminal activities. Over the next three years, the violence in the area was reduced to more manageable levels. There were 11 murders in Macao in 2000 and nine in 2001, down from 40 in 1999. According to Bertil Lintner, writing for the *Far Eastern Economic Review* (May 2007), in Macao the triads were long known to "manage VIP rooms, offer junket tours, and lend money to gamblers in need." Under Chinese control, Lintner continued, "in fact, the rules have been liberalized, enabling the triads to operate more legitimately," and less violently.

Unflappable about the handover of Macao to Chinese authorities, Ho was more concerned with the prospect of the cancelation of his gambling monopoly in 2001. STDM's exclusive rights to gambling in the region had been renewed for ten years in 1986; two years before that contract was to expire, it was extended for another five years, until 2001. Ho was initially resistant to the idea of allowing competitors to operate in

Macao, explaining to reporters that competition could lead to lower prices and lower gambling tax revenues for the Macanese government; by late 2000, however, Ho spoke in favor of increasing competition. "I think it is quite fair," he told Mike Chinoy for CNN's International News (December 18, 2000). "We had it for 40 years, and it's really high time … to make some small changes so that there will be more competition. And they are hoping that this is one form of progress of development for the gaming industry. We don't mind." Twenty-one companies, including companies from the United States and Britain, applied in 2001 for one of the three gambling licenses the Macanese government was granting.

"Gaming should never be a win–lose proposition. There can be multiple winners: casino operators, government and society."

In February 2002 officials announced the licensees: Ho and STDM; Wynn Resorts, a Las Vegas-financed company; and Galaxy Casino Limited, a company built with private funding from Hong Kong and Macao. The license allows Ho's gambling operations to run uninterrupted until 2020. Each of the licensees was allowed to bring in one sub-concessionaire, an arrangement that resulted in six gaming licenses being granted in all. In December 2002 the Venetian Group (Las Vegas Sands) was authorized to operate casino gaming in Macao under a subconcession from Galaxy. In April 2005 SJM signed a subconcession contract with MGM Grand Paradise, and in September 2006 Wynn signed a subconcession contract with Melco PBL Gaming of Macau. In 2014 the six official licensees were SJM; the partnership of MGM Mirage and Pansy Ho Chiu-king; Wynn Resorts; Melco Crown Entertainment, a partnership headed by Lawrence Ho Yau-Long; Galaxy Entertainment Group; and Las Vegas Sands. Thus Pansy Ho and Lawrence Ho, both children of Stanley Ho's second marriage, hold gaming licenses of their own.

While none of Ho's international operations proved as lucrative as his Macao holdings, he acquired an array of worldwide investments. He invested in gambling operations and real estate in Australia, Portugal, Spain, Vietnam, South Korea, North Korea, Indonesia, Iran, Hong Kong, and mainland China. Real estate in Hong Kong surged in 1987 after China announced that capitalism in the city would be maintained, and Ho, president of the Real Estate Developers Association of Hong Kong, made a significant profit. He was also chairman of several of Hong Kong's Jumbo floating restaurants, which were major tourist draws. In late 1999 he invested heavily in restaurants and hotels in the Philippines, and he moved one of his Jumbo floating restaurants from Hong Kong to Manila. The president of the Philippines, Joseph Estrada, encouraged Ho's plans of investing in gambling there, but many Filipinos were resistant to Ho, fearing the arrival of a depraved gambling culture in the image of Macao's—Macao also was known for its prostitutes—and wary of Ho's alleged crime connections. Matters were complicated when Dante Tan, Ho's business partner in the Philippines, was investigated for fraudulent stock price manipulation and Estrada was accused of pressuring the chairman of the Philippines's Securities and Exchange Commission to clear Tan. Estrada's implication in the scandal—one of many that would result in his eventual ouster—caused the president to tone down his favorable stance toward Ho's investment in the islands. With dwindling support, Ho announced that he would not include the Philippines in any future development plans.

For more than a decade Ho was the chairman of Semi-Tech Microelectronics, a Canadian company founded by James Wei Ting in 1981. After Ho became chairman, Semi-Tech bought out the Singer Sewing

Machine Corporation, with Ho personally guaranteeing a substantial portion of the purchase price. Semi-Tech's revenues proceeded to increase 18 percent a year in the following four years, and the company was taken public in 1991. It purchased a number of other companies over the next seven years, including Sansui Electronics. The Asian financial crisis of 1997–1998 eventually sank the overextended company with the failure in 1999 of its main subsidiary, music equipment manufacturer Akai, in Hong Kong's largest corporate collapse. It emerged that Ting had sold the remaining Akai assets to Grande Holdings, a company founded by Ting, Stanley Ho, and Christopher Ho (a partner unrelated to Stanley Ho) in 1987. In the aftermath Grande Holdings itself filed for bankruptcy protection.

Ho financed a successful Internet gambling site that operated out of Antigua. The site was run by his son-in-law Peter Kjaer, the husband of Angela Ho, a daughter of Ho's first marriage, to Clementina Leitão.

In March 2002 Stanley Ho named one of his daughters, Pansy Ho, as the heir to his empire, and she was subsequently voted to the board of directors by STDM shareholders. She was given the responsibility of overseeing STDM's preparation to fashion Macao into a family tourist destination. Part of this plan was to build a theme park and the Macao Tower, housing a restaurant, a department store, and an entertainment center. The Tower, which was completed in 2001, ranked among the world's tallest buildings.

In November 2001 Sociedade de Jogos de Macau (SJM) was incorporated as a limited liability company. As the operating entity of STDM, in March 2002 it signed a gaming concession contract valid with the Macao Special Administrative Region, extending to 31 March 2020. Its operations commenced with 11 casinos. In November 2002 Ho organized another rearrangement of his holdings, increasing Shun Tak's interest in STDM from 5 percent to 11 percent, which gave investors an opportunity to speculate on increased revenues from Macao's new "family" orientation. Share prices soared. SJM's Grand Lisboa landmark hotel opened in February 2007 and the Casino Ponte 16 exactly a year later. After it was decided to take SJM public, Winnie Ho, the estranged sister of Stanley Ho, unsuccessfully attempted to block the initial public offering in court. In July 2008 SJM was listed on the Stock Exchange of Hong Kong. The company then had, and still has, by far the largest number of Macao casinos and the biggest share of gaming revenue among Macau's six licensed casino operators. In 2008–2009, government visa restrictions had an enormous impact on gambling revenue, temporarily bringing at least one operator, Las Vegas Sands, to the brink of collapse. Citing the Asian financial crisis, in March 2009 SJM announced that it would abandon a plan to buy the Hotel Lisboa and another site for development from its parent, STDM.

In 2010 SJM's gambling revenue at its casinos (14 of which are franchised operations owned by third parties) rose 43 per cent over the previous year's total, to HK$18.14 billion, an almost fourfold increase in profit. For 2013, despite some relative weakness in the VIP sector, SJM reported that its net profit had increased 14 percent, to HK$7.7 billion (approximately U.S. $992 million), surpassing forecasts. SJM's 2013 operating results, publicly released in February 2014, amply illustrate the continued exponential growth of casino gambling in Macau: on gaming revenue of HK$86,956 million (US$11,220 million), the company reported a profit of HK$7,706 million (US$994,322,000), an increase of 14.2 percent over 2012 results. The company reported its market share as 24.8 percent.

According to Shun Tak's 2013 annual report, the company has three major development projects on the Chinese mainland: Beijing Tongzhou Integrated Development Phase 2 and Beijing Dong Zhi Men Commercial Land Use Project (renamed the Shun Tak Tower, Beijing) in Beijing and the Hengqin Integrated Development in Zhuhai, a city northeast of Macao. In Macau itself Shun Tak's "signature project" is Nova City, a mixed commercial and residential development now in Phase 5 of construction. Shun Tak is also active in Hong Kong. In March 2014 Shun Tak reported its profit in 2013 as HK$1,406 million (US$181,419,350).

Set to open in 2017, SJM's Lisboa Palace complex on the "Cotai Strip"—reclaimed land joining the two islands of Coloane and Taipa; the term was coined and patented by the Las Vegas Sands Corporation for its own developments but is widely used for the reclaimed land generally—will include three hotels: the 270-room Palazzo Versace Macao, designed by the Versace fashion house; another 270-room "fashion-branded" luxury hotel designed by Karl Lagerfeld, head designer and creative director for Chanel and Fendi; and the five-star Lisboa Palace, with more than 1,450 rooms. In all, the complex will include approximately 27,000 square meters of gaming facilities, 34,000 square meters of retail shops, and 36,000 square meters of restaurants and entertainment facilities. The allocation of the built portion of the 7- hectare (approximately 17-acre) site reflects the government's current regulations on casinos, intended to encourage a family orientation and to limit growth. In an article for Reuters (February 18, 2014), Farah Master explained that, "Casino operators' efforts to diversify are likely to be a key consideration in renewing gaming licenses which start to expire in 2020. … Under the new rules, Macau is only granting gaming tables to casinos based on their non-gaming facilities—the more activities they offer to general tourists the more tables they will be allotted."

Ho's seven-month hospitalization following a fall in August 2009 intensified investors' concerns about the future of his gambling empire and his other business ventures. His first wife, Clementina, had died in 2004, and their eldest son, Robert, and his wife Melanie had perished in an automobile accident in Portugal in 1981. A bitter internal struggle among Ho's surviving wives and children for control of his assets became public in January 2011. In December 2010 Ho had conveyed his 7.7 percent stake in SJM to Angela Leong, positioning her as a contender to control the casino gambling business. Countering this move, third wife Ina Chan un-chan and Pansy, Daisy, Maisy, Josie and Lawrence, the children of Ho's second marriage, to Lucina Laam, took control of Lanceford, which holds the largest stake in STDM, by issuing 9,998 new stock shares effective on January 24, 2011. The following day a lawyer acting for Stanley Ho produced a letter written in early January in which Ho said that he had not agreed to the issuance of the shares; the lawyer asserted that certain family members had effectively seized Ho's assets without his consent. Before the end of the day, however, a public relations firm representing Lucina Laam and Ina Chan un-Chan released another letter from Ho saying that the transfer of control was not fraudulent, and expressing a wish not to involve lawyers in "family affairs." On January 26 a frail Ho appeared on television and, reading from a white board at the home of Ina Chan Un-chan in Hong Kong, confirmed the validity of the transfer. Later that day, however, he filed a lawsuit charging his second and third wives and his five children with his second wife, as well as his banker, with illegally taking control of Lanceford. The dispute was resolved in March, when Ho relinquished control of SJM, splitting up his 31.66 percent stake in STDM among his families. Angela Leong On-kei, managing director of SJM, received 6 percent of STDM, with other family members dividing the remaining 25.5 percent. The terms of the settlement made it possible for Pansy Ho and Lawrence Ho to pursue their several casino and other business interests while retaining their stake in STDM, provided they did not directly or indirectly control STDM and the latter's Macao casino investments are confined to SJM.

Writing in *Asia Times* (January 28, 2011), Muhammad Cohen assessed Stanley Ho's business acumen, noting Ho's success in meeting the challenges posed by glossy American competitors in the Macau casino business and in responding to the 2008–2009 global recession: "SJM rebounded following business principles that are Ho's hallmarks: letting the market guide business, rather than trying to guide the market;

investing wisely; and building partnerships, not just to lessen risk but to spread the rewards and create more stakeholders in shared success." Cohen cited Ho's own words in accepting the Global Gaming Expo Asia Visionary Award in June 2009: ""Gaming should never be a win-lose proposition. There can be multiple winners: casino operators, government and society. … "From society to society: this is my long term vision."

Aside from his investments, Ho is a philanthropist. He funds scholarships and has made major contributions to cultural institutions such as art festivals and opera in Hong Kong and Macao. In 1994 he contributed money to build the Franklin Delano Roosevelt Memorial in Washington, D.C. (The gift was later investigated as a possible illegal campaign contribution to President Bill Clinton.) In the 1980s Ho was honored by Pope John Paul II for his community work in Macao (ten percent of Macao is Catholic, a vestige from its days as a Portuguese colony). Ho has honorary doctorates from Macao's University of East Asia (1984) and the University of Hong Kong (1987).

Ho, who lives in Hong Kong, has several colorful nicknames, including "Mr. Macao," "Wong Tai Sin," (meaning the "god who fulfills peoples' wishes") and "Sun Gor" (which translates as "Big Brother Sun"). He enjoyed bird shooting, swimming, tennis, ballroom dancing, playing bridge, attending opera, and collecting art and luxury cars. He never gambled. "I don't have the patience," he told Elaine Kurtenbach of the Associated Press (May 30, 2001). "Don't expect to make money in gambling. It's a house game. It's for the house." Since his fall in 2009 and subsequent hospitalizations, Ho has rarely appeared in public, his appearances during the succession struggle being notable exceptions.

Further Reading:

Asia Times May 14, 2010, Jan. 28, 2011

Asian Business p18+ Sep. 1996

Asiaweek p22 June 22, 2001

Associated Press May 30, 2001, with photo

Australian Finance p32 Dec. 10, 2001

Businessweek p98 Jan. 19, 1987, with photo Aug. 4, 2002

Far Eastern Economic Review May 2007

Financial Times IV p4 June 1, 1983, with photo

Forbes Jan. 8, 2014

Perspectives p4 Feb. 15, 1997, II p45 Oct. 11, 1997, with photo, p22 Jan. 13, 2001

Manila Standard Oct. 23, 1999

New York Times, March 26, 2014

South China Morning Post p1 Jan. 31, 1993, May 18, 2011

Business p2 July 4, 1994, with photo, p1 Aug. 10, 1996, p1 Mar. 14, 1998, with photo, p1 Sep. 6, 2001, with photo, p3 Feb. 9, 2002

Reuters Jan. 2, 2014, Feb. 13, 2014

Shun Tak Group website

[Hong Kong] *Standard,* Feb. 1, 2011

Toronto Star D p1 Feb. 11, 1990, with photo

Keller, Thomas

Chef, restaurant owner, cookbook author

Born: 1955, Oceanside, California, United States

"Eating at chef Thomas Keller's famed Napa Valley restaurant The French Laundry makes me think of watching Fred Astaire," the food critic Patricia Wells wrote for her eponymous website (February 24, 2004). "When you watch the master dance, you only think about how much fun he must be having, it all looks so easy, so natural. It never crosses your mind that he is working about as hard as a human being can work. The truth is, no matter how hard the modest, talented Thomas Keller works, you can be sure he is having fun at it." According to *Food & Beverage International Magazine* (April 10, 2000), he is the "most respected American-born chef cooking in this country today." Julia Moskin of the *New York Times* (May 15, 2012) called Keller "a calm and kingly figure, representing both ends of the transition that has transformed fine dining from formal French dinners to anything-goes performance art in just a couple of decades. His cuisine at Per Se and The French Laundry has feet in both worlds." According to Moskin, Keller "view[s] the goal of haute cuisine as a seamless fusion of pleasure and art."

Keller began his career at the age of 17 at the Palm Beach Yacht Club, in Florida, when, with virtually no experience, he began cooking for club members. He has never attended a culinary school; rather, he gained his expertise as a restaurateur while on the job at various eating places in the United States in addition to the yacht club and while working as an apprentice in a half-dozen restaurants in France. He also learned a great deal as the co-founder/co-owner/chef of a restaurant in Florida that closed after a short time in the early 1970s, and of another in New York City—the much-praised Rakel, which opened in 1985 and closed in 1990. Keller's skills, knowledge, boundless culinary creativity, and perfectionism turned the French Laundry into a restaurant that many publications (among them *Esquire, Gourmet, Bon Appetit, USA Today, Food & Wine,* the *New York Times,* the *Los Angeles Times,* the *San Francisco Chronicle,* and *Wine Spectator*) have ranked among the finest in the United States. Keller "never tires of coming up with new, surprising, and well-executed variations of the possibilities of something as simple as an egg or a tomato," Dana Cowin, the editor in chief of *Food & Wine,* told Peter Kaminsky for *New York* magazine (January 5, 2004). "He explores every facet of an ingredient in every possible way—playfully yet intellectually and dramatically. I get the sense that he tries new flavors and dishes because he wants to please himself." Recalling Keller's execution of a signature dish, Beets and Leeks, longtime French Laundry maître'd Larry Nadeau told Paolo Lucchesi of the *San Francisco Chronicle* (SFGate, June 10, 2014), "It was a focus that I still have never seen, and an intensity that is rare. He just moved with a confidence that is hard to match. You can make all these analogies that sound silly, like somebody playing a violin. … It was just these fluid movements whether he was filleting a fish or putting sauce down."

Beginning in 1998, relinquishing some of the hands-on control for which he had become well known, Keller opened four bistro-style restaurants, all called Bouchon: the first in Yountville, a short walk from the French Laundry, and the others in Las Vegas, New York, and Beverly Hills. He also launched a Bouchon Bakery next to the Bouchon bistro in Yountville, after which, according to the Bouchon Bakery page at the Thomas Keller Restaurant Group website, "we wanted to open one near our other restaurants in Las Vegas, New York City and Beverly Hills to bake the bread for them and to add an additional layer of cafe life to the areas that surround them."

In February 2004, in what was described as his most ambitious project to date, Keller opened another fine-dining restaurant, Per Se, in the new Time Warner Center, in New York City. In the highly anticipated inaugural Michelin Guide for New York City in 2005, he was awarded three stars for Per Se, and the following year the inaugural Michelin Guide to the Bay Area gave the same honor to the French Laundry, making Keller the first American chef to hold simultaneous three-star Michelin ratings for two different restaurants. In Yountville, in 2006, Keller opened Ad Hoc, which serves prix-fixe "comfort food, "family style."

Keller was honored two years in succession by the James Beard Foundation, which bestows awards that are known as the Oscars of the culinary industry: in 1996 he was named the best chef in California, and in 1997 he won the Outstanding Chef of the Year Award. *The French Laundry Cookbook* (1999), which he wrote with Michael Ruhlman, garnered awards as well. Among other honors, Keller was inducted into the French Legion of Honor in 2011.

Education and Early Career

Thomas Keller was born on October 14, 1955 in Oceanside, California, to Edward Keller, a U.S. Marines drill instructor, and his wife, Betty. During his childhood his parents divorced; his mother then raised him and his siblings (he has several older brothers and a sister) in southern Florida. Keller's father remained distant for decades, but father and son reconciled late in Ed Keller's life. Thomas Keller's mother, according to different sources, owned or managed restaurants or clubs, among them the Palm Beach Yacht Club. "If I wanted to see my mom after school, I went to the yacht club," Keller told Florence Fabricant for the *New York Times Magazine* (December 11, 1988). "I wound up washing dishes or peeling potatoes. Otherwise, it was go home and eat chili dogs with my older brothers. I hated the kitchen." Nevertheless, as Kim Severson of the *New York Times* (October 27, 2009) observed, Keller "has often credited his mother, Betty Keller, for much of his success. She got him into the restaurant business and gave him his sense of adventure, ambition and aesthetics." After he graduated from high school, Keller took a dishwashing job at the yacht club. When its cook quit, his mother "moved him to the stoves," as Joel Stein put it in *Time* magazine (September 17, 2001). Keller prepared simple fare—hamburgers, sandwiches, salads, eggs. Sometimes, when a customer wanted something he had never cooked before, he would call his brother Joseph for guidance. (Joseph Keller is also an esteemed chef.) During this period, according to Stein, Keller attended a Florida college for two years, majoring in psychology. Feeling that he was "in a rut," as he put it to Fabricant—"I'm easily bored," he told her; "That's one of the reasons I keep trying different things"—he ended his employment at the club.

Keller next worked in a succession of restaurants in various places, among them Newport, Rhode Island; Lake Park, Florida; New York City; and the Catskill Mountains region of New York State. In some of them, he got hands-on instruction. "It was very mechanical, learning how to make hollandaise [sauce]," he told Dave Welch of Powells.com (October 18, 2000). "But it was a challenge, trying to make it perfect every day." He also learned "by asking stupid questions," as he recalled to Marian Burros of the *New York*

Times (October 16, 1996). In a restaurant in the Catskills, every night for three summers, he singlehandedly cooked for 80 people; he thereby "learned great organizational skills because I had to do it all myself," as he told Burros. His approach to and understanding of cooking began to change in about 1977, after he met Roland G. Henin, who was then the chef at a private club in Rhode Island and later the corporate executive chef for the companies that manage the restaurants and other concessions in Yosemite National Park, California. Through Henin, who became his mentor, Keller came to realize that cooking is not "about mechanics" but "about a feeling, wanting to give someone something, which in turn was really gratifying," as he told Dave Welch. "That really resonated for me. I wanted to learn everything I could about what it takes to be a great chef. It was a turning point for me."

Earlier, at age 21, Keller, along with two men who had no experience in the field, opened a restaurant in southern Florida. "It was my first taste of responsibility, managing people and being critiqued and learning the why of cooking," he told Burros. The venture failed after 18 months. "I became more focused after that and … I understood that I needed to know much, much, much more," Keller told Hattie Bryant for PBS's Small Business School website. In the early 1980s he worked at Raoul's, an expensive French restaurant in New York City, and then moved to the Westbury Hotel's Polo Lounge, also in New York, which had been set up shortly before by the now-celebrated chef Daniel Boulud. Later, in a conversation with Peter Kaminsky, Boulud described the young Keller's way of working as "boom, boom, get the job done, like clockwork." Next, Keller spent one and a half years in France, serving as an apprentice in the kitchens of such top-ranked restaurants as Guy Savoy, Gérard Besson, Taillevent, Le Toit de Passey, Chiberta, and Le Pré Catelan.

In 1985, back in New York, after working for others (among them La Réserve and Raphael) for a year or two, Keller opened the restaurant Rakel, in collaboration with Serge Raoul (the owner of Raoul's), in a former factory building in Lower Manhattan. Rakel soon attracted wide attention for what John Mariani, in *Wine Spectator* (November 30, 1995), labeled Keller's "highly individualized work" and Florence Fabricant described as "his daring flights from the ordinary." Fabricant's article, published in the *New York Times Magazine,* included Keller's recipes for four items on the Rakel menu: rosemary tuiles (a type of cookie that is usually sweet rather than seasoned with herbs, as is Keller's version); medallions (small round or oval servings) of monkfish with lentils (preferably "imported French green lentils," as Keller advised); breast of lamb, braised, deboned, and grilled in the French manner; and lemon sabayon tart with pine-nut crust, a shell of baked dough filled with a whipped lemony mixture. Frequented by many Wall Streeters, Rakel fared well until the stock-market crash of October 1987. With its clientele shrinking, Raoul felt that the restaurant had to lower its prices by altering its menu. Keller, however, would not agree to cost-cutting measures that required a drop in standards; instead, in about 1989, he ended his partnership with Raoul. "It was heartbreaking, confusing," he told Burros. "It was torture. I was sad, depressed, embarrassed. Now I feel it was a great accomplishment to gain that experience at that age." In 1990 the restaurant went broke. "My credibility was low after Rakel failed," Keller told Terry McCarthy for *Time* (February 1, 2004). "I was labeled the chef who couldn't control food or labor costs."

At around this time Keller moved to Los Angeles, California, to assume the post of executive chef at the Checkers Hotel. His experience there was "disastrous," as he told Bryant, mainly because his many duties did not include cooking: "I found out that I was more miserable … in a kitchen environment and not being able to cook than I was not cooking." After 17 months Keller left Checkers. With a partner, he founded a small company, called Evo, that sold bottled olive oil. He also began seeking another opportunity to produce the kinds of meals he wanted to serve the public.

Later Career

While visiting Napa Valley, in California, in the late 1980s or early 1990s, Keller discovered the French Laundry, a restaurant surrounded by lush gardens and set up in a nineteenth-century, two-story stone building that had once housed a French steam laundry. "It was a magical place," he told Burros. "It reminded me of France." After its owners, Don and Sally Schmitt, put the restaurant up for sale, Keller told them that he wanted to buy it. For the next year and a half to three years (sources differ on how much time elapsed), the Schmitts waited patiently while Keller struggled to raise the $1.2 million purchase price. He achieved that goal by borrowing thousands of dollars on credit cards and in bank loans to finance his 70 percent share and by setting up a limited partnership with 48 others, who invested the remaining 30 percent. The French Laundry reopened in 1994 with seating for 62 people.

"My legacy is the restaurant. And to keep the continuity, the key is picking the right people and training them."

Over the first year the French Laundry developed a five-course menu—changed every day—with up to 45 dishes. The restaurant now offers two nine-course tasting menus—a "chef's tasting menu" and a "vegetable tasting menu"—each of which consists of very small, beautifully presented portions of a meticulously prepared dish, with no ingredients repeated over the courses. The meal is meant to be consumed slowly, over two and a half to four hours. "Our philosophy is simple," Keller told Hattie Bryant of PBS, explaining that it is based on "the law of diminishing returns—the more you have of something the less you want of it. So we want to give you just enough to where you get to the point where you've had that last bite and it's at the pinnacle of flavor, because your taste buds have reached that. They've gone through the kind of initial acceptance of the flavor, to the realization of the flavor, … to the point where all of a sudden, [your mouth] becomes saturated with the flavor and then it starts to go down. Well, we want to keep you at the top of the bell curve of your taste buds." The French Laundry website reiterates Keller's intention: "We want you to say, 'I wish I had just one more bite of that.'"

John Mariani, in an assessment representative of many, wrote, "Every item on the menu seems to have a reason for being there, with each dish balancing another, each flavor enhancing the last, each texture leading to the next. This is the true, modern fusion cuisine—a fusion of seasonal elements into perfect balance, every dish a coalescence of herbs, spices, meat or seafood into a splendid whole." Most of the ingredients for Keller's recipes come from the French Laundry's gardens, local farms, and specialty growers and producers, among them a commercial pilot who raises hearts of palm and a scholar who sends Maine lobsters using an overnight delivery service.

The French Laundry's three-acre garden, Paolo Lucchese says, is the primary influence on the restaurant's menu. The meticulous planning for a dish can begin months in advance, when seeds are planted for its ingredients. For Beets and Leeks, for example, five varieties of beets are planted. The beets will mature in approximately 60 days, but the leeks need almost double that time to reach harvest size, and culinary gardener Aaron Keefer must plan accordingly. Keefer, Lucchese says, "gives the kitchen an ingredient availability list every night after dinner service. At their late-night meeting, the chefs riff off the garden ingredients and write the next day's menu."

While Keller is deeply serious about his craft, he maintains that preparing and eating high-quality foods should not be elevated into a quasi-religious experience. To set diners at ease, the menu at the French Laundry often contains such familiar-sounding dishes as bacon and eggs, chips and dip, coffee and doughnuts, and macaroni and cheese, though each is far from the usual. The macaroni and cheese, for example, consists of orzo in coral oil with mascarpone cheese topped with lobster and a parmesan chip, while the coffee and donuts, Keller's signature dessert, is cappuccino semifreddo, a flavored mousse, topped with steamed milk and served with tiny cinnamon-sugar donuts. "Coming to a restaurant like this can be intimidating," Keller told Stein. "And that's the last thing I want. I don't want people to come here afraid, like it's some kind of temple of gastronomy. It's just a restaurant. Coffee and doughnuts on the menu should make you smile. It gets everyone laughing and in a good mood."

In 1999 Keller published *The French Laundry Cookbook,* co-authored by Michael Ruhlman, with photographs by Susie Heller and Deborah Jones. The book won an unprecedented three awards from the International Association of Culinary Professionals in 2000, for best book of the year, best first book (the Julia Child Award), and best-designed book. In addition to instructions for preparing 150 dishes served in the French Laundry, the book includes essays in which Keller discusses techniques, his love of particular foods, experiences that helped him develop as a chef, and his relationships with his food suppliers. According to a review on the Global Gourmet website, Keller's "creative process, reverence for ingredients, and deep respect for his purveyors, not to mention his wit and whimsy, come to life in a series of recipes and essays that make *The French Laundry Cookbook* more than just a cookbook. … This is a book driven by passion, a very personal book that reveals the soul of a chef."

In 1998 Keller opened the first Bouchon, down the street from the French Laundry. Five years later he opened a bakery on the same street and a second Bouchon, in the Venetian, a Las Vegas resort, hotel, and casino. In 2001 the offer of a site for a restaurant at the Times Warner Center lured him back to New York City. The center, which was then under construction, is at Columbus Circle, on the southwest corner of Central Park. As part of the deal, Keller secured a prime location for his restaurant, overlooking the park, and veto power over the installation of other potential eateries in the center. Built at a cost of $12 million, Per Se opened with 16 tables and offered a menu and service on a par with those of the French Laundry. Six weeks after its debut, in February 2004, a kitchen fire forced Per Se to close temporarily; it reopened the following May.

Keller spent 18 months training members of his French Laundry staff for the move to New York. He was determined to handle the expansion without sacrificing the high quality for which he had become known. Toward that end, he set up a six-member advisory board (including two bankers, an attorney, a restaurant consultant, an accountant, and a psychologist) and increased staff training. In addition, he installed a live video link between the kitchens of the French Laundry and Per Se, so that he could view the food preparation in either restaurant from the opposite coast. (There is a similar arrangement in place for the Bouchon locations.) A $1.8 million renovation of the French Laundry in 2004 was completed within six months. In 2006 Keller opened a branch of Bouchon Bakery in the Time Warner Center. A new restaurant, Ad Hoc, with a different fixed price comfort food dinner served family style every night, opened the same year, in Yountville.

The recipes in Keller's second cookbook, *Bouchon* (2004), are based on the less-complex dishes prepared in his bistro-style restaurants. (*Bouchon* means "cork" or "stopper" in French.) In 2008, for a very different audience, Keller published *Under Pressure,* a handbook of sous-vide cooking for professional chefs. *Ad*

Hoc at Home (2009) was intended for home cooks; Kim Severson of the *New York Times* (October 27, 2009) noted that this book, dedicated to Keller's brother Joseph, shows his "goofy" side. With Sebastien Rouxel, executive pastry chef for his restaurant group, Keller compiled *The Bouchon Bakery Cookbook* (2013), which won the 2013 IACP Cookbook Award for Food Photography and Styling.

In addition to his cookbooks, Keller launched a line of signature white Limoges porcelain dinnerware by Raynaud called Hommage Point, which he helped design. (The name refers to French chef and restaurateur Fernand Point; Keller wrote an introduction to a 2008 edition of Point's *Ma Gastronomie,* originally published in 1969.) In Yountville he opened Finesse, The Store, a retail business selling "hand-selected kitchen tools, apparel, gifts and accessories favored by Chef Thomas Keller and his restaurants."

Keller is the president of the Bocuse d'Or U.S. team, and the Yountville compound includes the Bocuse d'Or USA House, where chef candidates and their sous chefs train for that well known biennial competition, held in Lyon, France. Each competition cycle a candidate spends a week cooking for and being coached by a group of chefs assembled to evaluate the candidate's progress. Keller's father lived in this small building in his last years, from 2006 until his death in 2008. *Ad Hoc at Home* presents the recipes for the last meal Keller made for his father.

Keller served as a consultant for the Pixar animated film *Ratatouille* (2007), for which Pixar personnel prepared intensively. The producer interned at the French Laundry kitchen, and Keller developed a layered version of ratatouille, "confit byaldi," for the title character to cook in a climactic scene. In the American version of the film, Keller has a cameo, voicing a restaurant patron. (In the French version, one of Keller's mentors, chef Guy Savoy, takes this part; in the Spanish version the voice is chef Ferran Adrià's.)

The French Laundry is unusual for the calm and extreme neatness of its kitchen and the politeness that prevails among its workers—a far cry from the noise and frenzy commonly associated with restaurant kitchens. Keller himself, an acknowledged perfectionist with an obsession for even the smallest details, has checked his earlier tendency to explode in anger. He has connected his once-frequent outbursts to his father, who "used to tear people apart and then build them up again," as he told McCarthy. "I used to be like that. But now if I shout at someone, I get embarrassed." He also learned to temper his desire to control the behavior of others. That change has proved invaluable with the opening of Per Se and the second, third, and fourth Bouchon bistros, since Keller necessarily had to spend much of his time as an adviser rather than as a chef for the establishments distant from Yountville.

In addition to his awards from the James Beard Foundation, Keller has won Restaurants & Institutions's Ivy Award (1996) and the World Master of Culinary Arts Award (2002), and he was dubbed America's Best Chef by *Time* magazine. The French Laundry received the Smithfield Foods Outstanding Service Award in 2003 and occupied the top spot on *Restaurant* magazine's list of the "world's 50 best restaurants" that year. In March 2011, Keller became only the third American in the culinary field (the first two being Julia Child and Alice Waters) to be named a Chevalier of the French Legion of Honor, owing to his role in promoting French cuisine in America. Paul Bocuse, the acknowledged eminence among contemporary French chefs, bestowed the award.

Keller has been described as soft-spoken, gracious, and thoughtful. He has admitted that he sometimes enjoys dining at relatively lowbrow eateries. Soon after his father's death, he became engaged to his long-time girlfriend, Laura Cunningham, formerly general manager of the French Laundry and then director of operations for the Thomas Keller Restaurant Group; she is now brand director for TKRG. Christine Whitney of *Harper's Bazaar* (April 20, 2012) has called Cunningham the "curator of the Keller empire." (According to the same source, Cunningham has referred to herself as the "aesthetic police of the company.") Keller and Cunningham live in Yountville, in a Victorian carriage house in back of the restaurant, and have apartments in the Wall Street area in New York City and near Bouchon in Los Angeles.

Keller has attributed his drive to his desire to make his mark on the world, even beyond his lifetime. "Most people's legacy is their kids," he told McCarthy. "I don't have any kids, so my legacy is the restaurant. And to keep the continuity, the key is picking the right people and training them." One motivation for his restaurant expansion, Keller has said, is the desire to provide opportunities for advancement for talented staff in order to retain them. In June 2014, with an eye toward his legacy, Keller undertook a complete remodeling of his kitchen at the French Laundry. "I'm challenged emotionally," he told Amanda Gold of the *San Francisco Chronicle* (SFGate, June 9, 2014), "because I'm tearing down the last kitchen I ever worked in. But I have to do it to give this restaurant what it needs for the next 20 years. Otherwise it's going to be stagnant."

Further Reading:

Bloomberg Sep., 24, 2007

Gourmet p118+ Oct. 1999, with photo

Harper's Bazaar Apr. 20, 2012

Modern Maturity p26+ 88 Nov./Dec. 2000, with photos

New York p38+ Jan. 5, 2004, with photos

New York Times Magazine p97+ Dec. 11, 1988, p57+ Aug. 31, 1997, Dec. 12, 2004, Sep. 25, 2007, Oct. 27, 2009, May 15, 2012

New Yorker Sep. 5, 2005

PBS Small Business School, with photos

Powells website Oct. 18, 2000, with photo

San Francisco Chronicle (SFGate) Jun. 27, 2007, June 9, 2014

Time Sep. 17, 2001, Feb. 1, 2004

Selected Books:

Keller, Thomas, with Susie Heller and Michael Ruhlman, *The French Laundry Cookbook,* 1999

Keller, Thomas, *Bouchon,* 2004

Keller, Thomas, et al., *Under Pressure: Cooking Sous Vide,* 2008

Keller, Thomas, with David Cruz, et al., *Ad Hoc at Home,* 2009

Keller, Thomas, and Sebastien Rouxel, with Susie Heller et al., *Bouchon Bakery Cookbook,* 2012.

Matsuhisa, Nobu

Chef, restaurateur, entrepreneur, actor

Born: 1949, Saitama, Japan

The owner and founder of an elite global chain of Japanese restaurants, Nobuyuki Matsuhisa (nicknamed Nobu) has earned high critical praise for his numerous restaurants, which have become popular among jet-setters and celebrities and have inspired a slew of imitators. "Whether you're in London, New York, Japan or Milan, Nobu means the same [thing]," Caroline Roux wrote for the London *Guardian* (August 17, 2001). "It's international shorthand for toe-curlingly expensive, delicious dining in the company of said city's reassuringly glossy stars." Matsuhisa's success as a chef lies in his imaginative and innovative blend of Japanese food with South American flavors. Writing for the *Los Angeles Times* (March 5, 2000), S. Irene Virbila noted, "Traditional Japanese cuisine has an austerity and narrow range of flavors that can seem monotonous if you're not attuned to the nuances of texture and other subtleties. By introducing garlic, searing hot peppers, olive oil, even butter, [Matsuhisa has] raised the decibels on this quiet cuisine, playing hot against cool, raw against cooked. Above all, he seduces with the dramatic presentation. There's always an element of theater to any Matsuhisa restaurant." Matsuhisa told Richard Martin of *Nation's Restaurant News* (May 22, 1989) that empathy with his customers was one of the biggest keys to his success. "Always prepare food as if you were sitting on the other side," he explained. "That should be the spirit of the restaurant business."

Education and Early Life

Nobuyuki Matsuhisa was born on March 10, 1949, in Saitama, a suburb of Tokyo, Japan. His father was a timber merchant who died in a road accident when Matsuhisa was seven years old. Shortly afterwards, his older brother attempted to cheer him by taking him for his first meal at a sushi restaurant. Matsuhisa was entranced by the food. After graduating high school at the age of 17, he took a live-in job at a sushi restaurant in Tokyo. Instead of training as a chef, as he hoped, he spent the next two years performing such menial tasks as washing dishes, cleaning floors, and carrying baskets of fish from the market. He received only two days off a month and occasionally thought of quitting. "Sometimes I would think: 'Why am I here, washing dishes?'" he told Malcolm Macalister Hall for the London *Daily Telegraph* (August 31, 2002). "But I needed patience. I thought, 'Some day I'll get there—some day.'" In Matsuhisa's free time he imitated the sushi chefs by practicing their art on leftover tofu or pieces of cloth. Finally, in his third year, he was promoted to working behind the sushi counter.

After being appointed an assistant chef at the restaurant, Matsuhisa met a Peruvian man of Japanese descent who suggested they start a restaurant together in Lima, the capital city of Peru. The two opened the establishment in 1972. A critical and popular success, it attracted even visiting members of the Japanese imperial family. Matsuhisa experimented with traditional Japanese food there, adding elements of Latin American cuisine, especially garlic. His use of expensive ingredients led to friction with his business partner, who demanded that he trim the budget, and in 1975 Matsuhisa left to become the chef of a Japanese restaurant in Buenos Aries, Argentina. The restaurant did not do well, however. "In Argentina they mostly eat meat, and the fish is not as good," he told Florence Fabricant of the *New York Times* (August 10, 1994). Matsuhisa returned to Japan with his wife and daughter after one year but found he was no longer happy in his homeland. "I was so spoiled by the life in foreign countries," he told Fabricant. "I had a big house in Lima, but in Japan nothing seemed to fit for me now. I wanted more room." Matsuhisa moved his family to Anchorage, Alaska, where he went deep into debt to open the restaurant Kioi. The establishment was a success, but on Thanksgiving Day 1977 it burned to the ground in an electrical fire while Matsuhisa was elsewhere, celebrating Kioi's fiftieth day in operation. "I received a telephone call from my partner in the restaurant. 'Nobu, the restaurant's on fire! Come as quickly as you can,' he said in a panicky voice. I thought it was a sick joke and told him so, but he repeated. 'There's a fire. Really, there is.' As we talked on the phone, I began to hear sirens," Nobu recalled to Kirsten Dixon for the *Anchorage Daily News* (May 29, 2002).

Matsuhisa had taken out no insurance on Kioi and had no money to rebuild the restaurant. "I made up my mind to die, even thought of ways to kill myself: jumping into the cold seas, heading into the mountains with nothing to keep me alive, leaping off a cliff," he told Dixon. Matsuhisa recovered his will, however, and sent his wife and daughter back to Japan on borrowed money to live with relatives while he packed one suitcase and went to look for work in Los Angeles, California. He had $24 in cash. "This time I wasn't starting from zero, but from below zero," he recalled in *Nobu: The Cookbook* (2002), as quoted by Bob Krummert for *Restaurant Hospitality* (May 1, 2002). (Matsuhisa told the same story to Maggie Overfelt of *Fortune* magazine [March 26, 2009].) Matsuhisa was hired by Mitsuwa restaurant in West Los Angeles. "The owner made me work hard but taught me how to be American," he told Fabricant. Matsuhisa soon brought his family back to the United States, and within two years he received his green card. In 1980 he began work at O Sho Sushi in Beverly Hills, California. "That is where I found the roots of my style," he told Fabricant. "I was allowed to try my personal ideas, some of the South American ideas." Among those experiments was the ceviche and green mussels in chili-spiked salsa dressing that is one of his most popular dishes today.

Later Career

In 1987, with a $70,000 loan from a friend, Matsuhisa opened his own restaurant in Los Angeles, calling it Matsuhisa. There he established some of his most celebrated dishes, including Chilean sea bass with black bean sauce; black cod with miso; squid scored to look like shell pasta and cooked in a garlic and asparagus sauce; and sashimi accentuated with garlic, ginger spears, chives, toasted sesame seeds and soy sauce covered in hot olive and sesame oil. Each menu was accompanied by a 20-page glossary of terms and ingredients. His eclectic, high-quality food regularly brought gourmands and Hollywood celebrities to his restaurant, and in its second year Matsuhsia was named one of *Food & Wine* magazine's top-ten new chefs. After three years, he had repaid his friend's loan and doubled the size of his restaurant. Writing for *the Los Angeles Times* (April 5, 1987), Max Jacobson wrote, "Half the fun of eating here is watching [Matsuhisa] in action. While he's paring a cucumber thinner than you thought possible he'll be taking an order in Spanish over the counter, and keeping an eye on his assistants at the other end of the bar. Then, in a quick motion, he passes two pieces of yellowtail to an outstretched hand, shouts an order in Japanese to the back kitchen, and moves down the counter to another beaming customer. Toscanini couldn't conduct himself with more consummate skill." A 1993 *New York Times* article called the establishment one of the top ten restaurants in the world. Not all critics agreed, however. Virbila, for example, wrote for the *Los Angeles Times* (January 30, 1994) that the chef"'s "East-West juggling act too often results in muddled flavors."

One of Matsuhisa's celebrity regulars was the noted film actor Robert De Niro, who tried for several years to convince Matsuhisa to open a restaurant in New York City. In 1993 Matsuhisa finally agreed, going into business with De Niro and the restaurateur Drew Nieporent to open Nobu, located on Hudson Street in the Tribeca area of lower Manhattan. The restaurant took eight months to design and build—at a cost of $1 million—and opened in late August to instant success. In her review for the *New York Times* (October 7, 1994) Ruth Reichl wrote, "The new Nobu tries to fulfill every American's dream of a Japanese restaurant. In this bold space with its hand-glazed tiles and chairs with legs like chopsticks, the dishes are arranged with the spare elegance of Japanese flowers, the service is thoughtful and extremely gentle, and the food offers something for every taste." Although she noted that the restaurant was not always up to the high standards it set for itself, she praised the "raw fish of astonishing quality." Getting a reservation at Nobu quickly became a status symbol as wait lists for dinner extended to over a month. In one oft-repeated story, then-Secretary of State Warren Christopher was initially turned down for a table in 1995.

"Cooking is my life, and I enjoy watching my chefs grow."

While Matsuhisa focused on Nobu, his original restaurant, Matsuhisa, continued to get mainly stellar reviews. In 1995 the James Beard Foundation honored the restaurant with an award, and in 1997 it was chosen as one of the top-three restaurants in the Los Angeles area in a poll of *Gourmet* magazine readers. Pamela Robin Brandt, writing for In the November 1, 2001, *Miami New Times,* however, the "What I found at Matsuhisa … in 1996, was the usual when chefs become empire-builders: The food that had seemed so mind-blowing in 1991 was still good but less good than that at the newer New York Nobu, where the chef was personally concentrating his energies."

In 1998 Matsuhisa opened Nobu Next Door, a more casual version of Nobu that opened in an adjacent building on Hudson Street. Unlike its sister restaurant, it did not require reservations for parties of fewer than five people. In March 1999 Matsuhisa opened Ubon—Nobu spelled backwards—in Beverly Hills. Less expensive than his other restaurants, Ubon featured soba and udon noodles as well as Matsuhisa's other non-sushi dishes, and he hoped, fruitlessly as it turned out, that it would become a popular franchise. Virbila wrote for the *Los Angeles Times* (July 11, 1999) that Ubon "should satisfy many people with its casual ambience, quality ingredients and appealing array of dishes, not to mention its affordable prices." British critics were less impressed when Ubon by Nobu opened at Canary Wharf in London, in 2000. Matthew Fort wrote for the London *Guardian* (March 17, 2001) that Ubon by Nobu featured "food as fashion accessory," which, despite its "nice clean flavours," in the end is "disappointing and one-dimensional. It westernises Japanese food, taking out all the difficult bits and rounding off the edges, distracting from the play of textures and the subtleties of flavours." Toby Young, writing for the *London Evening Standard* (February 5, 2004), agreed. "The stuff we were given had a tired, mass-produced air, not so very different from the readymade sushi you can buy at every supermarket in the country."

Matsuhisa continued to expand at a fast rate, opening Nobu London at the Metropolitan Hotel on Old Park Lane in 1997, Matsuhisa Aspen in 1997, and Nobu Tokyo in 1998. In Tokyo Matsuhisa faced his toughest criticism. "Japan is very traditional. … In Japan, they don't like somebody doing something new," he told Virbila for the *Los Angeles Times* (January 2, 1999). "I believe in what I think is correct and do what I think is correct," Matsuhisa told Tetsuko Yoshida and Matthew Wiesner for the *Mainichi Daily News* (December 29, 1998). "Even if you receive criticism of your style of cooking at first, if you keep your way, some of your customers come back, then they gradually increase in number and eventually the food becomes popular and takes root with the public. I think that's how cooking styles undergo change and transition."

In 1999 Matsuhisa opened Nobu Las Vegas at the Hard Rock Hotel, a $2.8 million project, as well as Nobu Malibu (with the musician Kenny G as a partner). In 2000 he opened Nobu Milan, followed by Nobu Miami Beach in 2001. The increasing size and success of his restaurant empire brought Nobu $2.4 million in 2000 alone, and *Forbes* magazine ranked him number 100 on their list of the world's 100 richest and most powerful celebrities for that year. In 2001 Matsuhisa opened Nobu Paris; one of his few failed ventures, the branch soon closed. The following year Kodansha International published *Nobu: The Cookbook* to good reviews. "I can reveal my recipes, but nobody can steal what comes from my heart," Matsuhisa told Geoffrey Eu for the *Business Times Singapore* (March 2, 2001). He published his second cookbook, *Nobu Now,* in late 2005, followed by *Nobu West* (2007) and *Nobu Miami: The Party Cookbook* (2008). Also in 2005 Matsuhisa opened a Nobu in Dallas, Texas, followed by a Nobu in the Bahamas on Paradise Island. In London he opened a second Nobu, in Berkeley Street—this one a more casual restaurant cum lounge bar and club—and another Nobu on West 57th Street in midtown Manhattan. As of 2013 Matsuhisa had 26 restaurants in 13 countries. In March 2011 Caesar's Palace in Las Vegas announced that it would completely renovate its Centurion Tower as the Nobu Hotel, Restaurant, and Lounge; this was the first Nobu Hotel, a line Matsuhisa hoped to expand.

When Alison Beard of the *Harvard Business Review* (October 2013) asked him why he had opened so many restaurants, Matsuhisa responded, "I like teamwork, and my chefs give me a good education. My background is Japanese, but the people working in my kitchens are from London, New York, France, Italy, China, the Philippines, so I learn from them too. I like growing," he continued, "—when the quality is controlled."

Matsuhisa, who has also designed menus for Crystal cruise ships (the Crystal Serenity and the Crystal Symphony), was nominated as chef of the year at the prestigious James Beard Awards in 2001, 2003, and 2004. In 2002 he was inducted into the D'Artagnan Cervena *Who's Who of Food and Beverage in America,* which recognizes food professionals for significant and lasting achievements in the industry. He split his time among charitable events, television appearances, and his large franchise of restaurants, sometimes traveling among three branches in one day. "He's more like a chief executive of a company these days," Tracy Nieporent—the marketing director of Myriad Restaurant Group, which manages several Nobu restaurants—told Benjamin Genocchio for the *Australian* (June 6, 2003), "although he still sets the menu and is always developing recipes." "In all my restaurants," Matsuhisa told Virbila in January 1999, "I stay as long as possible at the beginning. I can't do it all myself—it has to be teamwork. … Cooking is my life, and I enjoy watching my chefs grow. By having so many restaurants, I can give a chance to them, too."

Matsuhisa appeared as a high-stakes gambler in the movie *Casino* (1995), which starred De Niro; as an evil scientist in the hit comedy *Austin Powers in Goldmember* (2002), which starred Mike Myers, another longtime customer; as a kimono artist in *Memoirs of a Geisha* (2005); and as Cho-Cho San's father in *The Girl from Nagasaki,* an adaptation of the classic Puccini opera *Madam Butterfly,* filmed in 3D. In 2003 Matsuhisa introduced his own line of dinnerware in partnership with Miyao Pottery of Japan. Although he acknowledges his level of fame, he hesitates to use such words as artist or master in describing his culinary talents. "I never think about that myself," he told Eu. "People respect me and people like my restaurant, so I'm very honoured. Happiness for me is when my customer compliments my food. I try my best, I never count food cost, worry about profit and so on. Money and success automatically follow."

When not traveling, Matsuhisa lives in Los Angeles with his wife, Yoko. They have two children. Matsuhisa claims to cook for himself only once a year, at his annual New Year's Day party.

Further Reading:

Business Times Singapore Mar. 2, 2001

(London) *Daily Telegraph* p7 Aug. 31, 2002

Fortune Mar. 26, 2009

Harvard Business Review Oct. 2013

Los Angeles Times p33 Jan. 30, 1994, F p1 Jan. 2, 1999, p29 July 11, 1999, F p59 Dec. 23, 1999, p32 Mar. 5, 2000

Nation's Restaurant News May 22, 1989, May 24, 1993

New York Times C p7 Aug. 10, 1994, with photo

Selected Books:

Nobu: The Cookbook, 2002

Nobu Now, 2005

Nobu West, 2007

Nobu Miami: The Party Cookbook, 2008

Muñoz Zurita, Ricardo

Mexican chef, educator, writer

Born: 1966, Coatzacoalcos, Veracruz, Mexico

"In order to make contemporary and nouvelle Mexican cuisine, you really need to know the roots of Mexican cooking," the Mexican chef, cookbook author, and cultural anthropologist Ricardo Munoz Zurita told Maria C. Hunt for the Copley News Service (April 14, 2003). "My duty, my commitment, is to show people how to do things the traditional way." Mexico possesses a rich and varied gastronomic tradition, but its traditional flavors and cooking methods have never been accorded the same worldwide respect as the cuisines of such countries as France and Italy. Even in Mexico, the idea of teaching Mexican cooking in professional culinary academies was long unexplored. But in 1993, at the Escuela Internacional de Turismo, Munoz Zurita taught the first professional cooking course on native Mexican cuisine. Munoz Zurita was repeatedly encouraged by his teachers at the world's finest culinary institutions to pursue a lucrative career in French or Italian cookery. However, a combination of cultural pride and intense curiosity drove Munoz Zurita to seek out the hidden gastronomic gems of his own nation. As both chef and culinary anthropologist, he has written seminal volumes on Mexican cooking, and is now considered the authority on this increasingly popular cuisine. Munoz Zurita, Bianca Vazquez Toness wrote for *Time International* (October 15, 2001), is a "prophet and preserver of a culinary tradition."

Education and Early Career

Ricardo Munoz Zurita was born on February 28, 1966 in Coatzacoalcos, Veracruz, Mexico. His father was an engineer for Benex, a major oil company. When Ricardo was eight, his parents opened a family restaurant in Xalapa, the capital of Veracruz, in order to earn enough additional money to send Ricardo and his six siblings to college. His father managed the restaurantand his mother handled the finances. Ricardo, his three brothers,and his three sisters helped out in the kitchen. Once a year, Ricardo's parents would take a month-long vacation, and one time during their absence the head chef called in sick. "We needed to have a menu and I decided I had to cook something and I did," Munoz Zurita told *Current Biography International* in an interview. "That's how I found out I liked cooking and that I had talent." Although he had never cooked before, Ricardo boldly tied on an apron and, for three days, ran the restaurant's kitchen and prepared meals. He earned high praise from the patrons, who willingly ate his improvised recipes. When Ricardo's parents returned, the restaurant staff and all six siblings kept his stint as chef a secret. Eventually, however, customers returned asking for more of the boy's cooking. The secret was out, and his parents allowed Ricardo to cook for the restaurant whenever he chose.

According to Munoz Zurita, the misconception that Mexican cooking is unsophisticated derives from the Mexican food served in America. "Traditional Mexican cuisine is very different from what is usually thought of [in the U.S.] as Mexican food," he told Kerry Webster for the *Seattle Times* (May 3, 1995). "What you have in North America is mostly what we would call 'Tex-Mex.'" Genuine Mexican cuisine is lighter, more delicate, and less heavily spiced than its American counterpart, according to Munoz Zurita. However, when he began his studies as a professional chef, he discovered, to his chagrin, that even his compatriots held biases against local food. In 1986 Munoz Zurita enrolled at the Escuela Internacional de Turismo (International University of Tourism) in Mexico City. (In the mid-1980s it was the only school in Mexico that taught cooking and restaurant administration; in the years since, however, the country was awarded a satellite campus of the elite French cooking academy L'Ecole Cordon Bleu.) During his time there, Munoz Zurita's teachers demonstrated French, Italian, Japanese, and Chinese cooking. "'When are we going to study Mexican cuisine?'" Munoz Zurita asked, as he recalled to Maria Hunt. "They said that Mexican cooking was not part of the education. They said you have that at home. . . . I was offended. Here we are, these stupid Mexicans studying this cooking from around the world, and we cannot learn about what is right here." Munoz Zurita later moved to San Diego, where he did coursework in French and Italian cooking at San Diego Community College, from which he graduated in 1989. Two years later he studied cooking at the world's most prestigious culinary institute, L'Ecole Cordon Bleu in Paris, France. Munoz Zurita finished his apprenticeship with a year of training at the Culinary Institute of America in Hyde Park, New York.

"I think that people in general don't understand the great gastronomic diversity of [Mexico]."

In 1993 Munoz Zurita returned to Mexico to teach a course in Mexican cooking at his alma mater, the Escuela Internacional de Turismo. It was the first university course of its kind in Mexico. He later created a more elaborate Mexican cuisine course at the Centro Culinario de Mexico. In about 1995 Munoz Zurita was hired by the Universidad Nacional Autonoma de Mexico (UNAM) to oversee the university's executive dining room. UNAM has more than 500,000 students, and its executive dining room is a major destination for world figures who visit Mexico. While head chef at UNAM, Munoz Zurita cooked for dozens of notable figures, from presidents to Nobel-prize winners to royalty. He published his first book on Mexican food, *Los Chiles Rellenos en Mexico* (*Stuffed Chili Peppers in Mexico*), in 1996. The book was a major success, selling tens of thousands of copies. His second book, 1998's *Verde en la Cocina Mexicana* (*Green in the Mexican Kitchen*), meticulously explored Mexican recipes with green ingredients, from tomatillos to cilantro to the Cesar salad, which was purportedly invented by Cesar Cardini, a chef in Tijuana, during the 1920s. Munoz Zurita left his position at the university in the summer of 1999 to become the head chef of the posh Nikko Hotel in Mexico City.

Munoz Zurita put 12 years of research into *Diccionario Enciclopedico de la Gastronomia Mexicana* (*Encyclopedia of Mexican Gastronomy*, 2000). When his schedule permitted, he traveled throughout Mexico, rescuing countless old recipes from extinction. To complete the mammoth 49-volume encyclopedia, Munoz Zurita studied such native languages as Zapotec, Huasteco, Tzozil, and Nahuatal, learning enough to decipher recovered texts. The *Enciclopedico* has already become a Spanish-language food writing classic. In 2001 Munoz Zurita published *Yucatan: Relatos para Disfrutar en la Mesa de los Almendros*, a book of stories and recipes from the Yucatan peninsula.

Later Career

Munoz Zurita has made it a point to take food lovers on gastronomic tours of Mexico, teaching them how to cook indigenous recipes in exotic locations using fresh, local ingredients. "I think that people in general don't understand the great gastronomic diversity of this country," he told Gabe Ulla in an interview that appeared on the Web site *Eater* (January 11, 2013). "There's almost every imaginable landscape here, and that gives way to different ingredients and styles of cooking." He also frequently works as a guest chef at fine restaurants all over the world, and teaches cooking classes at schools and food conferences. At one such course, Munoz Zurita had students sample one of the ancient Mexican recipes he had discovered. "Food that is not memorable is not good," he told them, as quoted by Maria Hunt. "When you put this in your mouth, think about a thousand years ago, and this is the same food that those people used to have." The fast-food chain Taco Belland Goya, a company specializing in Latin American food products, have both used Munoz Zurita as a food consultant. The Spanish version of *Los Chiles Rellenos en Mexico* is so popular that it has already been reprinted several times (and there is also an English version). "That's extremely unusual for a cookbook in Spanish in Mexico," Munoz Zurita told Dennis R. Getto in the *Milwaukee Journal Sentinel* (September 22, 1999). He has written extensively and although has made great progress in teaching the outside world about the delights of Mexican cuisine, "Mexicans are still far from recognizing that our own food is elegant," Munoz Zurita explained to Bianca Vazquez Toness for *Time International* (October 15, 2001).

Munoz Zurita lives in Mexico City. When he isn't in the kitchen, he enjoys listening to opera and classical music, and reading about Greek, Roman, and Mexican culture.

Further Reading:

Copley News Service Apr. 14, 2003

Eater (Jan. 11, 2013)

Milwaukee Journal Sentinel Food p1 Sep. 22, 1999, with photos

Time International p60 Oct. 15, 2001, with photo

Selected Books:

Los Chiles Rellenos en Mexico, 1996 [and subsequent English translation, 2010]

Verde en la Cocina Mexicana, 1998

Diccionario Enciclopedico de la Gastronomia Mexicana, 2000

Tausend, Marilyn, with Ricardo Munoz Zurita, *La Cocina Mexicana:Many Cultures, One Cuisine*, 2012

Larousse Diccionario Enciclopedico de la Gastronomia Mexicana, 2013

Nelson, Marilyn Carlson

Business executive

Born: 1939, Minneapolis, Minnesota, United States

Much has changed in the five decades since Marilyn Carlson Nelson worked briefly in the marketing department of the Gold Bond Stamp Company in 1964. Gold Bond—later called Carlson Companies and now known simply as Carlson—was once a mom-and-pop operation that sold trading stamps to local grocery stores, but it expanded to become a global leader in the travel, hospitality, and marketing industries. In 2012 Carlson, headquartered in Minnetonka, Minnesota, had earnings of some $37.6 billion, with 178,000 employees in 150 countries. Among the best-known of the Carlson companies are Radisson Hotels, Carlson Wagonlit Travel, Country Inns & Suites, Park Inn Hotels, and Park Plaza Hotels & Resorts.

The company was founded by Curtis L. Carson in 1938. Marilyn Carlson Nelson, his daughter, returned to the company in the mid-1990s, at her father's urging, and she led Carlson as chairwoman and chief executive officer (CEO), shepherding the company as it evolved from a mid-20th-century entrepreneur's vision to an enduring 21st-century conglomerate. Marilyn Carlson Nelson retired from the CEO position in March 2008 and from the chairmanship in 2013, but she remains on Carlson's board of directors.

Nelson assumed the company's helm in 1998, a few years after she rejoined the firm as a full-time employee. Thereafter she turned it into one of the 100 best companies for working mothers, according to *Working Mother* magazine, and transformed herself into one of the 100 most powerful women in the world, according to *Forbes*. Nelson has also followed in her father's philanthropic footsteps, working energetically for the United Way and the World Childhood Foundation, among other entities. In addition, she made her firm the first in the United States to refuse to conduct business with companies in the tourism industry that are known participants in the sexual exploitation of minors. Carlson lectures on corporate responsibility at the University of Minnesota's Carlson School of Management, founded in 1998.

Education and Early Career

The elder of the two children of Curtis L. Carlson and his wife, the former Arleen Martin, Nelson was born Marilyn Arleen Carlson on August 19, 1939, in Minneapolis, Minnesota. "In a sense, I was born a chauffeur's daughter because I didn't grow up wealthy," she told David Saltman for *Chief Executive* (August/ September 2003). Her birth occurred a little more than a year after her father sold his first set of trading stamps to a Minneapolis grocer. Known as Curt, he had then been working as a Procter & Gamble salesman servicing grocery stores; he had quickly made a name for himself by expanding the company's sales of soap into drugstores. While on his sales beat, he had noticed that a local department store was giving out stamps redeemable for gifts and cash, as a way to build loyalty and encourage return business. Curt, who had earned a bachelor's degree in economics from the University of Minnesota, adapted the department store's idea for the customers he had already cultivated. Using a $55 loan from his landlord, he had formed the Gold Bond Stamp Co. in 1938 and devoted nights and weekends to building it. His goal was to earn, as an independent entrepreneur, $100 a week, almost four times his Procter & Gamble salary. He began his company, Nelson told Ann Merrill of the *Minneapolis Star Tribune* (September 21, 1997), with the impetus provided by "two very powerful formative experiences"—growing up as the child of Swedish immigrants and living through the Great Depression from his mid-teens until his mid-20s.

Curt Carlson left Procter & Gamble when Marilyn was an infant. Gold Bond became his passion, and Nelson and her sister, Barbara, came to regard it as virtually a third sibling. "I learned the family business at the breakfast table, at the dinner table, on weekends," Nelson told David Saltman. She also told him, "We gave up dessert when I was in my formative years because we got a little speech about investing and return on investment. If we ate it, it'd be gone. If we put the money in the company, it would grow and we'd get a return." She told Ann Merrill, "The sense of valuing capital, leveraging capital, saving every penny, investing pennies, and recognizing the miracle of compounding was absolutely a driver for us."

Curt Carlson's conservative business methods produced impressive results. In 1953 one of the largest supermarket chains in the nation, Super Valu, began buying Gold Bond stamps, and other chains soon followed suit. In the 1960s, at the peak of the trading-stamp market, of which Gold Bond then controlled about a third, Carlson diversified, first buying Minneapolis's landmark Radisson Hotel and using its brand name to build a nationwide hotel chain, then, in the 1970s, acquiring established hospitality chains, such as T.G.I. Friday's, as well as travel agencies and cruise lines. From 1938 to 1978 Curt Carlson's eye for solid acquisitions and the tight control he maintained over his swelling enterprise produced an average annual rate of growth of 33 percent.

Curt Carlson publicly expressed consternation over not having a male heir, but as he navigated his company, Marilyn Carlson showed signs that she might be as capable as he was. At Edina High School, in a Minneapolis suburb, she was editor of the school paper, a member of the student council, and a popular cheerleader. She briefly considered a career in acting before enrolling at Smith College, in Northampton, Massachusetts, where she majored in international economics and minored in theater. She spent her junior year abroad, studying at the Sorbonne, in Paris, France, and the Institut des Hautes Études Economiques Politiques in Geneva, Switzerland. She graduated with honors from Smith in 1961. Shortly thereafter she married Glen Nelson, who went on to become a surgeon; he eventually became vice chairman of Medtronic Incorporated., which produced the first implantable pacemaker. She flirted with joining the diplomatic corps before deciding to enter the business world. Early in her marriage, she got a job with PaineWebber (then called Paine, Webber, Jackson & Curtis) as a securities analyst; she was the first woman to hold that position in one of the firm's offices in the Midwest (a fact the company apparently did not want to reveal: her supervisor told her to sign all documents as "M. C. Nelson" to hide her gender). Ten months into her tenure, she left PaineWebber, having become pregnant with her first child.

Nelson worked full-time for Gold Bond briefly in 1964. Following her departure from the company, during her third pregnancy, she devoted herself not only to motherhood but also to fund-raising for local organizations, among them the Minneapolis Symphony and the Minneapolis United Way, and she became a well-liked civic leader. In 1984 she was named the chairwoman of the Minnesota Super Bowl task force, formed to lobby the National Football League (NFL) to bring the championship game to their state in 1992. Nelson relentlessly pursued her task. In one attempt to woo the NFL, she sent life-size chocolate ducks to Tampa, Florida, for a meeting of all the teams' owners. The ducks—the best approximation that she could find of the loon, Minnesota's state bird—arrived with their necks broken. Enlisting the help of a chef at the hotel where she and the owners were staying, she made a paste out of sugar, flour, and water and worked all night to reattach the ducks' heads. To hide the scars, she tied around each duck's neck a ribbon bearing a message from her, and then had a duck placed on each team owner's pillow. The effort paid off: the NFL agreed to hold the 1992 Super Bowl in Minneapolis's Metrodome, and her community's regard for Nelson skyrocketed.

"I learned the family business at the breakfast table, at the dinner table, on weekends."

During this period Nelson, who had worked part-time for Gold Bond since the early 1970s, contemplated a run for the U.S. Senate, but her father strongly encouraged her to work for the family firm full-time. "He said: 'If you care about this company, you'll do it,'" Nelson told De'Ann Weimer for *BusinessWeek* (now *Bloomberg Businessweek*; August 17, 1998). She admitted to Weimer that she had felt reluctant to return to a full-time position, and his words had made her "uncomfortable." "I had my own opportunities," she explained to Weimer. "If I was going to be in the company, I needed a role where I was allowed to make an impact." Nelson agreed to her father's request after he named her co-chair of Carlson Holdings, Carlson Companies' parent company, and chair of the audit committee. "My father is tough but he's fair," Nelson said to Khoi Nguyen in 1992. "Above all, he's my father, and he's in his advanced years. It's invaluable that I can run across the hall to ask his advice. And later on, I'm sure I will even miss all the times when he comes parading in my office to tell me what to do."

After her promotion Nelson immediately began studying family-owned firms to identify problems prevalent among them. Her research led her to advise her father to bring in outside directors to offer fresh perspectives and stabilize the company during the transition when, at an as yet undetermined date, Curt Carlson would retire. She also discovered a serious lack of internal financial regulation, common in privately held companies because they do not have to disclose profits publicly. In 1993 she helped to recruit Martyn Redgrave from Pepsico to fill the position of chief financial officer (CFO), with responsibility for implementing a stricter accounting system, one more in line with those used by public corporations.

Meanwhile, a year or so before Nelson had rejoined the company full time, Curt Carlson had had to undergo heart surgery and had named as CEO Edwin C. "Skip" Gage, his daughter Barbara's husband, who had worked at the company for about 20 years. After he recovered, however, Carlson, who was known for watching the bottom line with an eagle eye and managing with an iron fist, clashed with Gage over business philosophies and softening revenues. In 1991 Gage resigned, bought three Carlson marketing companies, and set up the Gage Marketing Group. (He remained a Carlson board member.) Many observers speculated that Carlson would choose Juergen Bartels as Gage's successor. During his tenure as head of Carlson Hospitality Worldwide, Bartels had made his division Carlson's most profitable business segment. Bartels, however, increasingly chafed under Carlson's hands-on management, and he resigned in 1995 to become chairman and CEO of Westin Hotels.

Beyond the unpleasantness connected with Gage's and Bartels's respective departures, these events highlighted a larger problem with which Carlson Companies—and many other family-owned firms—have grappled: the steady loss of top executives who see little chance for advancement. For his part, Carlson settled the issue by grooming Marilyn Carlson Nelson to take over. In 1995 he hired a succession consultant, Barbara Hauser, as vice president of financial and tax planning for Carlson Holdings Incorporated. Hauser's assignments included structuring the company's stock, all of which was owned by Curtis Carlson, so that it could be sold only to the company. Within two years Carlson named Nelson chief operating officer (COO), relinquishing all of Carlson Companies's day-to-day operations to her. In March 1998, at Carlson Companies's sixtieth anniversary celebration, in Las Vegas, Nevada, Carlson appointed his daughter CEO and president of the firm. He himself retained the title of chairman until his death, in February 1999.

Later Career

After she took the rudder at Carlson Companies, Nelson sought to change its corporate culture. "I want to lead with love, not fear," she told De'Ann Weimer. In the conviction that an inspired and dedicated workforce was necessary if the company was to grow and remain strong, she expanded bonus programs and profit sharing, including "phantom stock," a system of bonuses tied to revenue growth, as well as flextime and day care for children—perks that Curt Carlson had resisted. Over time she increased the representation of women in the company's executive ranks; by the time Nelson stepped down as chairman, it had reached 49 percent. (In 1989 the figure was 8 percent.) Nelson also instituted training programs to encourage workers to prepare themselves for executive positions.

Above all, her goal was to lead by example. Drawing on a skill she developed while working with volunteers whom she did not have the power to hire or fire, she tried to build consensus among her executives so that they felt they had influence on business decisions. Nelson also spearheaded many projects that had deep and long-lasting effects on the organization of Carlson Companies. As COO she brought the technology infrastructure under her aegis, with the aim of bringing improved technology and increased efficiency to all Carlson units. This enabled the units to track, for instance, a frequent business traveler's preferences.

In the wake of the September 11, 2001, terrorist attacks on the United States and the resultant slump in travel and tourism, Nelson reevaluated Carlson's business model and processes and then restructured them to increase efficiency and profitability. Her analyses saved tens of millions of dollars in operating and other costs. She also worked with government officials and the media to launch a public-relations campaign to encourage people to travel. "One out of every seven jobs in America is connected to the travel industry," Nelson observed to David Saltman. "People don't realize that when the travel industry slumps, there's a huge ripple effect in the construction industry, in agriculture, in all sorts of seemingly unrelated businesses."

According to the LeighBureau, an international speakers' bureau, "Under Ms. Nelson's leadership, often referred to as the firm's "Golden Decade," systemwide sales nearly doubled to $40 billion and the corporate culture was transformed into a true meritocracy where today 49% of upper management positions are held by women." In 2010 Carlson announced its "Ambition 2015" global growth strategy, projecting a $1.5 billion investment focused on the improvement and positioning of Radisson as a globally consistent first-class brand. The company set a goal of 1,500 hotels in operation and under development by 2015. This intensive focus led Carlson to shed some of its noncore operations. In May 2014 it announced that the TGI Friday's restaurant chain would be sold to Sentinel Capital Partners and TriArtisan Capital Partners.

Nelson herself experienced succession turmoil at Carlson. Her son, **Curtis Carlson Nelson**, was the company's president and chief operating officer, but he left Carlson in 2006 after he was passed over for promotion and in 2007 sued his mother and Carlson Companies. According to Jane Levere, writing in the

New York Times (February 24, 2008), "The company and a spokesman for Mr. Nelson both said that all legal issues had been resolved. The company would not comment further." Curtis Carlson Nelson later filed for bankruptcy. Hubert Joly became Carlson's president and chief executive officer in 2008 and served in this capacity until August 2012, when he resigned suddenly to become CEO of Best Buy and was succeeded by Trudy Rautio, who had previously served as the company's CFO. In May 2013 Marilyn Carlson Nelson's daughter Diana Nelson took over as chairman of Carlson.

Recognized as a worldwide business leader, Marilyn Carlson Nelson, according to her Carlson website, currently serves on the boards of United Nations Global Compact, the Committee Encouraging Corporate Philanthropy, the National Endowment for Democracy and the Kennedy Center for the Performing Arts. She is past chair of the Mayo Clinic Board of Trustees and a former board member of ExxonMobil. In 1999, with Queen Silvia of Sweden, Carlson co-founded the World Childhood Foundation to aid abused and sexually exploited children around the world. The Carlson website explains that the foundation "supports more than 100 projects in 17 countries, working with children who are victims of abuse, families at risk, children in alternative housing and street children."

A graduate of Smith College, Nelson earned a degree in international economics and studied at the Sorbonne. Her profile at LeighBureau notes that she is a member of the World Economic Forum's International Business Council, serves on the steering committee of the WEF's Aviation, Travel & Tourism Governors, and is co-founder and advisory board member of the WEF's Women Leaders Program. In 2004 she co-chaired the World Economic Forum's annual meeting in Davos, Switzerland. Nelson was appointed by President George W. Bush in 2002 to chair the National Women's Business Council, which advises the White House and Congress on public-policy issues that affect female business owners.

Noteworthy among the many honors accorded Marilyn Carlson Nelson are the 2000 Woodrow Wilson Award for Corporate Citizenship and her induction into the Sales and Marketing Executives Hall of Fame. In 2006 H.E. Jean-David Levitte, French Ambassador to the United States, inducted Nelson in the French Légion d'Honneur. *Ethisphere Magazine* named her one of the "100 Most Influential People in Business Ethics" in 2007. In 2013 the Women's Foundation of Minnesota gave Carlson Incorporated the Champion for Equality Award because the company has so many women in upper management. Also in that year, President Barack Obama bestowed on the company the inaugural Presidential Award for Extraordinary Efforts to Combat Trafficking in Persons.

Nelson's book *How We Lead Matters* (2008) was characterized in the *New York Times* as a "series of short, personal essays on her life as a businesswoman, wife, mother and grandmother, introduced by quotations from everyone from Percy Bysshe Shelley to Judy Garland." Among Nelson's favorite poets are Rainer Maria Rilke and Carl Sandburg (a Midwesterner of Swedish descent, as is Nelson).

The Nelsons' eldest daughter, Juliet, died in a car accident in 1985, a week after leaving for college. "I don't know if I'll be here tomorrow," Marilyn Nelson told David Saltman. "I know that today is a day I have and I've often said that what [Juliet] taught me was that each day should be a day I would sign my name to and that we should live as a kind of artist, because that may be the last day." In addition to their son Curtis and daughter Diana, the Nelsons have another surviving daughter, Wendy Nelson, who served as an executive with various Carlson business units beginning in 2003. Wendy Nelson is now a member of the Carlson board, as are Barbara Carlson Gage's husband Edwin C. Gage and two of her sons, currently Geoffrey C. Gage and Richard C. Gage. There are 6 family seats on the 11-member board. In a May 2014 press release,

Diana Nelson announced that Richard Gage would replace his brother Scott, as part of the family's plan to rotate third-generation Carlson family representation on the board every three years.

Further Reading:

BusinessWeek p52+ Aug. 7, 1998, with photos

Carlson Incorporated website

Chief Executive Aug./Sep. 2003, with photos

LeighBureau website

New York Times Sep. 30, 2001, Oct. 10, 2004, Feb. 24, 2008, Aug. 9, 2008, Nov. 8, 2012

[Minneapolis, Minnesota] *Star Tribune* D p1 Mar. 14, 1997, with photo, D p1 Sep. 21, 1997, with photo, A p1 Mar. 24, 1998, with photos, S p16 Sep. 26, 2003

Town & Country p85+ Aug. 1992

Selected Books:

How We Lead Matters: Reflections on a Life of Leadership (2008)

Nooyi, Indra

President and CEO of PepsiCo. Inc

Born: 1955, Chennai, India

On October 1, 2006 the 51-year-old Indra Nooyi succeeded Steve Reinemund as chief executive officer (CEO) of PepsiCo Inc., one of the world's largest food-and-beverage companies. In doing so she not only entered the rarefied group of female heads of *Fortune* 500 companies, but shattered the glass ceiling for minority advancement, becoming the most prominent Indian-born executive in the United States and PepsiCo's first Indian-born CEO.

Nooyi immigrated to the United States in 1978 to study business at Yale University's prestigious graduate school of management. She held high-level positions at the Boston Consulting Group, the Motorola Corp., and Asea Brown Boveri in the 1980s and early 1990s before beginning her tenure at the Purchase, New York-based PepsiCo in 1994, as the company's senior vice president for corporate strategy and development. Among other successful moves there, in 1997 Nooyi persuaded then-CEO Roger Enrico to divest the company of its restaurant chains--Taco Bell, Kentucky Fried Chicken, and Pizza Hut--and refocus its mission on its core business:snack-and-beverage brands such as Frito-Lay corn chips and multiflavored soft drinks. Nooyi later became the chief architect behind PepsiCo's $3.3 billion purchase of the Seagram Co.'s Tropicana juicesin 1998, and its $13 billion acquisition of Quaker Oatsin 2001--key mergers that diversified the company's product portfolio in the United States and increased its presence overseas. In 2000 she became chief financial officer (CFO) of PepsiCo, and in the following year she took on the additional duties of president, teaming with the new CEO, Reinemund, to enlarge the company's global profile and work to surpass its archrival, the Coca-Cola Co.

As a result of their partnership, PepsiCo significantly increased its profits and nearly doubled the value of it shares., Nooyi told a writer for the *Hindu* (January 2, 2001), "Much like GE was one of the most admired companies in the 20th century, we want people to look back and say PepsiCo [was] the defining corporation for the way they treated their employees, the way they created shareholder value and the way they thought about growth. We do want to set the standards for being the greatest corporation in the 21st century." Known for her singular style, Nooyi has enlivened PepsiCo's conservative corporate culture with her sense of humor and bicultural ethos, frequently wearing a flowing scarf and a sari (a traditional Indian dress) to PepsiCo functions and promoting a "be yourself" atmosphere among her colleagues.

Education and Early Career

The second of three children, Indra Krishnamurthy Nooyi was born on October 28, 1955 in Chennai (formerly known as Madras), India's fourth-largest city, located in the southeastern state of Tamil Nadu. Her father was an employee at the State Bank of Hyderabad, her mother a homemaker. Her aunt, Aruna Sairum, is a renowned singer. Nooyi had a strict but supportive upbringing in a conservative Hindu family that valued religious faith, academic excellence, and a strong work ethic. Nooyi recalled, as quoted in an online transcript from the question-and-answer portion of a lecture she gave at the Tuck School of Business at Dartmouth College (September 23, 2002), "My grandfather, who was very tough on us, said, 'The only thing that matters in life is grades.' As long as you got good grades you were okay. If you didn't get good grades you were not worth it." Nooyi's mother often gave her and her older sister, Chandrika, speaking exercises that called for them to articulate their career aspirations in creative ways. The better speaker was rewarded with chocolate. "It didn't matter what they said, but it instilled in them a sense of pride and the urge to dream big and chase that dream. It made them achievers," one family friend told Nandini Lakshman for *Daily News & Analysis* (August 14, 2006)

In the early 1970s Nooyi enrolled at Madras Christian College (MCC), one of the oldest colleges in India, where she studied chemistry and physics and quickly impressed her teachers and peers with her intellectual drive and quick wit. V. J. Phillip, a former principal of the college, told Lakshman that Nooyi was "always a go-getter who had the capacity to rally around people and get them excited." Nooyi participated in a host of extracurricular activities, serving as captain of the women's cricket team and playing guitar for an all-girls rock band. After earning her bachelor's degree from MCC in 1976, Nooyi enrolled at the prestigious Indian Institute of Management (IIM) in Calcutta, as one of only six women in the incoming class. She earned her master's degree in business administration from IIM in 1978 and then worked briefly for Mettur Beardsell, a British textile company in India, before assuming the post of product manager at Johnson & Johnson, a global consumer-products company, in Mumbai. As product manager, Nooyi helped launch Stayfree, a brand of sanitary pads, by generating awareness among female consumers through an innovative marketing strategy. "It was a fascinating experience because you couldn't advertise personal protection in India so you had to go from school to school and college to college teaching people," Nooyi told Sarah Murray in the *London Financial Times* (January 26, 2004). "And it was very embarrassing to put out personal care items in retail stores. So even persuading retailers to carry it was difficult. But it was terrific and I learned a lot."

During her tenure at Johnson & Johnson, Nooyi happened upon a magazine advertisement that featured Yale University's newly launched graduate school of management. She applied to the program "on a whim," as she said to Murray, and was accepted and offered financial aid. Nooyi then faced the task of persuading her family to let her pursue higher education in the United States. "It was unheard of for a good, conservative, south Indian Brahmin girl to do this. It would make her an absolutely unmarriageable commodity after that," Nooyi told Murray. But to her astonishment, her parents were already softened to the idea of her relocation, since their elder daughter, Chandrika, had left India to work for Citibank in Beirut, Lebanon.

Nooyi enrolled at Yale in 1978 and covered her expenses by working odd jobs, often wearing a sari out of necessity. "When you don't have a safety net, when you don't have money to buy clothes for interviews and you are going to a summer job in saris, all of a sudden life gives you a wakeup call and you realize that you have got to work extremely hard to make it happen in this country for you," Nooyi said to the students at the Tuck School of Business. At Yale, in addition to her traditional seminars in business-case study, Nooyi took mandatory courses in organizational behavior, which left an indelible impression on her. Courses in communication were also a part of Yale's curriculum. "That was invaluable for someone who came from a culture where communication wasn't perhaps the most important aspect of business, at least in my time," Nooyi told Sarah Murray. Nooyi graduated from the Yale School of Management in 1980 with a master's degree in public and private management. She then joined the Boston Consulting Group (BCG), where she directed international corporate-strategy projects. In 1986 Nooyi went to work at the Motorola Corp., a mobile-communications company, where she was vice president and director of corporate strategy and planning. In the early 1990s she briefly held a senior-level post as vice president of corporate strategy and strategic marketing at Asea Brown Boveri Group (ABB), a Connecticut-based engineering firm. When Nooyi left ABBin the mid-1990s, she declined a job offer from Jack Welch, the legendary CEO of General Electric, to instead join PepsiCo. Her decision was influenced by PepsiCo's then-CEO, Wayne Calloway, who said to her, as quoted by Nandini Lakshman, "Jack Welch [is] the best CEO I know, and GE is probably the finest company. But I have a need for someone like you, and I would make PepsiCo a special place for you."

"At the end of the day, don't forget that you're a person, don't forget you're a mother, don't forget you're a wife, don't forget you're a daughter."

Nooyi became PepsiCo's senior vice president for corporate strategy and development in 1994. She helped to transform the company, which had seen lagging sales, from an ill-focused conglomerate to a company specializing once more in beverages and so-called convenience foods, such as Frito-Lay corn chips, which PepsiCo had owned since 1965. Nooyi particularly impressed CEO Roger Enrico, the successor to Wayne Calloway, with her ability to "look over the horizon," as he told Diane Brady for *BusinessWeek* (August 14, 2006). In 1997 Nooyi initiated PepsiCo's spin-off of its fast-food restaurant chains, including Kentucky Fried Chicken, Taco Bell, and Pizza Hut., Under Nooyi's influence PepsiCo similarly spun off its bottling operation.,

Beginning in 1998, Nooyi served as the chief negotiator in a number of key PepsiCo acquisitions, which positioned the company atop the snack-and-beverage industry. She aggressively pursued the Seagram Co.'s Tropicana juice line, recognizing the enormous potential of the Tropicana brand in the evolving consumer market that, as market researchers had forecast, favored fruit juices and functional drinks (energy drinks for athletes) over carbonated beverages. Faced with skepticism from PepsiCo's executive board, Nooyi pressed forward and enlisted Enrico's support to execute the $3.3 billion acquisition. The success of the Tropicana acquisition contributed to Nooyi's promotion to chief financial officer (CFO) of PepsiCo in February 2000. As Nooyi pointed out, the Quaker bid announced PepsiCo's further expansion into the snack-foods industry. "For any part of the day we will have a little snack for you," Nooyi quipped to Nanette Byrnes for *Business-Week* (January 29, 2001). In August 2001 PepsiCo sealed the $13.8 billion takeover deal, acquiring Quaker Oats's cereals and breakfast bars and its well-known sports drink, Gatorade.;

In the spring of 2001, meanwhile, Enrico had resigned from his post as CEO, naming Steve Reinemund as his successor. At Reinemund's invitation, Nooyi also moved up, becoming the company's president while retaining her position as CFO. Betsy McKay noted in the (California) *Contra Costa Times* (December 10, 2000) that Nooyi tried in a variety of ways to keep the office mood light. She was known to sing around her colleagues, for example, and "once kept a 'yes' man statuette on her desk at work; when touched, it made ingratiating utterances." The Reinemund-Nooyi partnership ushered in a new age for PepsiCo, as the two executives tried to integrate PepsiCo's Tropicana and Quaker brands through a profitable, seamless sales and marketing strategy. The Frito-Lay division also thrived, while the successful launches of the beverages

Mountain Dew Code Red, Aquafina water, Lipton flavored iced tea, and Pepsi Blue gave the company an ongoing competitive edge over its rival soft-drink makers.

In 2003 Nooyi helped implement an even broader marketing strategy, one that differentiated PepsiCo's products portfolio into three parts:"fun for you" products (Pepsi soft drinks and Lay's potato chips), "better for you" products (Baked Lay's and Rold Gold Pretzels), and "good for you" products (Tropicana juices and Quaker Oats)--which enabled the company to leverage its more nutritious offerings. The strategy earned plaudits for putting PepsiCo "closer to being a friend rather than a foe of the health community with moves like switching its chips from oils containing trans-fats to more heart-healthy versions," as Diane Brady noted for *BusinessWeek* (October 20, 2003).

Later Career

In 2006 Nooyi succeeded Steve Reinemund, who had announced his early retirement from the company, to become the fifth CEO in PepsiCo's 41-year history. With her appointment Nooyi also became the highest-ranking Indian-born executive in the United States and joined an small, exclusive group of other women who preside over *Fortune* 500 companies.

Nooyi assumed the post of of PepsiCo's CEO on October 1, 2006. Asked by one of the Tuck students what lessons she had learned as a woman in the business world, Nooyi replied, "I will tell you one thing which some of you women may not like to hear, but accept it for whatever it is. The fact is that if you are a woman and especially a person of color woman, there are two strikes against you. Immigrant, person of color, and woman, three strikes against you. I can go on. If you want to reach the top of a company, . . . you have got to start off saying that you have got to work twice as hard as your counterparts. If you decide to get on a crusade and argue for equality and some kind of promotion, you could be on that crusade forever."

Nooyi remains an idiosyncratic and distinctive addition to the boardroom: part of a

growing number, as Anand Giridhardas has written in the *New York Times* (May 16, 2010), of "an emergent breed of hybrid leaders." PepsiCo, John Seabrook has written in *The New Yorker* (May 6, 2011), "is the largest food-and-beverage company in the United States," with tens of billions of dollars in revenue. Yet, as Michael Useem relates in *U.S. News & World Report* (November 19, 2008), its CEO has kept in mind that "at the end of the day, don't forget that you're a person, don't forget you're a mother, don't forget you're a wife, don't forget you're a daughter."

Nor has she forgotten her all-important roots. Nooyi is quoted in Gary Burson's book *No Fear of Failure* (excerpted in *Fast Company*, April 29, 2011): "I have an immigrant mentality, which is that this job can be taken away at any time, so make sure you earn it every day."

A hybrid leader tends to have a different outlook. "And in perhaps the ultimate heresy for a soda company," Stephanie Strom wrote in the *New York Times* (March 12, 2012), "Pepsico in 2010 decided not to advertise... its Pepsi Cola brand during the Super Bowl. It instead gave away money in grants awarded for charitable ideas selected through a contest on Facebook..."

Nooyi makes her residence in Greenwich, Connecticut, with her husband, Raj K. Nooyi, a management consultant, and their two daughters.

Further Reading:

Chicago Tribune p1 Dec. 5, 2000

Dartmouth College Tuck School of Business Web site

(India) *Daily News and Analysis* Aug. 14, 2006

Fast Company Apr. 29, 2011

(London) *Financial Times* p3 Jan. 26, 2004

The New Yorker May 16, 2011

New York Times May 6, 2010, March 12, 2012

U.S. News & World Report Nov. 19, 2008

Oliver, Garrett

Beer expert, brewmaster, writer, lecturer

Born: 1962, New York City, New York, United States

"When people say they don't like beer, they almost certainly have never tried the real thing," the beer expert Garrett Oliver told Damaso Reyes of the New York *Amsterdam News* (July 24, 2003). "Saying 'I don't like beer' is like saying 'I don't really care for food.' Beer has that wide a range." As a world-recognized authority on traditional American-made beers as well as a professional brewer whose original recipes have earned the company for which he works—Brooklyn Brewery—international praise, Oliver has presided at more than 800 beer tastings, dinners, and cooking demonstrations in the United States and overseas, according to the Brooklyn Brewery website. The food writer Mark Bittman noted for the *New York Times* (June 16, 2004) that Oliver "has become widely acknowledged as an expert not only in making beer, but in tasting it, pairing it [with foods] and talking about it."

Oliver worked for the Manhattan Brewing Company as an assistant brewmaster for about two years and as brewmaster for about one. In 1994 he was hired by the Brooklyn Brewery, one of the approximately 1,500 craft breweries now operating in the United States; unlike the so-called industrial beer makers, each of the craft breweries produces a strictly limited number of barrels of beer and usually tries to make its beers distinctive. As the brewmaster and vice president of production at Brooklyn Brewery, Oliver is responsible for developing recipes and overseeing all aspects of the production of the firm's beers. He told *Current Biography,* "The brewmaster is essentially the 'chef' of the brewery." In an article for the *New York Times* (October 19, 2007), Oliver described as "watery" the beers that have dominated the American market for several decades. Referring to the period (1920–1933) known as Prohibition, when the manufacture and sale of all alcoholic beverages were illegal in the United States, as well as the large number of craft breweries that operated in the United States in the nineteenth- and early twentieth century, he added, "If we truly want to restore the vibrant beer culture that flourished in this country before Prohibition, craft brewers need to retain the values and goals—creating beers that are flavorful, interesting to drink and made from proper beer ingredients—that put us on the map in the first place. Let's not undo American beer again."

Education and Early Career

Garrett Oliver was born on July 29, 1962, in the New York City borough of Queens. His mother was the membership director for the New York Academy of Sciences; his father helped to develop television commercials for the advertising firm Young & Rubicam. An excellent cook, his father sparked Garrett Oliver's interest in pairing beer with fine food. "That certainly influenced me," Oliver told *Current Biography.* "I could write a book on my parents' influence. … I can certainly say that they both stressed the importance of education."

Oliver attended Boston University, in Massachusetts, where he majored in broadcasting and film. After he graduated, in 1983, he got a job with the Home Box Office (HBO) TV network. Later that year he moved to London, where he became a stage manager for rock groups. At his first visit to a London pub, he ordered a glass of the local English bitter. "I wasn't even sure that I liked it," he told Damaso Reyes, also remarking that until that time, he was not partial to beer and had mostly drunk brands not known for their quality. During his stay in London, he grew fond of traditional English beers, especially the Fuller's line, which includes, most notably, London Pride, ESB, and Chiswick Bitter. After a year Oliver left England to travel on the European continent, tasting many other beers along the way. He "really fell in love" with some of them, as he recalled to *Current Biography.*

On his return to the United States, Oliver found that the light taste of the American beers he bought at the supermarket no longer satisfied him. At that time (and now) the American beer market was dominated by such mass-market beers as Coors and Anheuser Busch's Budweiser—beverages that Oliver described to Damaso Reyes as "yellow fizz," because they tasted so watered down. "That's why I started home-brewing," he told *Current Biography.* "It wasn't that I was interested in brewing—I started brewing in order to have some real beer." After producing a series of unsatisfactory beers, he consulted other home brewers, and his skills improved. In the mid-1980s, he founded the New York Home Brewers' Guild, and at one of the group's meetings, he befriended Mark Whitty, the former head of the Samuel Smith Brewery, in Yorkshire, England, who now had the same position in New York City with the Manhattan Brewing Company. Oliver called his first successful homemade beer Blast!, the name of a magazine edited by the British writer and painter Wyndham Lewis (1882–1957). Oliver told *Current Biography,* "Amateur brewers are not allowed to sell their beer. Home-brewing is a great hobby, but it's a hobby. It bears little resemblance to professional brewing, just as being a chef is very different than being a home cook. That said, you can make great beer and great food at home. I made a wide variety of styles, but probably more English-style pale ales than anything else." He also noted that the brewing process "is certainly time-consuming. At its simplest, it can involve using a pre-made syrup; that's what I call the 'Betty Crocker' version. Starting from scratch is much more elaborate, and involves the full brewing process, including sugar conversion and extraction, etc. It can easily take all day."

When he returned to the United States, Oliver had been rehired by HBO and assigned to produce short films. He quit the network in 1987 to take a position at a law firm. In 1989, after the assistant brewmaster of the Manhattan Brewing Company left, Mark Whitty offered Oliver the position. One of the first working breweries to open in New York City in decades, the Manhattan Brewing Co. had started to produce beer—and opened a pub in which to serve it—in 1984 in Lower Manhattan. Oliver was given the freedom to work on his own recipes, and Whitty imparted to him his wealth of knowledge of brewing.

Produced for at least 8,000 years, beer is an alcoholic beverage made from grain, or cereals: barley (primarily), wheat, corn, rice, or oats. Water, yeast, hops, and occasionally fruits or other ingredients are added; in large quantities, beer is manufactured in breweries. Yeast is a microscopic organism that consumes the sugars in grain and converts them into alcohol and carbon dioxide; hops, the female flowers of the hop vine, add a bitter flavor and act as a preservative. The manufacture of beer involves many steps; differences in ingredients and fermentation and in the time spent in carrying out various steps account for differences in appearance and flavor. The main types of beers are ale (brown ale, porter, stout) and lager (pale lager, pilsner, light lager, and dark lager). Some beers are produced year round, while others are manufactured only during one or another season. Draft (or draught) beer is usually defined as beer that is dispensed from kegs or other large containers, as in a saloon, rather than from cans or bottles.

In 1991, for financial reasons, the Manhattan Brewing Company closed. To support himself, Oliver wrote articles about beer and conducted beer tastings. Then, in 1993, a group of business partners reopened the brewery and hired Oliver as brewmaster, with control of the firm's products. Within months Oliver had created five new, traditional-style beers with both U.S.- and British-grown ingredients. His beers included a brown ale, a golden ale, a British amber ale, an extra stout, and an Indian pale ale. Reviewing the beers for the London *Guardian* (September 25, 1993), Roger Protz wrote, "The Brown Ale … packs a greater punch than the average English mild and has great toasted-malt character from the use of roasted barley." He also noted that Oliver's British amber ale "has a fine bitter-sweet nutty palate and a dry, hoppy finish" and that the extra stout "tastes the way dry Irish stouts did until the mass marketing mentality took over and squeezed the roasty, hoppy character out of them. . . . The aroma and palate are rich with bitter chocolate and coffee and the long finish is bitter-sweet, with developing hop notes." Oliver told Protz that he made beers that appealed to him. "When I agreed to become brewmaster, I told the partners it was important I should like the beer," he said. "If the customers like it, but I don't, the beer gets dumped."

Later Career

In 1994 Oliver left Manhattan Brewery to become the brewmaster at Brooklyn Brewery, which had been founded ten years earlier by Steve Hindy, previously an Associated Press correspondent, and Tom Potter, a onetime lending officer at a bank. At first Hindy and Potter had sold their two varieties, a lager and a brown ale, from the back of a truck, going store to store. Their limited resources forced them to have their beers manufactured at the F. X. Matt Brewery in Utica, New York. After Oliver arrived, he reformulated both beers and set up facilities for brewing the beers in a warehouse in an industrial section of the Williamsburg, Brooklyn, neighborhood. There, he began to craft new year-round beers for the company. Currently, the company produces "perennial" Brooklyn Lager, Brooklyn Pilsner, Brooklyn Brown Ale, Brooklyn East India Pale Ale, Brooklyn Pennant Ale '55 (named for the Dodgers baseball team, which played in Brooklyn until 1957 and won the World Series in 1955), and Brooklyn Blast. Oliver also developed "seasonal" beers, among them Brooklyn Summer Ale, Brooklyn Winter Ale, Brooklyn Oktoberfest, Brooklyn Post Road Pumpkin Ale, Brooklyn Black Chocolate Stout, and Brooklyn Dry Irish Stout. The Brooklyn Brewery has the largest bottle re-fermentation program in the United States; using this technique of re-fermenting beer 100 percent in the bottle, it produces Brooklyn Local 1, Brooklyn Local 2, Brooklyn Silver Anniversary Lager, Sorachi Ace, Brooklyn Greenmarket Wheat, and Brooklyn BAMboozle. The Brooklyn Quarterly Experiment program makes a new bottle-conditioned beer available for just a few months. The Brewmaster's Reserve Program releases Oliver's "one-time only creations" on a limited basis to what the Brooklyn Brewery website calls "our favorite" bars and restaurants.

Critics generally praised Oliver's Brooklyn Brewery creations. The Boston-based beer connoisseurs Jason and Todd Alstrom, who own the popular rating site beeradvocate.com and publish the magazine Beer Advocate, gave Brooklyn Brewery's flagship beer, Brooklyn Lager, a "B" rating. Jason Alstrom described it as "a good solid brew, the only thing that bothered me about it was the hop flavour seems to be too much and the beer is not as crisp as you would expect a lager to be." They gave Oliver's winter seasonal beer, the Brooklyn Black Chocolate Stout, "A-"; Todd Alstrom wrote that it was "an incredibly tasty and powerful stout" and represented the "best use of chocolate malt that I've ever seen for the style." The article in the

Jersey Journal noted that Brooklyn Summer Ale is "a refreshing thirst quencher," adding, "This beer is not too heavy, except in flavor. Excellent with salads, seafood, and quiches, it's good for brunches and light lunches during the summer months."

"If we truly want to restore the vibrant beer culture that flourished in this country before Prohibition, craft brewers need to retain the values and goals—creating beers that are flavorful, interesting to drink and made from proper beer ingredients—that put us on the map in the first place."

Oliver is also recognized for his ability to pair particular beers with particular foods to best effect. He told Mark Bittman, "To me, beer and wine are both beverages meant to be served with food. And good beer, real beer, often offers things that most wine does not, like carbonation and caramelized and roasted flavors—aspects that sometimes make beer the preferable choice. And the most wonderful thing about beer is that it has that ability to 'reset' your palate"—that is, remove whatever taste remains in the mouth from whatever was eaten last. He also said that with food, wine "contrasts" better, while beer "harmonizes" better, giving as an example the traditional pairing of chocolate cake with port, a wine produced in Portugal: "You like the idea of the port, but you don't taste anything. But if you eat that cake with the right beer--a framboise, or a chocolate stout—it dovetails beautifully. Unfortunately, people don't necessarily think in that direction." Oliver has demonstrated his pairing abilities and skill as a beer taster at sites in many parts of the world. He has hosted tastings and given talks about beer at such prestigious venues as the James Beard House, Gramercy Tavern, the Waldorf-Astoria Hotel, the Sommelier Society of America, and the American Institute of Wine and Food, all in New York City, and the Culinary Institute of America, in Hyde Park, New York. Overseas, he has presided at events in cities including London and Leeds, in England; Copenhagen, in Denmark; and Rio de Janeiro and Sao Paulo, in Brazil. He spoke at the 2004 International Association of Culinary Professionals (IACP) conference, in Baltimore, Maryland; the 2006 Cape Wine Conference, in South Africa; and the 2008 Good Experience Live (GEL) conference, in New York City. He has also hosted tastings and lectured at such institutions as the Museum of Natural History and the Jewish Museum, in New York City; the Smithsonian Institution, in Washington, D.C.; and MassMOCA, the Massachusetts Museum of Contemporary Art, in North Adams.

Oliver produced the *Good Beer Book* (1997) with the help of Timothy Harper, a freelance writer. In an undated review for Booklist, as quoted on Amazon.com, Ray Olson wrote, "Harper and Oliver's beer book is twice good: it is about good—flavorful, zesty, attractive—beer, and it is a good—amusing, informative, lively—book. It covers beer history, how and of what beer is made, the major styles of lagers and ales, the rebirth of American craft brewing, the rise of brewpubs, big brewers' response to craft brewing, and proper beer handling and tasting, and it provides advice on beer and food, annotated lists of outstanding American and European breweries, a little gazetteer of brewpubs and beer bars, some home brew recipes, online and periodical resource lists, and a glossary. Other books are more comprehensive on one or another, even several, of these matters (for example, there are book-length beer gazetteers), but none treats them all so well at so reasonable a price." Damaso Reyes wrote that Oliver's next book, *The Brewmaster's Table: Discovering the Pleasures of Real Beer with Real Food* (2003), "gives insight to both the history of beer from ancient times … to the present day. After reading the lively and well-written book you will not only know just about everything there is to know about beer, but also how to match beer with food, something the Europeans have been doing for centuries but we are still learning about here in America. According to Oliver it is the variety and flexibility of beer that makes it, much more so than wine, the perfect companion to foods from Chinese to Thai to American BBQ." *The Brewmaster's Table* won an International Association of Culinary Professionals (IACP) Book Award in 2004 and, also that year, was a finalist for a James Beard Foundation Book Award. Oliver was commissioned by Oxford University Press to act as editor in chief for the *Oxford Companion to Beer,* which appeared in 2011. The book won the 2011 André Simon Book Award in the Drinks Category and placed first in the 2012 Gourmand Award for Best in the World in the Beer category.

Oliver has served for 20 years as a judge for the Professional Panel Blind Tasting of the Great American Beer Festival. He has also been a judge at the annual Great British Beer Festival competition and the Brewing Industry International Awards competition. Oliver has been a guest on National Public Radio (NPR) programs and on television news shows on CBS, CNN, ABC, PBS, the History Channel, the Travel Channel, and A&E

Oliver's honors include the Russell Schehrer Award for Innovation and Excellence in Brewing (1998) from the Institute for Brewing Studies and the 2003 Semper Ardens Award for Beer Culture (2003), a Danish prize. He was named the *Cheers* Beverage Media's "Beverage Innovator of the Year" in 2006. In 2007 *Forbes* named him one of the top-ten tastemakers in the United States for wine, beer, and spirits. Oliver's page at the Brooklyn Brewery website recounts that he was a founding member of the board of Slow Food USA and later served for five years on the board of counselors of Slow Food International. In May 2014 Oliver won the James Beard award in the category of Outstanding Wine, Beer, or Spirits Professional.

A few years ago, when Josh Abraham, writing for gothamist.com (May 31, 2005), asked Oliver to name his favorite beer, he responded, "I'm sure I've had close to 1,000 different beers. So I have too many favorites to list. I have a particular love for the more complex Belgian styles and for British cask-conditioned ales when they're done properly." He told *Current Biography,* "Any time you can take a hobby and make it into your job, it's a wonderful thing. I've had the opportunity to meet people and to brew all over the world. I'm a very lucky man."

Further Reading:

(New York) *Amsterdam News* July 24, 2003

Brooklyn Brewery website

First We Feast website, Sep. 17, 2013

garrettoliver.com

(London) *Guardian* Sep. 25, 1993

(Hudson County, New Jersey) *Jersey Journal* June 7, 2008

Selected Books:

Oliver, Garrett, and Timothy Harper, *The Good Beer Book,* 1997

Oliver, Garrett, *The Brewmaster's Table: Discovering the Pleasures of Real Beer with Real Food,* 2003

Oliver, Garrett, ed., *Oxford Companion to Beer,* 2011

Otis, Clarence, Jr.

Business executive

Born: 1956, Vicksburg, Mississippi, United States

Many people who have never heard of Darden Restaurants Inc. have eaten at one or another of the company's 2,100 restaurants, which bear the names Red Lobster, Olive Garden, LongHorn Steakhouse, the Capital Grille, Bahama Breeze, Seasons 52, Eddie V's, and Yard House. Unlike fast-food outlets, the restaurants in those chains provide full service, complete with waiters or waitresses and menus with a wide variety of items, and Darden owns its restaurants rather than operating them as franchises. Clarence Otis Jr. is the chairman and chief executive officer (CEO) of Darden, which is headquartered in Orlando, Florida. In July 2008, in its annual report, Darden—a holding company whose subsidiaries operate its restaurants— described itself as the largest company-owned and company-operated full-service restaurant business in the world. Darden and its founder, William H. "Bill" Darden, are acknowledged to be among the pioneers of what is known as casual dining.

Otis arrived at Darden as treasurer in 1995, some 27 years after Bill Darden opened the first Red Lobster restaurant. Raised in a poor, high-crime area of Los Angeles, California, Otis earned undergraduate and law degrees with the help of scholarships. For 15 years, beginning in 1980, he worked as a lawyer and then as an investment banker. When he rose to the top executive post at Darden, in 2004, only six other African Americans headed Fortune 500 companies. In a brief essay for *BusinessWeek* (August 20, 2007), he wrote, "I always believed major companies had significant leverage and that they could make profound differences. So if you had the ability to shape the direction of a major company, then you could make a social difference." In an interview with Adam Bryant for the *New York Times* (June 7, 2009), Otis said, "Leaders really think about others first. They think about the people who are on the team, trying to help them get the job done. They think about the people who they're trying to do a job for. … You think last about 'what does this mean for me?'"

Education and Early Career

The oldest of the four children of Clarence Otis Sr. and his wife, the former Calanthus Hall, Clarence Otis Jr. was born on April 11, 1956, in Vicksburg, Mississippi. Along with two brothers and a sister, he was raised in Watts, a poor, black section of Los Angeles. His father was a janitor employed by the city. His mother, a homemaker, took an active role in the Otis children's education, volunteering at their schools, attending meetings of each school's parent-teacher association, and making sure her sons and daughter did their homework carefully. "Would Clarence have turned out as good as he did, a straight arrow, without his mother? I don't know. I doubt it," Felix Grossman, a lawyer who served as a recruiter for Williams College, and who met Otis as a teenager, conjectured to Sarah Hale Meitner for the *Orlando* [Florida] *Sentinel* (December 26, 2004). Around the time Otis started school, he developed a love for reading. He would go to the local library a few times a month and check out a big stack of books. By the time he started high school, he had read most of the biographies and novels in the library.

Otis experienced the Watts riots of August 1965. The riots were triggered by a traffic arrest that inflamed years of growing animosity, fear, and rage that residents of Watts felt toward the virtually all-white police force; fights, arson, and looting continued for six days, resulting in more than 30 deaths and 1,000 injuries, nearly 4,000 arrests, and the destruction of vehicles and hundreds of stores and other buildings. "I can still see the National Guard, with bayonets at the end of their rifles," Otis wrote in his *Business Week* essay. Even on ordinary days Watts was plagued by gang activity, drug peddling, shootings, and other forms of violence as well as stop-and-frisk searches and other tension-filled encounters with police officers; as a teenager Otis himself was once "pulled over by the police, guns drawn, [and] told to get on the ground," he recalled for *Business Week*. He always tried to avoid danger or potential trouble, however, and he became adept at dealing with many sorts of people. Thanks to his father, he observed firsthand some of the radical differences between Watts and wealthy neighborhoods: on weekends Clarence Sr. would often take his wife and children for a drive to see the beautifully maintained houses, manicured yards, and clean sidewalks of Beverly Hills and experience the atmosphere of calm that prevailed there. "Those drives showed me how the other half lived," Otis told Bruce Horovitz for *USA Today* (November 27, 2006). "They made me believe another life was possible."

The summer before his senior year at the David Starr Jordan High School, in Watts, Otis fractured his hip. He spent the next few months bedbound in a body sling. Determined not to fall behind in his schoolwork, he studied, got tutoring, completed homework assignments, and took tests, and he graduated with his class, in 1973. He accepted a scholarship to Williams College, a private liberal-arts school in northeastern Massachusetts, where he concentrated in economics and political science. In his senior year Otis won the school's prize for political-science writing. He graduated magna cum laude with a B.A. degree in 1977; he was also elected to the honor society Phi Beta Kappa. By then he had developed an interest in law, and, again with the help of a scholarship, he enrolled at the Stanford Law School, in California. To cover his expenses he worked as a waiter. He earned a J.D. degree in 1980. He told Adam Bryant that what had prepared him "the most" for his career in management were his experiences as an actor in student plays in high school, college, and law school, "and even for a couple of years after law school," because in each production the cast had to function as a team: "I would say that probably is the starkest lesson in how reliant you are on others, because you're there in front of an audience. It's all live, and everybody's got to know their lines and know their cues and know their movement, and so you're totally dependent on people doing that."

After he graduated from Stanford, Otis moved to New York City, where for four years he practiced law, specializing in securities litigation and mergers and acquisitions. His first employer was the firm Donovan Leisure Newton & Irvine; the second was Gordon, Hurwitz, Butowsky, Weitzen, Shalov & Wein. Having found that he was more fascinated by finance than law, in about 1984 he joined the investment-banking firm Kidder, Peabody, & Co. (now defunct), where he served as a vice president. In 1987 he left that company to become a vice president at another investment firm, First Boston Corporation, where his work involved real estate. In 1990 he changed jobs again, moving to Giebert Municipal Capital as a managing director; his focus there was public and government finance, which concerns the collection of taxes and uses of tax monies. Then, in 1991, he joined the Chemical Banking Corporation (now JPMorgan Chase & Company), a holding company for Chemical Bank, first as a vice president and then as managing director of public finance. During his four years with Chemical, Otis contributed to "the turnaround of the company's struggling public-finance division," according to various sources, and he reinforced his reputation as an astute leader.

Later Career

In 1995 a recruiter from Darden tapped Otis for a newly created job at the company—that of treasurer. During his interviews with Darden representatives, Otis wrote for *BusinessWeek*, "I felt, here's an organization that is pretty multidimensional compared to Wall Street. I liked the mass appeal of the brands, the fact that they really were pervasive. And you've got this broad employee base that was diverse in every respect, in an industry where folks can really go from entry level to the top. And it was an organization that was earnest. It had a humility that I was comfortable with." Earnestness and humility were said to be traits that characterized Bill Darden, who opened his first eatery in Georgia in 1938, when he was 19 years old. It was a tiny luncheonette called the Green Frog, whose motto was "Service with a hop." In subsequent years Darden became the owner or part-owner of 20 Howard Johnson franchises and a seafood restaurant in Orlando, among other properties. The first Red Lobster opened in Lakeland, Florida, in January 1968. Darden insisted that no more than ten minutes elapse between the time customers placed their orders and the time their food reached their tables, and on each table he left a card on which customers could assess the Red Lobster's service and food. Immediately the "response was so overwhelming that even Darden and his investor partners had to work full shifts just to get the food out," Bill Carlino wrote for *Nation's Restaurant News* (February 1996).

In 1970, after two additional Red Lobster restaurants had opened— two more were under construction— the food giant General Mills bought the chain; as a General Mills employee, Darden supervised the chain and set up a Red Lobster headquarters in Orlando. Thanks to financing from General Mills, the business expanded enormously: within a decade some 260 Red Lobster restaurants were operating. The first Olive Garden restaurant opened in 1982. In a profile of Red Lobster for the *New York Times* (April 23, 1989) when the chain had 513 restaurants, Douglas C. McGill wrote that its success could be attributed to various factors, among them its emphasis on friendly, helpful service and comprehensive training of new waiters and waitresses; its frequent surveys of customers, awareness of trends, and rapid responses to changes in customers' preferences; a customized computer system that enabled management to keep track of every order in every restaurant and thus see which items were selling well or poorly; and a worldwide system for purchasing seafood from thousands of fishing operations, large and small. "We believe there is a science to running dinnerhouse restaurants," Joe R. Lee, then the president of General Mills restaurants, told McGill. "We believe there is a science to determining consumer needs, and a science to answering those needs, in a disciplined manner, on a massive scale." Lee, a protégé of Bill Darden, had begun his career with Darden Restaurants as the manager of the first Red Lobster restaurant. "Experts in the industry largely credit Mr. Lee with providing the vision that has guided Red Lobster's growth," McGill wrote.

When Bill Darden died, in 1994, there were 675 Red Lobsters and 458 Olive Gardens. That year General Mills began the process of divesting itself of Darden Restaurants; it was the anticipation that the company would become independent of General Mills that led to the creation of the treasurer post. Otis was present at the New York Stock Exchange when, on May 30, 1995, Darden became a publicly traded firm. Otis remained treasurer until, two years later, he was named senior vice president of investor relations. In 1998 he became senior vice president of finances, and in 1999 he was promoted to chief financial officer. Beginning in 2002, he took on the post of president of Smokey Bones Barbeque & Grill, a chain launched in 1999. In December 2004 Otis was appointed Darden's CEO. Otis succeeded Joe R. Lee, who had retired.

In his interview with Adam Bryant, Otis identified Lee as the person who "reinforced" the philosophies of management and service that have guided him at Darden. As an example of Lee's wisdom and humanity, Otis told Bryant that on September 11, 2001, after they learned about the terrorist attacks in New York City and Washington, D.C., "we had an all-employee meeting, and Joe started to talk. One of the first things he said was, 'We are trying to understand where all our people are who are traveling.' The second thing he said was: 'We've got a lot of Muslim teammates … who are going to be under a lot of stress during this period. And so, we need to make sure we're attentive to that.' And that was pretty powerful. Of all the things you could focus on that morning, he thought about the people who were on the road and then our Muslim colleagues." In speeches and interviews Otis has also cited curiosity—the desire to seek out truths that are not immediately obvious—as one the most essential characteristics of a leader.

"I always believed major companies had significant leverage... If you had the ability to shape the direction of a major company, then you could make a social difference."

In November 2005 Otis assumed the chairmanship of Darden Restaurants Inc., while remaining CEO. Noteworthy events since then include Darden's acquisition in 2007 of Rare Hospitality International, which owned the 288 restaurants in the LongHorn Steakhouse chain and the 29 restaurants in the Capital Grille chain. In the same year Darden sold the Smokey Bones chain. Despite the economic recession that began in the United States in December 2007, Darden as a whole continued to prosper. In a report filed with the Securities and Exchange Commission in March 2009, the company reported that sales for the nine months that ended on February 22, 2009, totaled $5.24 billion, up from $4.80 billion during the corresponding nine months one year earlier. In a striking indication that Darden had fared better than many other firms during the economic downturn, the company was ranked 374th on the 2009 Fortune 500 list of the nation's largest businesses that year, with annual sales of $6.747 billion and a profit of $377.2 million; on the 2008 Fortune 500 list, the company ranked 415th, with annual sales of $5.925 billion and a profit of $201.4 million. At the time Chuck Salter wrote about Darden for *Fast Company* (July 1, 2009), Darden was the twenty-ninth-largest employer in the United States, in terms of the number of people on its payrolls. In fiscal year 2013, Darden had sales of $8.5 billion and served 425 million meals annually; Darden Restaurants employed more than 200,000 people. According to Theresa Johnston, writing in *Stanford Lawyer* (June 2, 2013), "Share prices have roughly doubled since Otis took over Darden's helm in 2004." Clarence Otis's biography at the Darden website reports that in 2014, his most recent year as chairman and CEO, Darden appeared on *Fortune* magazine's "100 Best Companies to Work For" for the fourth year running.

In late 2013, however, Darden, as reported in RestaurantNews, announced that it would embark on a "comprehensive plan to enhance shareholder value, address changing industry dynamics in the casual dining sector and leverage the benefits of the Company's position as the premier casual dining restaurant company." The company planned to "separate the company's Red Lobster business," either by spinning Red Lobster off to its shareholders or selling the chain outright. "Our industry is in a period of significant change, with relatively low levels of consumer demand in each of the past several years for restaurants generally, and for casual dining in particular," Otis declared, noting that the "operating priorities, capital requirements, sales and earnings growth prospects, and volatility profiles of the two parts of the business" were "increasingly divergent." In May 2014 Darden sold its Red Lobster unit to Golden Gate Capital for roughly $2.1 billion.

Otis is a trustee of Williams College and sits on the boards of directors of Verizon Communications, the apparel giant VF Corporation, and the Federal Reserve Bank of Atlanta. He received the International Foodservice Manufacturers Association's Silver Plate Award in 2012; the award recognizes outstanding achievement and innovation in the foodservice industry.

Otis has been married since 1983 to Jacqueline Bradley, who has a master's degree in business from Columbia University; Bradley is a former vice chairperson of the Greater Orlando Aviation Authority, which manages Orlando International Airport, and secretary of the Florida Council on Arts and Culture. Otis and Bradley own one of the most extensive collections of African American art in the United States; the couple are listed among the nation's 100 top collectors of art of any kind. The paperback book *Crossing the Line: African American Artists in the Jacqueline Bradley and Clarence Otis, Jr. Collection*, edited by E. Luanne McKinnon, was published by Rollins College in 2007; it contains introductions by both Otis and Bradley. The Otis-Bradley Fund provides grants through the Community Foundation, which seeks to address central Florida's most pressing needs.

In October 2010 Otis won the Leadership Award of the Business Committee for the Arts, a division of Americans for the Arts, a national nonprofit. The BCA award recognized Darden's $5 million commitment to the Dr. Phillips Center for the Performing Arts in Orlando. In granting the award, the Business Committee for the Arts also cited Darden's support for Central Florida arts groups through its Good Neighbor program. Among Darden's beneficiaries are the Orlando Philharmonic, Orlando Ballet, Orlando Shakespeare Theater, Orlando Repertory Theatre, the Zora Neale Hurston Festival and the Mennello Museum of American Art.

Clarence Otis and Jacqueline Bradley have three children, Calvin and twins Allison and Randall. They reside in Windermere, Florida.

Further Reading:

Black Enterprise p28 Nov. 2004, p114 Feb. 2005

BusinessWeek p54+ Aug. 20, 2007

Fast Company July 1, 2009

Los Angeles Times Sep. 10, 2010

New York Times Business p2 June 7, 2009, Feb. 10, 2007

Orlando [Florida] *Sentinel* A p1 Dec. 26, 2004, Oct. 20, 2010

RestaurantNews website, Dec. 19, 2013

Stanford Lawyer June 2, 2013

USA Today B p1 Nov. 27, 2006

Oudolf, Piet

Landscape architect

Born: 1945, the Netherlands

"A plant should look good when it's dead," Piet Oudolf has often said. A leader in so-called new wave gardening—or new perennial gardening, or the Dutch Wave—Oudolf has earned renown as one of the world's most innovative landscape designers. A native of the Netherlands, he is associated with what is sometimes referred to as the European wild style, in part because of his inclusion of wild and little-known plant species in gardens and his preference for relaxed and eclectic arrangements. Eschewing the flowering plants common in seasonal gardens, in which there is often little of interest visually by late summer, Oudolf fills gardens with perennials, which keep their looks all year round. "Perennials lend so much excitement to the garden that I can't do without them," Oudolf has said, according to Yvonne Cunningham in *Gardening Life* (Fall 2002). "All my work is related to trying to re-create [the] spontaneous feeling of plants in nature. The idea is not to copy nature, but to give a feeling of nature."

Oudolf, who has studied and worked with plants for more than 30 years, emphasizes form and texture rather than color. "If the structure is right, the garden works—it doesn't matter what colors you use," Cunningham quoted him as saying. Oudolf routinely disregards convention; for example, he has often placed tall plants (albeit slender ones) in the front of a border rather than the back. He typically uses "see-through" plants, such as ornamental grasses, to add to a landscape a sense of depth as well as light and motion. "Oudolf's gardens may build on tradition, but they never look backward," the garden writer Noël Kingsbury explained in the London *Financial Times* (September 30, 1995). "They are a strong breath of fresh air for those of us tired of the constant historical references of much contemporary British work." In *Horticulture* (October 2002), Kingsbury, who was Oudolf's co-author on several books, noted the "remarkable combination of naturalistic abandon and contemporary formality" in Oudolf's work. Oudolf, he wrote, is "a rare example of a high-profile designer who combines a strong sense of architecture with a genuine love and knowledge of plants and their natural beauty." Writing in the *New York Times* (January 31, 2008), Sally McGrane asserts that Oudolf's "understanding of plants is generally acknowledged to be unrivaled among designers and has been a key, he said, to his ability to compose a garden where the plants work well together year round (or, as Mr. Oudolf put it, throughout the phases of birth, life and death)."

In the early years of his career, Oudolf worked on private gardens; later he also designed public parks in Germany, Sweden, the United Kingdom, and the United States. In January 2003 the Battery Conservancy of New York City chose Oudolf to design the Gardens of Remembrance, a tribute to the victims of the September 11, 2001, terrorist attacks on the World Trade Center and the Pentagon. "I try to make more beautiful gardens, more sensible gardens, more sensitive gardens [where] people can experience something in a more spiritual way," Oudolf told Sally Ruth Bourrie of the *Oregonian* (March 23, 2000). "It's more that I follow my heart." Oudolf subsequently worked with the landscape architects James Corner Field Operations on the High Line park in New York City, the first section of which opened in 2009. Oudolf is also a respected plant breeder; his nursery became world famous as the source of unusual perennials.

Education and Early Career

Piet Oudolf was born in about 1945 in the Netherlands. He studied architecture as it applies to buildings but never entered that field. For a few years he assisted his parents at the restaurant they owned. Finding little pleasure in that work, at the age of 26 he began taking courses in landscape design and served as a gardener with a series of firms. At age 31, in partnership with Romka Van de Raat, he started a small landscape-gardening business in Haarlem, not far from Amsterdam, the Netherlands' capital. He and Van de Raat, a former head gardener for the British writer and garden expert Christopher Lloyd, collaborated for five years.

By his own account, Oudolf developed his style through trial and error. Having concluded that clearing away the lifeless debris from annuals each fall was largely a waste of time, he came to prefer certain perennial plants that he left uncut in the winter. The stalks that remained, in Oudolf's view, looked dramatic all year round. In the London *Daily Telegraph* (November 4, 2000), James Bartholomew noted that Oudolf's designs stir "our subconscious awareness that gardens can be atmospheric and compelling, even on dull days and without lively color." Unlike many traditional European gardeners, Oudolf makes sparing use of shrubs and avoids roses altogether in his designs. "Shrubs take up too much space," he told Noël Kingsbury. "Roses have a poor form and their foliage is not interesting enough." Many of Oudolf's outdoor compositions contain plants that grow to heights of at least five feet. "You feel different when you have a tall plant around you," he told Sally Ruth Bourrie. "If you have only small plants, you have the feeling always that you rule the garden, and if you have tall plants, it's like the garden rules you."

In 1982, feeling increasingly frustrated about the difficulty of acquiring the plants he wanted for his clients' gardens, Oudolf and his wife, Anja, opened their own plant nursery. Located on farmland in Hummelo, a village some 60 miles southeast of Amsterdam, the property "took us five years to get … back into shape," as Oudolf told a writer for Genootschap Nederland-Engeland (Netherland-England Association). The unusual plants the Oudolfs began to raise attracted much publicity. Described by Steve Whysall for the *Vancouver Sun* (August 4, 2000) as a "plant-lover's paradise," the nursery—which was managed mainly by Anje Oudolf—was "one of the most exciting sources of new herbaceous perennials in Europe," according to Kingsbury. The Oudolfs closed the nursery in 2010 but continued to work on what Piet Oudolf called plant "experiments." Oudolf's business Future Plants markets the cultivars Oudolf has developed for his own use.

Later Career

For some years Oudolf concentrated on designing gardens for private residences and organizations. Thanks to media attention and the growing popularity of his work, in the 1990s he began to get commissions for public gardens. In 1996 he created a garden in the center of Enkoping, Sweden, using 240 species of plants and featuring a meandering strip of blue salvia, whose blossoms survive for an unusually long time. "People walk through [the garden] on their way to work," Stefan Matzon, Enkoping's superintendent of parks, told Anne Raver of the *New York Times* (January 16, 2003). "We call it the Dream Park, because we want people to put their dreams there." In other public projects, in England, Oudolf designed borders for the Royal Horticultural Society's garden at Wisley, in Surrey, and the Millennium Garden at the Pensthorpe Waterfowl

Trust, in Norfolk. He also designed gardens for the new offices of the global financial firm ABN AMRO in Amsterdam and the Hogeland Multifunctional Social Centre in Beekbergen, also in the Netherlands.

At the 2000 Chelsea Flower Show—one of the most prestigious outdoor garden events in England (Queen Elizabeth and members of her family attend every year)—Oudolf and the London-based garden designer Arne Maynard captured the "best in show" award and a gold medal for their joint exhibit, called Evolution. It was the first time that a non-British citizen had won first prize. More than two years in the planning, the garden measured about 30 feet by 70 feet and took three weeks to set up. According to the Genootschap Nederland-Engeland website, the design combined "classic elements, such as clipped hedges, with modern forms: stainless-steel flower boxes and red brick seating."

"All my work is related to trying to re-create [the] spontaneous feeling of plants in nature. The idea is not to copy nature, but to give a feeling of nature."

In January 2003 the Battery Conservancy, a nonprofit organization, announced that Piet Oudolf had been commissioned to design the Gardens of Remembrance in Battery Park, at the southernmost tip of Manhattan, to honor the victims of the September 11, 2001, terrorist attacks and provide a haven for reflection for their survivors and others. Oudolf's proposal won out over those of 17 competitors, including such heavyweights in the field of landscape architecture as Margie Ruddick and Michael Van Valkenburgh. "Piet has an incredible instinct for how plants entice us and envelop us," Warrie Price, the founder and president of the Battery Conservancy, told Anne Raver. "He knows how to make gardens look great in all four seasons." Planting of the Gardens of Remembrance began in spring 2003. The 10,000-square-foot garden—Oudolf's first garden in the United States—runs parallel to the water to the west of the Castle Clinton National Monument (once the country's official immigrant processing center). To the east of the monument, Oudolf subsequently (2003–2005) created the 53,000-square-foot Battery Bosque, featuring 140 mature London plane trees, and 34,000 perennials, according to Francis Morrone in *Guide to New York City Urban Landscapes* (2013). Amenities include "old fashioned … lamp standards, world's fair-type benches, winding paths, a sleek circular fountain of polished granite," a playground, and food kiosks. Morrone called it "one of the most ambitious additions to an existing New York City park in decades." For his part, Oudolf told Anne Raver, "It's very busy along the water. People are moving all the time. I want them to stand still, and feel what is happening."

Owing to its location, Oudolf's Battery Park gardens sustained major damage during Hurricane Sandy in October 2012. In an interview for *New York Cottages & Gardens* (March 2013), Warrie Price outlined for Alejandro Saralegui the catastrophic extent of the damage and the conservancy's efforts to address it: "The saltwater came up 13 feet over the seawall, and we had to flush out not just the salt, which is harmful to plants, but contaminants as well. We lost our last American elm, near the playground." (Price added that the conservancy's offices were so heavily damaged that the conservancy lost its "archives, library, founding papers, videos … everything!") The conservancy, Price said, "immediately reached out to horticulturalists in New Orleans to learn from their experience with Katrina, and they recommended that we rinse out the saltwater from the plants and soil. … We saved all the plants we could." Asked how the conservancy planned to handle future storms, Price said: "Nature is always in charge, and while the gardens were planned to withstand flooding, we will look for even better salt-tolerant plants. Once we go through a whole year's growing cycle, we'll assess what survived best and take it from there."

Together with the landscape artist Kathryn Gustafson and the lighting and set designer Robert Israel, Oudolf won an international competition to create the Lurie Garden at Millennium Park for the City of Chicago. Known colloquially as the Shoulder Garden (from Carl Sandburg's poem "Chicago," in which he referred to Chicago as the "city of the big shoulders"), the five-acre, four-season garden was completed in 2004. A 15-foot-high "shoulder hedge" on two sides protects the garden's perennials. Collaborator Kathryn Gustavson told Anne Raver that Oudolf "has an innate, visceral understanding of plants."

Oudolf returned to New York City for the High Line project, designing plantings for the former elevated rail bed that preserved the self-seeded nature of the existing landscape while giving the city a brilliantly successful and unique four-season public garden. The first section, Gansevort Street to 20th Street, opened in June 2009, and the second section, to 30th Street, opened two years later. The High Line at the Rail Yards, the garden's third, northernmost section, is set to open in fall 2014. The Friends of the High Line website explains that the "plantings on the High Line are meant to change. They mimic the dynamics of a wild landscape. Plants out-compete one another, spread or diminish in number. … The High Line's beds are planted in what Piet Oudolf calls a 'matrix' style. A mix of several dominant species, usually grasses, acts as the matrix that supports dots and drifts of other plants—generally the wildflowers, trees, and shrubs. Over the years, some species have disappeared from one area only to self-sow into another place. … The gardeners edit to maintain Oudolf's ratio of matrix plants to accent species, and to keep the dominant plants themselves planted in the right proportions. " Oudolf's vision for the High Line—"keep it wild"—was sustained in part by the Green Corps, a community-oriented, paid internship program involving local teens in the High Line garden.

Oudolf's later projects included the planting design for Swiss architect Peter Zumthor's *hortus conclusus* ("enclosed garden") in Kensington Park, London, the Serpentine Gallery Pavilion for 2011. The Serpentine Gallery Pavilion project is an annual temporary installation open from June until October. The pavilion is the venue for Park Nights, an annual series featuring live art, poetry, music, film, literature, performance and theory. Thereafter, over 2013–2014, in Somerset, England, Oudolf developed gallery landscaping for contemporary art dealers Hauser & Wirth as well as a 1.5-acre rectangular garden on the property. The freestanding garden displays what Tim Richardson of the London *Telegraph* (August 13, 2013) called "Oudolf's signature style, which [Oudolf] describes as 'romantic, nostalgic, not wild, organic, spontaneous.'" According to Richardson, the "overall plant choice indicates that Oudolf is adding more complexity and detail to his designs, in tune with the general trajectory of planting design at the moment." Richardson noted that Oudolf's work had been criticized for "its lack of application in domestic gardens"; matrix planting is, of course, most effective on a large scale.

Oudolf again collaborated with James Corner Field Operations and leading landscape architects on Queen Elizabeth Olympic Park, developed on the site of the main pedestrian plaza for the 2012 Olympics and Paralympic Games. The concept was the familiar garden "rooms," devoted here to play, music, theater, and "water." The park opened in March 2014.

Oudolf's book *Gardening with Grasses,* which he wrote with the garden designer Michael King, was published in 1998. It contains information about 150 varieties of grasses and grass relatives (in particular, sedges and bamboos), including cultivars (plants that do not exist in nature but, rather, are the creations of breeders), and describes ways of creating pleasing harmonies or dramatic contrasts by juxtaposing grasses and other species. The book also advises on uses of grasses in different spaces, ranging from a single container to plots of diverse shapes and sizes. "This is one of the most inspiring books to come out of new naturalistic gardening, but it is also an invaluable reference work," a reviewer for the website Sunday Books wrote; according to JoAnn Turner, in an assessment for the website Into the Garden, the lavishly illustrated book is a "sumptuous feast for the eyes."

Oudolf wrote *Designing with Plants* (1999) with Noël Kingsbury. In the section called "Planting Palettes," the authors discussed plant forms, textures, and colors; they then described how to combine those elements to create gardens that are distinctive in terms of atmosphere as well as appearance. For example, as Oudolf explained to Steve Whysall, a garden that was designed as "a paradigm of creation," in which "the human role with it … [is] a minor one," may stimulate in the visitor a "spiritual experience where one feels at one with the whole of creation." A review for the British website Garden Books by Post judged *Designing with Plants* to be an "informative and visually breathtaking study of Piet Oudolf's planting theory and practice, and it provides all the necessary advice to create the same effects in your own garden." In a critique for the website of the Chicago Botanic Garden, Julie Siegel declared, "Of service to both professionals and amateurs, this book's highly useful lists, superb photographs and modern design complement its innovative concepts."

In 2000 Oudolf published *Dream Plants for the Natural Garden.* Written with the Dutch gardener Henk Gerritsen, the book identifies and recommends some 1,200 plants suitable for temperate-zone sites. In a review for *Booklist* (December 15, 2000), Alice Joyce wrote, "Inquisitive gardeners will savor the engagingly wry tone and provocative opinions contained in this fine compendium"; in the *New York Times Book Review* (December 3, 2000), Verlyn Klinkenborg wrote, "The inattentive gardener, who by definition doesn't want to spray or stake or mollycoddle, will find a terrific guide to plants with a Shakerish self-reliance in *Dream Plants for the Natural Garden."*

With Noël Kingsbury, Oudolf wrote *Landscapes in Landscapes (2011) and Planting: A New Perspective (*2013). In a thoughtful review of *Landscapes in Landscapes* posted on Amazon.com, Alan Chandler remarked that on studying Oudolf's garden plans in that volume, "It's extraordinary to see quite how structured they are" despite looking so natural. The book is not organized chronologically, but rather by garden size. Chandler nevertheless noted Oudolf's "progression over time from perennial plantings with grasses used as accents to plantings today consisting of 75% grasses with a few forbs; moving from planting in blocks, to blocks, blended drifts and islands with scattered accent plants, to matrix planting with accents in thematic schemes." The Lurie Garden in Chicago, in Chandler's view, was a turning point for Oudolf, marking the first time he "used blocks and drifts with accent plants using a large percentage of local wild flora. … The hidden narrative of the book is [Oudolf's] movement over time towards increasingly complex and subtle plantings producing a more naturalistic look, with reduced reliance on a contrast with sculptural clipped hedging in the traditional Dutch manner." Of *Planting: A New Perspective,* Carol Haggas wrote in *Booklist* (December 15, 2012), "Faced with concerns such as sustainability, biodiversity, nature deficit, and water reclamation, [Oudolf and Kingsbury] extol high-performance designs that aim to collaborate with nature rather than control it. In truth, their gardens are paragons of apparent spontaneity, exhibiting an exuberance that seems neither forced nor contrived."

Among the plants that Oudolf considers garden essentials are the calico aster, the garden orache (also called mountain spinach), feather reed grass, sea holly, bronze fennel, purple moor grass, and the giant polygonum. "You look for the wildness in a plant," he told Jane Powers for the *Irish Times* (January 15, 2000), "but you also look for its 'well behaviour.' You look for plants that have personality or character. Every plant you meet … I call it 'meet the plant,' you see it as a character or person, and you want to know it and grow it and see the positives and negatives." Oudolf and his wife have bred cultivars of masterwort, prairie mallow, meadow sweet, bergamot, and salvia. According to Powers, "All share a certain guileless quality that gives an abandoned and nature-let-loose look to Piet Oudolf's magnificent plantings."

Photos of Oudolf's nursery and garden designs have appeared in such publications as *Gardens Illustrated, House and Garden,* the [London] *Independent, Perspectives,* and *Marie Claire Maison.* In June 2003 the Royal Horticultural Society awarded Oudolf the Gold Veitch Memorial Medal for his work toward advancing and improving the science and practice of horticulture. In addition to his Chelsea Flower Show medal, his other significant awards include the Award for Excellence in Design from the Art Commission of the City of New York (2003); the Award of Distinction from the Association of Professional Landscape Designers (2010); the Lucy G. Moses Preservation Award (2010), ecognizing his work on the High Line; the European Garden Award (2010), for the High Line and his work on Trentham Gardens, Stoke on Trent, England; and the Prince Bernhard Cultural Foundation Award (2913), bestowed by Queen Maxima of the Netherlands. Oudolf figures in *Elevated Thinking: The High Line in New York City,* a PBS documentary released in June 2014. He is the subject of Thomas Piper's forthcoming documentary *Piet Oudolf: Fall, Winter, Spring, Summer, Fall,* scheduled for mid-2015, which promises an "intimate view of Oudolf's process, from landscape blueprints to theories on beauty."

Further Reading:

Booklist Dec. 15, 2000, Dec. 15, 2012

Chicago Tribune D p2 May 9, 1999

[London] *Daily Telegraph* p20 Nov. 4, 2000, Aug. 13, 2013

Gardening Life p24 Fall 2002

Irish Times p75 Jan. 15, 2000

(London) *Financial Times* p7 Sep. 30, 1995

New York Cottages & Gardens March 2013

New York Times F p11+ Jan. 16, 2003, with photos, Jan. 31, 2008, with photos, Feb. 9, 2011, with photos

T Magazine Apr. 10, 2013

Oregonian p24 Mar. 23, 2000

Vancouver Sun E p3 Aug. 4, 2000

Books:

Dickey, Page, *Breaking Ground,* 1997

Richardson, Tim, *Futurescapes: Designers for Tomorrow's Outdoor Spaces,* 2011

Lynn, Robin, and Francis Morrone, *Guide to New York City Urban Landscapes,* 2013

Selected Books:

Oudolf, Piet, and Michael King, *Gardening with Grasses,* 1996

Oudolf, Piet, with Noël Kingsbury, *Designing with Plants,* 1999

Oudolf, Piet, and Henk Gerritsen, *Dream Plants for the Natural Garden,* 2000

Oudolf, Piet, and Henk Gerritsen, *Planting the Natural Garden,* 2003

Oudolf, Piet, and Noël Kingsbury, *Landscapes in Landscapes,* 2011

Oudolf, Piet, and Noël Kingsbury, *Planting: A New Perspective,* 2013

Petrini, Carlo

Activist, nonprofit director, publisher, writer, lecturer

Born: 1949, Bra, Italy

"Taste is the highest expression of a nation," Carlo Petrini, the founder of Slow Food, an increasingly popular international organization that fuses gastronomy with environmentalism, told Nicholas Lander for the *Financial Times* (November 21, 1998), "yet in the history of mankind we have never spent so little time or money as a percentage of our income on food as we do today. We must preserve the umbilical cord between the farmer, the producer and the consumer and make today's young aware that good food comes from the land, not an industrial zone." The Slow Food movement began in Italy, when, as a reaction against the intrusion of international "fast food" chains such as McDonald's, Petrini and his compatriots formed an organization dedicated to preserving local gastronomic traditions they perceived as threatened by the food industry's push for convenience.

Such traditions not only included the foods that people eat, but the style in which they eat them: Petrini lamented the threat to the hours-long meal that had been a longstanding tradition in many cultures, including those of much of Western Europe. "Behind the philosophy of Slow Food is the philosophy of slow life," Petrini told Susanne Fowler for the *Chicago Tribune* (November 13, 1998). "Slowing down becomes a homeopathic medicine. Every day we are able to slow down, we are able to relax, to think instead of run. There is one universal truth—we all end up in the same place. It's better to go there slowly." In the years since its inception in 1986, Slow Food has evolved from a movement advocating the preservation of regional customs, foods, and wines into one that binds gourmands and environmentalists into a powerful alliance based on good-tasting, aesthetically pleasing food produced in an Earth-friendly manner.

Education and Early Career

Carlo Petrini was born on June 22, 1949, in Bra, in Italy's Piedmont region. He attended Italy's University of Trento, a newly founded institution known for its social activism, where he pursued a sociology degree but also studied history, human sciences, and food culture. He never graduated, but he was known as a campus firebrand and was reputed to be an active member of the Communist Party. "I was trained on the barricades of 1968," Petrini said, as quoted by Florence Fabricant of the *New York Times* (November 15, 1989), referring to student revolts of that year that occurred at several Italian universities. ("Now I'm older and wiser," he added. "I'm not trying to overthrow the system but I'm hoping we can offer an alternative to the fast life. We won't throw bombs at McDonald's. Maybe handfuls of tagliarini.") In the 1970s Petrini used a Korean War-surplus transmitter from a U.S. tank to start a pirate radio station, Radio Bra Onde Rosse ("Red Waves"), in the Piedmont region, broadcasting his leftist political views. Within several years, however, he began to curtail his outspoken activities. "I came to understand that those who suffer for others do more damage to humanity than those who enjoy themselves," he reflected to Corby Kummer for the *Atlantic Monthly* (March 1, 1999). "Pleasure is a way of being at one with yourself and others."

In 1977, according to the Slow Food USA website, Petrini became an adviser to the mayor of Bra. The website credits Petrini, as an adviser, with organizing the Piedmont's Cantè j'euv, a week-long, Medieval era–inspired folk revival at which hundreds of European and North African musicians performed. Also in 1977 Petrini began working as a journalist, writing columns and restaurant reviews for several local magazines and newspapers, including *L'Espresso* and *La Stampa*. According to Alison Leitch, in "Slow Food and the Politics of 'Virtuous Globalisation'" (published in *Food and Culture: A Reader* [2013]), among the magazines Petrini contributed to was *La Gola*, which she describes as a "magazine published in Milan by a group of young intellectuals—philosophers, artists, and poets—dedicated to epicurean philosophy." Around this time, Petrini also became an event organizer for the Italian Recreation and Cultural Association (ARCI), a nonprofit organization responsible for promoting a wide array of cultural, sporting, and social events. In 1983 Petrini and several colleagues founded Arci Gola (a name that has been translated as "big gullet"), a Bra-based branch of ARCI devoted solely to gastronomy. The group elected Petrini as its president at the inaugural meeting and regularly re-elected him to that position in subsequent years. "With a few friends I started to think about an association based on the concept of pleasure and taste, and on the importance of good food and wine in life," Petrini explained to Christine Failla of *Art Culinaire* (Winter 2001). "We were very passionate on the matter and wanted to join as many people possible to share the pleasure. I traveled a lot and met a lot of people with the same passion. In the beginning, it started to grow as a net of Italian gourmets. The next step was the formation of Arci Gola." Three years later, in 1986, Petrini began editing "Gambero Rosso," a section of the national Communist newspaper *Il Manifesto* that was focused on wines.

Because ARCI was plagued by a multimillion-dollar debt—Petrini blames the politics of decision making for the debt accumulation—Arci Gola, as a subsidiary, was also strapped for funds. To fund his fledgling organization, Petrini edited a wine guide called *Vini d'Italia* ("Italian Wines") in 1987. He and his gastronome contemporaries named the publishing house through which *Vini d'Italia* was produced Gambero Rosso, after the *Il Manifesto* wines section, although Arci Gola was also credited as a copublisher. The guide, immediately successful, appeared annually and was edited by Petrini for more than a decade. (Aside from jointly publishing the wine guide, Gambero Rosso and Slow Food have no direct connection to each other.) By 1990 the book had become the leading wine guide in Italy.

Later Career

Meanwhile, the Slow Food movement evolved directly from Arci Gola. While the movement was officially launched in 1989, at the Opéra Comique in Paris, the year of its origin is often cited as 1986. After learning that year of a plan to open a 400-seat McDonald's fast-food restaurant in Rome's Piazza Navona—including display of the franchise's trademark yellow "M" (also known as the "golden arches")—Petrini organized protests against what he perceived to be the desecration of a landmark. Protesters adopted the name "Slow Food" for their cause in order to point up the contrast with McDonald's organizing principle. "There was a lot of public opinion that this was an invasion of a historical region, in one of the most beautiful sections of the city," Petrini told Dan Berger of the *Los Angeles Times* (April 8, 1990). (McDonald's opened the Rome franchise, but because of the popular support received by Petrini's demonstrations, the chain agreed to refrain from marking the building with the instantly recognizable "golden arches.") In about May 1989, Petrini began forming local support for Slow Food in Bra, mostly through word of mouth, and its adherents began to publish a monthly newsletter. On November 10, 1989, at simultaneous news conferences in such cities as New York, San Francisco, Rome, Paris, Zurich, Brussels, Copenhagen, Stockholm, Vienna, Caracas, and Fez, Slow Food spokespersons announced the organization's formation and the publication of its manifesto. Co-written by Petrini and Folco Portinari, a poet and close friend, the manifesto was an indictment of fast-food chains as emblematic of the problems of an efficiency-crazed society: "We are enslaved by speed and have all succumbed to the same insidious virus: Fast Life, which disrupts our habits, pervades the privacy of our homes and forces us to eat Fast Foods," it states, as reprinted from a Slow Food website. "A firm defense of quiet material pleasure is the only way to oppose the universal folly of Fast Life. May suitable doses of guaranteed sensual pleasure and slow, long-lasting enjoyment preserve us from the contagion of the multitude who mistake frenzy for efficiency." The movement adopted the snail as its symbol.

For several months following Slow Food's official founding, Petrini toured parts of the world to promote the movement. Slow Food inherited the 20,000 members of Arci Gola and by April 1990 could claim chapters—called "convivia," a reference to the dinner-table conviviality they hope to restore—in 26 countries. Membership fees were $55 a year, for which patrons received a bimonthly newsletter (*Slow: The International Herald of Taste,* which later became a quarterly published in English, Italian, German, French, and Spanish), an ID card, and a snail pin. The organization established a publishing wing, Slow Food Editoire, in 1990. The first International Slow Food Congress convened in Venice, Italy, in January 1991.

In the 1990s Slow Food members were frequently depicted by the press as food connoisseurs rather than activists. In 1996 the group organized its first five-day food fair, called Salone del Gusto ("Hall of Taste"), featuring foods from around the world; the Salone del Gusto became a biennial event. Later that year the movement began to incorporate more political elements into its overall philosophy, aimed at preserving biodiversity and ensuring the future of a wide array of foods—many of which tasted, at least to gourmands, superior to standardized varieties. (Petrini often explained that at the turn of the 20th century there had been 200 varieties of artichokes grown in Italy, while there were currently only 12.) By 1998 the organization urged its members to pursue and eat "endangered foods," on the assumption that demand would increase supply—these were not endangered species, but rather foods that standardization had abandoned—and compiled such foods in an "Ark of Taste," a list that also included recipes and wines.

The preservation of such foods often coincided with efforts to preserve the environment, an overlap which Petrini called "eco-gastronomy." "[Eco-gastronomy is] the transformation that Slow Food has undergone in these last four years," he told Tom Bates for the *Oregonian* (October 12, 1999), explaining his organization's newfound activism. "From gastronomic association, it has changed into an eco-gastronomic group. Why? Because we realized that the situation in the food world is dramatic—that species are dying. We don't want to be gastronomes who eat garbage." In response to the accusation that Slow Food living was only affordable to the elite, Petrini often countered by declaring that on average, people spend proportionately less money on food currently than they have at any other time in history. Petrini and other Slow Food advocates did not denigrate those who enjoyed fast food; rather, they openly advocated a world where a "Slow" life was possible. "If people want McDonald's, they should be free to go there," Petrini told a correspondent for the *Suddeutsche Zeitung,* as reprinted by the Global News Wire (November 11, 1998). "Everyone should live as they wish." In 1998 Slow Food claimed 60,000 members; a year later that number had increased to 70,000. During 1999 Petrini conducted an eight-state, 13-city tour of the United States (where he became fond of several "Slow" beers) and also toured Australia.

To aid its activist efforts, Slow Food opened an office in Brussels in about 2000, specifically to lobby at European Union (EU) headquarters. The office gathered about 500,000 signatures on a petition opposing the hygienic standards the EU was considering; such standards heavily favored mass-produced food products while potentially disenfranchising smaller producers, who, aside from making sacrifices in the taste of their foods, faced overwhelming costs to abide by the new standards. (In one case, the EU sought to require the makers of Roquefort cheese—who were known to ripen the cheese in limestone caves that naturally encouraged penicillin growth—to use caves or rooms lined with ceramic.) Because of such efforts, Slow Food secured exemptions from the standards for thousands of small producers. Slow Food also created an organizational wing, called the Presidia, to fund financially precarious businesses whose gastronomical practices exemplified Slow Food principles. Slow Food has also funded farmers' markets in the United States and Europe, as well as a hospital kitchen, in the Amazon rainforest, that uses regional foods.

"Gastronomy is holistic... If we adopt this vision of gastronomy, our relationships with food and each other change."

The first Slow Food awards—Petrini refers to them as the "Nobel prizes for food," according to Dale Curry of the New Orleans *Times-Picayune* (July 6, 2000)—were bestowed in October 2000 and honored producers of delicacies that preserved traditional techniques or created new means to make good food while maintaining biodiversity. The 2000 Salone del Gusto had considerable press coverage, and attracted about 100,000 attendees. (Today, the Salone del Gusto remains the largest international food and wine exhibition.) Prior to 2000 the conference concentrated on renowned master chefs, but the 2000 conference featured lesser-known regional products of small communities. At the 2000 Salone, the first 92 recipients of Presidia funds were announced. They included growers of the San Marzano tomato and producers of cured goat's thigh. "A gourmet who isn't interested in environmental issues is pathetic," Petrini told Fred Bridgland for the London Independent (September 7, 2001). "Equally, an environmentalist who doesn't appreciate good food is sad."

The Slow Food Foundation for Biodiversity was established in 2003 to support the Slow Food Award, the Presidia, and the Ark of Taste. That year the Slow Food International Congress attracted delegates from more than 50 nations. The launch of the Terra Madre Foundation in 2004—the first of its biennial World Meeting of Food Communities conferences was held in Turin in October 2004—was something of a watershed in the evolution of the "Slow" movement. In a conversation with Mark Bittman of the New York Times (March 26, 2013), Petrini recalled, "When we began Terra Madre, we were joined by Asians, Africans and Latin Americans, and we realized that 'gastronomy' was perceived by everyone in different ways, because our histories and conditions are different. But we all realized we had something in common, and that this fraternity was an important value." "Gastronomy," he continued, "is holistic. It's not only recipes and cooking but agriculture, physics, biology, genetics, chemistry, history, economy, politics and ecology. If we adopt this vision of gastronomy, our relationships with food and each other change."

Slow Food, which in 2014 claimed 150,000 members and 2,000 food communities (convivia) located throughout more than 150 countries, has continued to strengthen its activist operations, particularly through lobbying. It is occasionally referred to as the gastronomical equivalent of Greenpeace, although it is clearly less militant. In keeping with its dedication to local food traditions and production, Slow Food has conducted advocacy work in favor of sustainable agriculture and against genetically modified crops.

One of the most frequently encountered criticisms of the Slow Food movement is that it is elitist. Mark Bittman ascribes this perception to its early "narrow" focus on the taste and quality of food. He regards Slow Food as now "probably the only international organization that integrates concerns about the environment, tradition, labor, health, animal welfare … along with real cooking, taste and pleasure." Petrini himself acknowledged that the orientation of the organization has changed. He told Andra Zeppelin, as recounted in her guest blog at the *Denver Post* (May 2, 2013), "I believe that the real revolution is evolution. … We grew in a fluid manner and that is where our success comes from. We are now present in some of the poorest countries and there, we talk about gastronomy because even the poorest countries have gastronomy. It is that conversation that connects the population to the farmers, the fishermen, the food processors."

The Slow Food organization has also sent its representatives to classrooms to educate children about the cultural and ecological importance of the food they eat, and in about 2000 began planning for the opening of a university dedicated to the principles of Slow Food. That project, a brainchild of Petrini, came to fruition in October 2004, when 72 students from around the world, selected from thousands of applicants, began taking classes at the University of Gastronomic Sciences, at campuses in Parma and the Piedmont village of Pollenzo (a suburb of Bra). Administrators claim to have developed a highly academic curriculum for their students, who can earn a degree in three years and a master's degree after an additional two years. Students are enrolled in courses that cover the history of food and drink, food law, the semiotics of food, and the anthropology and sociology of consumption—subjects that are not usually offered at culinary schools. The curriculum also includes local and international travel and tastings intended to refine the pupils' palates. The university publicizes its program as a training ground for those seeking jobs in journalism, marketing, public administration, or the food industry. The Italian education ministry formally recognized the university in July 2004.

As editor in chief at Slow Food Editoire, Petrini oversaw the publication of a wide range of books, including cookbooks and guides to food, travel, wines, and inns. He published a book outlining the history and tenets of the Slow Food movement, *Slow Food: Le Ragioni del Gusto,* in 2001; it was translated by William McCuaig and published in English as *Slow Food: The Case for Taste* in 2003. The few reviews of its English translation criticized the tone of the book rather than its content. "Unfortunately, the passionate subjects of taste, seasonality and the true pleasure of eating are rendered dry as day-old toast in Petrini's slight, scholarly book," Anne Hurley wrote in her review for the *Seattle Times* (July 6, 2003). Most reviewers compared the book unfavorably to Eric Schlosser's 2001 condemnation of the fast-food industry, *Fast Food Nation,* in which many similar points were made. His later books included *Slow Food Revolution: A New Culture for Eating and Living* (2006); *Slow Food Nation: Why Our Food Should Be Good, Clean, and Fair* (2007), published in Italy as Buono, pulito e Giusto; and *Terra Madre: Forging a New Global Network of Sustainable Food Communities* (2010).

The International Wine and Spirit Competition honored Petrini as the Communicator of the Year for 2000, and he was featured as an "Innovator" in Time International's "European Heroes 2004" edition (October 11, 2004). He continues to travel the world promoting Slow Food's various initiatives. In May 2012 Petrini became the first guest speaker in history at the UN Permanent Forum (UNEP) on Indigenous Issues, and he was the co-laureate of the UNEP's 2013 Champions of the Earth Inspiration and Action prize.

Petrini lives in Bra and speaks fluent Italian and French. While he can no longer drink wine (which he once declared made meals whole), owing to a rare liver condition he contracted, Petrini has embraced alternatives: "Now I feel I have a new spirit," he told Nicholas Lander of the *Financial Times* (June 10, 2003), "[it] has been the experience of my life to survive this and, although I have had to give up wine, I have come to learn and appreciate the culture of tea."

Particularly appalled by acute hunger in the world in the midst of plenty, Petrini told Mark Bittman, "The main difficulty is that politicians don't understand that we need a new paradigm. They continue with the old ones: finance, production, consumption and waste. So we're producing enough food for 12 billion people, yet 1 billion out of our 7 billion aren't eating enough. And we hear that because there will be 9 billion people in 2050, we must produce more. But more production creates more environmental problems and more waste." "We can access a new vision," Petrini added, "but it will take patience. Politics is a problem, but you can already see the way. It's straight and determined, but this is a slow revolution. Slow. Slow."

Further Reading:

Art Culinaire p2 Winter 2001

Fast Company p194 May 2000

[London] *Independent* Dec. 10, 2009

Los Angeles Times H p1 Apr. 8, 1990 *Nation* p11 Aug. 20, 2001

New York Times C p10 Nov. 15, 1989, B p9 July 26, 2003, with photo, Mar. 26, 2013, May 1, 2013

Slow Food website

Books:

Andrews, Geoff, *The Slow Food Story: Politics and Pleasure*, 2008

Leitch, Alison, "Slow Food and the Politics of 'Virtuous Globalisation,'" in *Food and Culture: A Reader*, ed. by Carole Counihan and Penny Van Esterik, 2013

Selected Books:

Petrini, Carlo, *Slow Food: The Case for Taste*, 2003

Petrini, Carlo, with Gigi Padovani, *Slow Food Revolution: A New Culture for Eating and Living*, 2006

Petrini, Carlo, *Slow Food Nation: Why Our Food Should Be Good, Clean, and Fair*, 2007

Petrini, Carlo, *Terra Madre: Forging a New Global Network of Sustainable Food Communities*, 2010

Poon Tip, Bruce

Trinidadian-born Canadian travel executive

Born: 1967, Port of Spain, Trinidad

"I understand the craze for reality television," Bruce Poon Tip told Laura Pratt for the *National Post* (August 18, 2001), a Canadian newspaper. "It falls in line with my company offering reality travel. People want real experiences these days. They don't want fluff." Poon Tip's renown as the founder and CEO of the largest adventure tour company in Canada--Toronto-based GAP Adventures, Inc.--led producers of the successful CBS reality show *Survivor* to request his advice when planning their Australian Outback series. He has co-planned several seasons of *Survivor* since then, in such locations as the Serengeti desert and the Amazon jungle. Poon Tip's company also produced its own, self-titled reality series, which covered several of GAP's exotic adventures. His involvement in television, though, is a mere by-product of the enormous success he has experienced with GAP, which he founded while in his early 20s. The company offers tourists an environmentally and culturally sensitive travel experience--one with a closer adherence to such doctrines as sustainable development than more traditional, Westernized tours. "Poon Tip's firm envisions adventure travel as a grassroots, low-impact activity that encourages participants to travel responsibly and use locally owned accommodation," Paul Luke wrote for the *Vancouver Province* (October 27, 2002). "GAP clients mingle with local people and soak up exotic cultures, but there are few amenities--forget about five-star hotels and leave your hair dryer at home," Tamara Gignac wrote for the *Calgary Herald* (July 25, 2004).

Motivated more by his company's professed ideals than by profit, Poon Tip has twice been in Beijing on behalf of the World Bank and the United Nations Educational, Social and Cultural Organization (UNESCO) to address the Chinese government on the preservation of the country's cultural heritage, and he has spoken about ecotourism and sustainable development at the U.N. He also appears regularly on Canada's college-lecture circuit--offering his business knowledge to students in an effort to improve what he believes is a sub-par national support system for entrepreneurs. Today, G Adventures (the name changed in 2011, in part because of a lawsuit initiated by the Gap clothing-store chain))--a frequent recipient of national business awards--employsroughly 2,000 people, offers hundreds of tours on all seven continents, and is used by more than 100,000 tourists each year. While Wayne Lilley asserted in an article for the *National Post Business Magazine* (December 1, 2002) that "GAP's" marketing materials are full of exuberance that flirts with hyperbole, such as the boast that the company 'shocked the world' by winning a business award seven years in a row," Poon Tip's success is nonetheless noteworthy--a reflection of both the "entrepreneurial bravado" and "smart strategic moves" that Lilley attributed to him. "Every day is an adventure with Bruce," one frequent GAP customer told the *Calgary Sun* (September 9, 2004). "Being within a foot of a mountain gorilla in Zaire--that was beyond belief. What Bruce tells you may sound like an exaggeration, but every bit of it is true."

Education and Early Career

Bruce Poon Tip was born on March 15, 1967 in Trinidad. His father is of Chinese descent, and his mother is of Guyanese and Spanish descent. The family moved to Calgary, in Alberta, Canada, when Poon Tip was still a young child. There, his father operated a string of gas stations. Poon Tip has told journalists that he was considered a troublemaker while growing up. In the seventh grade, for example, he was suspended from school after getting in a dispute with a teacher who defended the absence from a classroom map of Tibet and Belize, saying they did not exist as countries. Poon Tip told Luke, "My logic was, 'How would you feel if you were Tibetan? How would you feel if you were Belizean?'" At around age 15, Poon Tip manufactured and sold more than 5,000 "Weather Worms"--temperature-sensitive bookmarks--with help from Junior Achievement (JA), a global non-profit agency providing business education to young people. The bookmarks, for which he was paid a dollar each by a local drugstore, were made from special yarn that turned pink when hot and blue when cold. Poon Tip, who had previous managerial experience from subcontracting his various paper routes, employed fellow students to help produce them. "I couldn't get the bookmarks out fast enough. It was a sweat-shop--almost every kid in the neighborhood started skipping school and staying up late to make these things," he told Gignac.

Poon Tip had difficulty adjusting to his earliest jobs working for others. He was fired two weeks into his first position, at a Denny's restaurant, after refusing to do another server's work in addition to his own. He was then let go from a training program at McDonald's, after telling his supervisor to "stuff it," according to Philip Jalsevac, writing for the Kitchener-Waterloo, Ontario, *Record* (March 17, 1999), and declining to wear a hair net. "I had barely any hair and I said it wasn't necessary and I wouldn't wear one," he told Luke.

In 1989 Poon Tip took a backpacking trip to Thailand, traveling on a budget of about $10 a day and staying with local tribes. There, he "saw travelers driving around in air-conditioned coaches, staying at the local Best Western and hiring North American guides," he told Gignac. "I developed a real attitude about it--these people were going home and telling their friends they visited Thailand, Malaysia or Peru, but they really didn't see the country at all." Poon Tip reckoned that others, like him, would appreciate being offered a more authentic, culturally sensitive brand of travel. In 1990, after finishing business classes at Calgary's Mount Royal College (some sources say the University of Canada), and some night-school courses in tourism and travel, he moved to Toronto, where he used his personal savings (including his bookmark revenues), loans from family and friends, and credit cards to start GAP. Early on, he had trouble finding business advice or funding from banks. "There was just no avenue for me to meet someone who had done something like this," he told Laura Pratt for the *National Post* (January 3, 2005). "There was no support system." Living modestly--for a time, in a converted garage--and operating out of what he described to Jalsevac as "a windowless office in an old warehouse" in Toronto, Poon Tip eventually gathered enough money to produce a brochure and buy canoes for trips he advertised to Ecuador and Belize. "It was hard to take seriously," he told Jalsevac. "Somebody actually wanted to pay money to go on this trip I just put together on a scrap of paper."

While the Ecuador trip went smoothly, at Belize's Macal River, Poon Tip told Gignac, "Our whole group got arrested because nobody had seen tourists there before [and] they didn't know what we were doing with these canoes." Poon Tip eventually reached a deal with the country's minister of tourism to allow GAP travelers to be taken in canoes paddled by select Belizean locals, but Gignac noted that even in recent years, "GAP's low-impact doctrine of travel occasionally causes rifts with local governments and tourism boards." The company policy of dealing almost exclusively with local communities, as opposed to governments, has contributed to such difficulties. However, "the flip side means GAP is able to fly under the radar and operate without interference in politically sensitive regions--such as Cuba--while bigger operators face restrictions," Gignac wrote. GAP experienced modest sales of $108,000 in 1991. That figure rose to $500,000 in 1994 and to $7.8 million in 1997. By 1999 GAP had reached almost $13 million in sales and had made many consecutive appearances on *Profit* magazine's list of the fastest growing companies in Canada.

Later Career

At the launch of the U.N.'s International Year of Ecotourism, in 2002, Poon Tip, the only tour operator invited to speak at the event, explained some of ecotourism's tenets. "See, study and understand the country and its people in their natural, day-to-day state without disturbing them or changing them," he said, according to the *Canada Newswire* (January 24, 2002). "Your presence shouldn't adversely impact human, plant or animal life or the environments in which they live." To protect the ecosystems and community infrastructures of the areas they tour, GAP's groups are were kept small, even though this could lessen sales. "Some of our trips are sold out months in advance, but we don't add more departures," Poon Tip explained to Gignac. "It opens us up to competition, but when you're dealing with countries like Tibet and Guatemala--fragile areas--we don't want to expand just for the sake of it." Additionally, Poon Tip has scaled back or discontinued trips that didn't meet the company's standards for sustainability. "I can't even begin to add up the losses" created by such measures, he told Hilary Davidson for *Profit* (May 2000). "We're bottom-line driven, we're profit-driven. But we don't only consider the bottom line. It's a question of what's right."

Though G Adventures',tours avoid artificial, Westernized environments, Poon Tip says that the quality of its activities and accommodations remains equal to those of other companies. "You're seeing what every other mainstream tour would offer, but you're seeing it from a different perspective," he said at the U.N., as reported by the *Canada Newswire*. "It's up to the traveler to choose a more rustic or comfortable trip." While some observers assumed that ecotourism would generate fewer economic benefits to the local community than mainstream tourism, Poon Tip argued, "Staying in a small hotel or with a family in a village will cost less than a five-star hotel, but ecotourists tend to stay longer and the money gets straight to the people."

G Adventures offers a huge amount of trips and its scope ranges worldwide. Lilley wrote, "Poon Tip's approach has been to adapt a mode of travel usually associated with young people on shoestring budgets to make it appealing to more affluent clients. While GAP tours feature some of the ad hoc elements of backpack travel, such as ample free time, they also include accommodation and transportation arrangements, as well as trained local guides."

Poon Tip would sometimes travel on tours himself and has mentioned Bhutan and Pakistan as favorite destinations. Lilley recounted that Poon Tip once "attempted to do some internal market research by going incognito on a GAP safari in Eastern Africa. Toward the end of the trip, the tour leader, a local GAP employee who had never met his boss, pulled out a brochure to recommend the company's other excursions." Poon Tip told Lilley, "My picture was on the brochure, but I'd told the others on the trip I was a waiter. . . . They were so angry they didn't invite me to the group farewell dinner."

Poon Tip's involvement with reality television began in 2000, when the producers of *Survivor: The Australian Outback* contacted him for advice before taping their show. "They wanted to know areas and ideas to look at," he said, as Sarah Kennedy reported for the *Calgary Sun* (November 18, 2004). Kennedy wrote that the producers sought "places that were rustic enough to make interesting television, but also include facilities and amenities for the show's host and crew." During tapings in Australia, GAP's local office managed the ground operations and oversaw transportation for the television company. In return, the producers granted GAP the use of the property so that *Survivor* fans could experience firsthand what the show's contestants had. (Poon Tip later admitted to Lilley that these adventures, aimed at executives, "didn't sell.") Poon Tip told Pratt, in 2001, "*Survivor* is really interested in perceived risk as opposed to actual risk. They want something that's fairly challenging, but don't want to put their survivors in life-threatening situations." After the Australian series, the producers proposed a series in the Amazon jungle, but Poon Tip suggested Kenya instead. "The floors of the Amazon are alive," he explained to Pratt. "There are bugs. Disease. It's tropical, it's hot, it's humid. . . . Kenya is the place, for sure. Visually, the Serengeti is stunning. It is a dry climate and the country is more developed as a tourism destination." The producers took Poon Tip's advice, filming their third season in Africa, and delayed the Amazon adventure until season six, allowing Poon Tip adequate time to formulate plans for the contestants' safety and the crew's comfort.

"See, study and understand the country and its people in their natural, day-to-day state without disturbing them or changing them."

Cast members from the Africa, Amazon and Marquesas (French Polynesia) *Survivor* series have all co-led trips with GAP tour guides. Poon Tip's company also produced its own, self-titled reality series, broadcast on Canada's CTV beginning in 2005. Poon Tip has appeared on an ABC program, hosted by Diane Sawyer, on unusual weddings. The show documented his marriage, in 2000, to his wife, Roula, in the Ecuadorian rain forest, where Quechua-speaking indigenous groups gave the couple an impromptu ceremony the day after the formal wedding. Grateful for years of GAP's tourism dollars, the tribesmen enthroned the couple, painted their bodies, and paraded them along the river on specially built boats festooned with elaborate floral garlands.

In 2002 Poon Tip was named a Canadian entrepreneur of the year, a prestigious award given by Ernst and Young, a financial-services company. GAP was on both *Profit* magazine's list of Canada's 50 fastest growing companies and the list of top-100 companies for five consecutive years; in May 2002 the magazine also recognized Poon Tip as entrepreneur of the decade. He is said to refuse any prize sponsored by a bank, because of the resentment he feels at being denied start-up loans or advice for his fledgling company; he has joked that executives from Visa, the credit-card company, were the only ones who exhibited faith in him. Poon Tip's other extensive honors include GAP's recognition, in 2006, by an independent business panel as one of Canada's 50 best managed companies and one of the 10 best employers for young people. He is the recipient of an award from the British Columbia Ethics in Action Society for the community development work his company has done in small villages. (He has told journalists that this is the honor of which he is the proudest.) Working with the World Bank, Poon Tip has helped impoverished villages to finance tourist lodges and has helped several communities reduce dependence on logging and the drug trade by profiting from tourism.

Bruce Poon Tip remains an avid traveler himself, although sometimes his work prevents him from visiting everywhere he'd like. "I booked three different canoe trips [at Gros Morne National Park, in Newfoundland, Canada] that I've had to cancel because of work commitments," he told Paul Luke. "I wander around Mongolia thinking, 'Boy, I wish I could go to Newfoundland.'"

In 2013 he authored a book, *Looptail: How One Company Changed the World by Reinventing Business.* Poon Tip, a deep admirer of the Dalai Lama, met the Tibetan spiritual leader, who agreed to write the book's foreword—an unprecedented endorsement for a business book.

Further Reading:

Calgary Herald F p1 July 25, 2004

Calgary Sun p52 Nov. 18, 2004

(Canada) *National Post* Aug. 18, 2001

(Canada) *National Post Business Magazine* p100 Dec. 1, 2002

Canada Newswire Jan. 24, 2002, Oct. 18, 2005

(Kitchener-Waterloo, Ontario) *Record* F p1 Mar. 17, 1999

Profit p25 May 2000, p84 Dec. 2003

Vancouver Province C p3 Oct. 27, 2002

Book:

Bruce Poon Tip, *Looptail: How One Company Changed the World by Reinventing Business* (Business Plus/Hachette, 2013)

Robinson, Jancis

Oenologist, writer, editor, lecturer

Born: 1950, Kirkandrews-on-Eden, England, United Kingdom

"The world of wine changes so rapidly, it has new vintages every year, the people change, people are interesting and lively, wine is produced in beautiful places, and it just tastes so good," Jancis Robinson, the author of more than two dozen books about wine; a frequent contributor to newspapers, magazines, and television shows; and one of the editors of the highly regarded *Oxford Companion to Wine,* told Susan Jung of the *South China Morning Post* (January 30, 2002). "I can't believe I have this lovely job." Since beginning her professional involvement with wine in 1975, Robinson has gained a reputation as a wine populist. A gifted taster and the first person outside the wine-selling trade to pass the Institute of Masters of Wine's extraordinarily challenging Master of Wine exam, Robinson "doesn't make grand pronouncements about wines and producers," Christopher Waters wrote for the Ontario *Standard* (October 20, 2001), "choosing instead to throw open the door of the wine world to all comers."

Robinson's enthusiasm for educating the wider public about wine and her commanding knowledge of the subject have won her both a wide readership and the nearly universal respect of her peers. The wine writer Andrew Jefford singled Robinson out in an article for the London *Evening Standard* (October 10, 1997) as being "almost alone among wine writers in never having produced mediocre work, and never … having compromised herself for commercial expediency or to satisfy grasping publishers." Gregg Stacy, in a piece for the Auckland, New Zealand, *Sunday Star-Times* (November 24, 1996), dubbed her "the people's hero," "Britain's vino supremo," and "the world's best-selling authority on the subject." Robinson told Stacy: "I really hate the role that wine has come to play in modern society. People use it as a way of signalling their status, throwing their weight around. Just because they know a little bit about wine they think it gives them the right to make other people feel small. The point of wine is not to terrorise your friends who happen to know less than you do. If only everyone could remember that wine is not a serious subject. It's there to give pleasure. Anyone who thinks otherwise should be treated with scorn."

Education and Early Career

Jancis Robinson was born on April 22, 1950, in the tiny hamlet of Kirkandrews-on-Eden, near Carlisle, in Cumbria, England. Her father, Thomas Edward Robinson, was the director of the Carlisle Racecourse, a horse-racing track; her mother, the former Ann Conacher, was an antiques dealer. (Robinson's rarely encountered first name—misspelled Jancice on her birth certificate—was taken by her mother from the name of the protagonist of the 1924 novel *Precious Bane* by the once-famous Shropshire writer Mary Webb.) An outstanding high-school student, Robinson matriculated, in 1968, to St. Anne's College, part of the University of Oxford. One night, while dining near Oxford with her then boyfriend, Robinson, whose family showed little interest in wine when she was growing up, sampled a glass of red Burgundy: a 1959 Chambolle-Musigny from "Les Amoureuses," considered that area's third-best vineyard. (The best is Musigny, the extraordinary spot that made the village of Chambolle famous, closely followed by the slightly less-perfumed but equally commanding Bonnes Mares.) In her autobiography, *Tasting Pleasure: Confessions of a Wine Lover* (1997), Robinson recalled that pivotal experience, writing that she "was overwhelmed by a clean, sweet perfume so ineffably more real, more vivid, more of the earth than the factory, than any wine I had ever come across before. ... This was brazen and fleshy and each mouthful entranced me, even if I found it impossible to describe." Although she had already been writing about food and wine for *Isis,* an independent magazine run by Oxford students, Robinson left Oxford with no intention of writing professionally about wine. "I was greedy and I cared about what I ate and drank," she told Brenda Polan of the London *Guardian* (April 20, 1988). "But, at that time, those were not respectable interests; they were completely tangential to the serious things in life."

After earning two master's degrees from Oxford—one in math and the other in philosophy—in 1971, Robinson spent three years coordinating ski trips with the company Thomson Holidays before moving to Provence, France, where she passed a year in a farmhouse, ostensibly studying French but in fact learning about the more intricate aspects of food and wine. She told Susan Jung, "That's when I realized how important it is to have a job that you like. I wanted to have a job in food or wine, I didn't mind which." In 1976, after working a series of odd jobs, Robinson applied for the position of assistant editor of the British trade magazine *Wine & Spirit* (not to be confused with the American wine magazine *Wine and Spirits*). In *Tasting Pleasure* Robinson recalled the magazine's publisher telling her that the many applicants for the position could be broken into two categories: "Either they're wine experts and we have to teach them how to write, or they're trained journalists and we have to teach them all about wine." "I was neither," Robinson told Jan Moir for the London *Guardian* (November 9, 1994), "but they knew I could organise myself into being both." Toward that end Robinson began taking classes in wine at the Wine & Spirit Education Trust and making important contacts within the wine industry. In 1979 she published *The Wine Book,* her first of many volumes on the subject.

In 1980 Robinson started writing about wine for the London *Sunday Times,* and two years later she published *The Great Wine Book,* which highlights 37 wines from around the world, each of which Robinson considered "great." Writing for the *Financial Times* (November 27, 1982), Edmund Penning-Rowsell praised Robinson's ability to put each of her chosen wines in a wider context, adding: "Moreover, not only is real information given about those selected, but the wine-makers and proprietors are allowed to speak for themselves, so that the flavour and style that inspires each is conveyed. ... For such rare and necessarily sometimes rather costly wines Jancis Robinson's cheerfully but not frivolously written record makes a worthwhile contribution to available wine literature."

In 1983, after publishing a guide to tasting called *Masterglass* ("I must claim personal responsibility for the grimace-worthy title," Robinson wrote in her autobiography), she launched what is considered the first-ever television show about wine, a six-part series called *The Wine Programme,* broadcast on the U.K.'s Channel 4. The show proved to be a success, and a second and third series of *The Wine Programme* were aired in 1985 and 1987, respectively. Discussing the show with Nicholas Wroe of the London *Guardian* (December 24, 2005), the novelist Julian Barnes, who worked as a television reviewer when Robinson's program debuted, said, "The production values were terrible, but she was an absolute natural. For so many years the wine trade was stuffed with chinless pinstripes who rippled with snobbery and pushed expensive bad wine with good names. Jancis, without it seeming to be part of her programme, has been a deeply democratic force working against all that."

In 1984 Robinson became the first wine journalist to become a Master of Wine, a nonacademic title obtained from the Institute of Masters of Wine, in London, only after taking a test that is, as Eric Asimov noted in the *New York Times* (November 1, 2006), "oral, written, and imbibed." The difficulty of the Master of Wine exam ("like a combined M.D. and Ph.D. program," Asimov quipped) means that, as of June 2014, only 313 people in the world are allowed to hold that title. Robinson, who took the tasting part of the exam while pregnant, described the experience to Larry Walker in *Wines & Vines* (November 1, 2006) as "a bit like climbing Everest—a huge challenge but deeply satisfying on a personal level once you've done it."

During the second half of the 1980s, Robinson's name became increasingly connected with the science of wine. *Vines, Grapes & Wines,* released in 1986, focuses on ampelography, the study of grape varieties, which at that time was still relatively fresh terrain for wine writers, who had traditionally viewed the subject as a geographical phenomenon, writing more about Burgundy, for example, than about the region's two most important grapes, Chardonnay and Pinot Noir. A reviewer for the *Economist* (September 17, 1986), called it "the most important book about wine since … Hugh Johnson's *The World Atlas of Wine,*" while Frank J. Prial, reviewing the book for the *New York Times* (December 17, 1986), described it as "very good." Prial noted that "in Europe, where grape varieties are considered less important than they are here, it is novel. … I'm not sure it's for all wine fans, but it will interest those ready to move beyond the geographic approach to wine." In 1988 Robinson published *The Demon Drink: A User's Guide* (also known as *Jancis Robinson on the Demon Drink*), which was billed, according to Brenda Polan, as "an objective assessment of alcohol from someone who loves it." After researching the scientific literature on alcohol and its long-term health effects, Robinson came to the conclusion, she told Polan, "that the truth is neither black nor white. On the one hand I think that … we have a confused attitude to drink and deceive ourselves about how much we drink and its effects. … On the other hand, as a social problem for Britain, it is probably rather less serious than we have been led to believe over the last few years. We are, however, appallingly ignorant about a drug which the vast majority of us consume very regularly." Murray Philippa, in an article for the Hobart, Australia, *Mercury* (May 30, 1988), praised Robinson's "frank and courageous manner" of writing and noted: "The book does not draw hard conclusions. It is a balanced, well-researched work which seeks to set down all the arguments without the hype."

The same year that *Demon Drink* appeared, Robinson was appointed by Oxford University Press to be the consultant editor for the *Oxford Companion to Wine,* a new addition to the publisher's well-established reference series. The appointment, T. J. Foderaro wrote for Newhouse News Service (January 5, 2000), confirmed "Robinson's stature as an international authority" on wine. Robinson spent about five years preparing the book, writing about half of its text and working with a host of other respected authorities to sharpen its thousands of entries. Jan Moir described the final product, which appeared in 1994, as "the most comprehensive book on wine ever compiled." Judging the book "highly recommended," Wendy Miller wrote for *Library Journal* (December 1994): "This essential addition to reference collections breaks new ground. … About 3,000 alphabetically arranged entries range from the most familiar topics, such as 'California,' to the quite obscure (e.g., 'Xynisteri,' a white grape grown on Cyprus). Yet those less interested in the esoterica of wine will surely find the information they seek, as about 70 percent of the book is concerned with specific wines and areas of wine production. There is also practical guidance on such matters as serving wine and matching the right wine with the right food. … While erudite, this book is not dry; historical anecdotes abound." G. S. Howell, writing for *Choice* (April 1995), was similarly emphatic, calling the book the "best general book on grapes and wine that this reviewer has ever read." Howell added: "Robinson brings together more than 80 contributors whose names read like a who's who in viticulture and enology, and the result is at once erudite and beautiful. It is a joy to read clear and accurate commentary about such diverse subjects as 'crop thinning,' 'malolactic fermentation,' and 'pearl glands' and to find accurate, unbiased descriptions of the potential value of 'hybrids.'" A second edition followed in 1999, and by the time of the third edition, published in 2006, the book had been enshrined as an "essential" volume for "anyone in the wine industry," according to Larry Walker, writing in *Wines & Vines* (November 2006), and Robinson as the "preeminent English-language wine journalist at the moment," according to Patrick Comiskey of the *Los Angeles Times* (February 22, 2006). A fourth edition of the *Oxford Companion to Wine* is scheduled for October 2015.

Robinson had maintained a steady stream of television appearances since *The Wine Programme* first aired, writing and hosting such shows as the ten-episode series *Jancis Robinson Meets...* (1987); the six-part series *Matters of Taste* (1991) on food writer Elizabeth David, which Robinson produced; and *Vintners' Tales* (1992), which she also produced, all of which were broadcast on British television. In 1994 and 1995, Robinson ventured onto American television as the co-host (with Frank J. Prial) of *Grape Expectations,* on the Food Network. But perhaps Robinson's most highly regarded series—as writer, presenter, and producer—was the BBC2's ten-episode *Jancis Robinson's Wine Course* (1995), which offered a comprehensive introduction to wine, with an emphasis on the most popular and important grape varieties. (The eponymous companion volume to the series appeared the same year.) While it won high marks from viewers and continues to circulate as a set of DVDs, the show also gave Robinson seemingly her only brush with public criticism. Since part of the onus for paying for the series fell on Robinson directly, as producer, she sought out a sponsor, eventually settling on the dominant British supermarket Sainsbury's. In exchange for Robinson's endorsement of a selection of Sainsbury's wines, she was given £50,000 toward the show, a quarter of the total amount that she shouldered. "Even before the series had begun, a row had broken out about the commercialisation of a BBC programme," Tim Atkin wrote for the *London Observer* (October 29, 1995). Atkin also noted that Robinson "would clearly prefer to have avoided any link with Sainsbury's": "As a journalist I agree with some of the reservations that have been expressed," she told Atkin. "But I'm also a television producer. Telly is just very, very expensive." Robinson was a wine consultant for British Airways from 1995 until 2010.

In 1997 Robinson published *Tasting Pleasure: Confessions of a Wine Lover,* an autobiographical account of the impact of wine on her life. The book received divided reviews, with many American critics finding the emphasis on the British wine business off-putting and a few commenting negatively on Robinson's writing style. On the other hand, Mary Dowey, writing for the *Irish Times* (October 18, 1997), described the book as "another gem" from Robinson and added: "It might have been otherwise. The story ... could have become little more than an inflated chronicle of memorable bottles ... except that Jancis Robinson's luminous intelligence and almost fierce common sense have enabled her to tell a much broader and more balanced tale, full of insight and self-deprecating humour. If it were a wine, you'd undoubtedly describe it as well structured but wonderfully approachable."

In 2000 Robinson served as the consultant editor for the *Oxford Companion to the Wines of North America,* and in 2001, with Julia Harding, she trimmed the larger *Oxford Companion to Wine* to create *Jancis Robinson's Concise Wine Companion.* Also in 2001 Robinson published a revised edition of *Masterglass* as *How to Taste: Jancis Robinson's Wine Tasting Workbook,* and she joined the noted wine writer Hugh Johnson to revise his acclaimed reference book *World Atlas of Wine* for a fifth edition. First published in 1971, the book contains extensive geographical information, including maps, of all the major areas where wine is produced and also features short but thorough essays on the various areas. Richard Kinssies described the fifth edition of the book, which featured all new maps and expanded coverage of new growing areas, for the Seattle *Post-Intelligencer* (January 2, 2002) as "nearly an entire wine library between two covers." A sixth edition was published in 2007 and a seventh in 2013. The seventh edition grappled with the growing effects of climate change on the wine industry, again expanded the maps, and added to the coverage of wine regions in China, Australia, and North America. Meanwhile, the *Concise World Atlas of Wine* was issued in 2009. Next Robinson collaborated with Julia Harding and José Vouillamoz on *Wine Grapes; A Complete Guide to 1,368 Varieties, Including Their Origins and Flavours* (2012), and with Linda Murphy, Robinson wrote *American Wine* (2013).

Robinson has continued to work on the Oxford Companion to Wine while also developing a strong online presence with her website JancisRobinson.com, which debuted in November 2000 and offers subscribers access to her tasting notes and comments on past and future vintages. She writes a newspaper column syndicated around the world.

In 2004 Robinson became embroiled in a major controversy in the wine world when she feuded briefly with the wine critic Robert Parker. Robinson had negatively reviewed the 2003 vintage Château Pavie, an expensive and prestigious Bordeaux, describing it, according to Roger Voss of the *San Francisco Chronicle* (May 27, 2004), as having "completely unappetizing overripe aromas" and being a "ridiculous wine more reminiscent of a late-harvest Zinfandel than a red Bordeaux with its unappetizing green notes." Parker, like many other American writers, had enthusiastically received the same wine and responded to Robinson's note by posting a defense of it and its producer, Gérard Perse, on his official website: "I had [that vintage of] Pavie four separate times, and, recognizing everyone's taste is different, Pavie does not taste at all (for my palate) as described by Jancis." Parker went on to claim that Robinson "has a lamentable and perplexing history of disliking" Perse's wines and those of related winemakers and suggested that her comments merely echoed those made by "reactionaries in Bordeaux." Robinson fired back with a post on her own website, noting that she had tasted the wine blind—that is, without seeing the bottle—and writing, "Am I really not allowed to have my own opinion? Only so long as it agrees with Monsieur Parker's it would seem. I do wish we could simply agree to differ." To many the debate was indicative of a wider battle in the wine world over the homogenization of wine styles. Tom Doorley, writing for *Business and Finance* (December 2, 2004), defended Robinson, writing that Parker "needs to lighten up. If Jancis Robinson tells you that the wine you rave about is grossly unbalanced … then you really do have to take stock of your taste in wine."

Robinson lives in England with her husband, the food critic and restaurateur Nick Lander. The pair have three children, Julia, William, and Rose. Robinson has written a weekly column for the *Financial Times* since 1989 and has received dozens of awards for her work, including an honorary doctorate from the Open University and a James Beard award for Best Television Food Journalism (for *Jancis Robinson's Wine Course*), both in 1997. She was named an officer of the Order of the British Empire in 2003 and since 2004 she has served as a member of the Royal Household Wine Committee, "advising on the Queen's cellar," as she reports at her website. Wine tastings are an inevitable part of her work; Robinson posts wine reviews to her website daily and often samples hundreds of wines in one day. "I'm very lucky, but I do work awfully hard," Robinson told Susan Jung. "I know it looks as if I just swan around, but writing reference books is hard work."

Further Reading:

(London) *Daily Telegraph* p1 Nov. 27, 2004

(London) *Guardian* Apr. 20, 1988, T p12 Nov. 9, 1994, p28 Sep. 16, 1995

JancisRobinson.com

(London) Observer p47 Oct. 29, 1995

(London) Times Oct. 26, 1995

New York Times C p16 Dec. 17, 1986, F p1 Nov. 1, 2006

Selected Books:

As author:

The Wine Book, 1979

The Great Wine Book, 1982

Masterglass, 1983, rev. as *How to Taste,* 2001

Vines, Grapes & Wines, 1986

The Demon Drink, 1988

Vintage Timecharts, 1989

Jancis Robinson's Wine Course, 1995, 2d ed., 2003

Jancis Robinson's Guide to Wine Grapes, 1996

Tasting Pleasure: Confessions of a Wine Lover, 1997

The World Atlas of Wine (with Hugh Johnson), fifth ed., 2001, sixth ed., 2007, seventh ed., 2013

The Concise World Atlas of Wine (with Hugh Johnson), 2009

Wine Grapes; A Complete Guide to 1,368 Wine Varieties (with Julia Harding and José Vouillamoz), 2012

American Wine (with Linda Murphy), 2013.

As editor:

The Oxford Companion to Wine, 1994, second ed., 1999, third ed., 2006

The Companion to the Wines of North America, 2000

Robuchon, Joël

Chef, restaurateur, author, television chef

Born: 1945, Poitiers, France

Widely considered to be the best chef in France—if not the entire world—Joël Robuchon made his name through a painstaking attention to detail that elevated even simple dishes such as salads and mashed potatoes to remarkable heights. "The way [Robuchon] trimmed the edges of the oysters with scissors or how precisely he cut the red peppers represents an extra zone of perfection that few people are obsessed with," David Bouley, a chef and former employee of Robuchon's, explained to Florence Fabricant of *the New York Times* (November 6, 1991). "I watched the way he takes notes on so many things and the keenness of his perception. He's like a Swiss watchmaker." Over the course of his career, the "famously over-achieving" Robuchon has established and run numerous world-famous restaurants, published an autobiography and several cookbooks, and hosted a popular cooking show on French television.

Robuchon told Megan Willett for AP (as published in *Business Insider,* March 28, 2014), "I never try to marry more than three flavors in one dish. I like walking into a kitchen and knowing that the dishes are identifiable and the ingredients within them are easy to detect. My role as a chef is respecting the produce. Why should I change and mask the original flavors of the produce that I'm utilizing?"

Robuchon has restaurants in Hong Kong, Las Vegas, London, Macau, Monaco, Paris, Singapore, Taipei, and Tokyo; among them, as of June 2014, they have earned him 25 Michelin stars, the most garnered by any chef in the world. He expects to open several more establishments in the near future. Robuchon regularly visits all of his restaurants, which have their own distinguished chefs. "I have a good team and you must keep questioning yourself and learn from past experience. Opening a restaurant is like raising a child, you must be involved," he told Rebecca Lynne Tan of the Singapore *Straits-Times* (March 31, 2011).

Education and Early Career

Joël Robuchon was born April 7, 1945 in Poitiers, France. His father was a stonemason, his mother a housewife. At age 12 Robuchon entered seminary school to become a priest. There, he often helped the nuns prepare meals, an experience that left a lasting impression. When his parents divorced in 1960, he was obliged to leave the seminary to support his mother. At 15 he got a job as an apprentice cook at Relais de Poitiers, a local hotel restaurant. He spent much of his time there cleaning, mopping, and scrubbing, but he also learned the foundations of classical French cooking and performed all the other minor duties of a large kitchen. The time spent cleaning was not lost on the apprentice chef. "Once you've washed pots and polished copper for someone else, you'll never treat pots the same, even once someone else is cleaning them for you," he told Patricia Wells in their joint cookbook *Simply French.*

In 1963 Robuchon left Relais de Poitiers to become a compagnon of the Tour de France, a program that sends aspiring chefs around the country to learn their trade working in various restaurants. Altogether he spent ten years as a *compagnon,* or journeyman, working in restaurants in Paris and across the French provinces, as well as competing in cooking contests, in which he garnered numerous bronze, silver, and gold medals. "As a compagnon," Robuchon told Patricia Wells, "I learned that no matter how well we think we do something, we can still do it better. And that there is no greater personal satisfaction than in giving the very best of yourself each day." In 1974 Robuchon was appointed head chef of a restaurant in the Hotel Concorde-Lafayette, in Paris, managing 90 other chefs who cooked for an average of 3,000 customers per meal. His care and precision proved well-suited to the monumental task. In 1976 Robuchon won the Meilleur Ouvrier de France, the country's highest culinary honor, in a national competition. Two years later, he took over the kitchen of the restaurant at the Paris Hotel Nikko.

"I learned that no matter how well we think we do something, we can still do it better."

In December 1981 Robuchon opened his own restaurant, Jamin, located on Paris's Rue de Longchamp. Although the restaurant accommodated a maximum of 40 guests, he hired 40 employees, including 15 chefs. A "maniac for neatness and cleanliness," as Patricia Wells characterized him, Robuchon ordered the kitchen cleaned from top to bottom twice a day. Jamin quickly earned a reputation for excellent, unobtrusive service and for food that approached perfection. In particular Robuchon's buttery potatoes and flawless salads made him a cooking celebrity. Before long the restaurant had become a Paris institution, with reservations often required months in advance. After only three years of operation, Jamin earned a three-star rating from Michelin, the famously selective restaurant guide—the fastest rise in Michelin history. (Few establishments earn even a single Michelin star, and only two or three dozen in the world earn three stars in any given year. Upon learning of Jamin's superlative rating, Robuchon remarked to Patricia Wells that the accolade "does not mean I merit three stars. … It only means that now I have the right to merit them.") Robuchon's cooking later earned a 19.5 rating (out of 20) in the Gault Millau guide, and he went on to win the Pierre Taittinger Prize, a prestigious culinary award.

Speaking with Patricia Wells, Robuchon explained his culinary philosophy: "You have an obligation to respect the flavor, the essence, the authenticity of ingredients. You don't have the right to alter them. … When you cook a mushroom, you don't have the right to make it taste like anything other than a mushroom." At times this approach stands in contrast to the traditional methods of French cooking, in which the natural flavors of ingredients are sometimes masked and altered by herbs, spices, cream, and sauce. While Robuchon does make use of spices and sauces, he does so only to enhance the ingredients' inherent flavors. "In order to feed yourself, you are always killing something else, whether it's a vegetable, fish, lamb or lobster," he explained through a translator, as quoted by Scott Warner. "Once you understand that, you are obliged to respect the nature of that ingredient—and you cook with much more love."

In 1991 Patricia Wells published *Simply French,* an English-language presentation of Robuchon's cuisine. *Simply French* drew excited praise from American food critics. "Despite—or perhaps because of—its complexity and rigorous nature, 'Simply French' is an exciting cookbook," Jocelyn McClurg wrote for the

Hartford Courant (December 25, 1991). "There is a sense of newness, of freshness and adventure about Robuchon's cuisine." Robuchon later expanded upon his culinary ideas in *Joël Robuchon: Cooking through the Seasons* (1995), *La Cuisine de Joël Robuchon: A Seasonal Cookbook* (2001), and *The Complete Robuchon* (2008).

In 1993 Robuchon closed Jamin in order to open Restaurant Joël Robuchon, a larger, more formal establishment which soon surpassed Jamin in popularity. "It's the best presented, most expertly prepared and well-thought-out repast I've experienced," Jerry Shriver wrote for *USA Today* (April 14, 1995), "a testament to artistry, and almost worth the money." (Shriver noted that he had paid $391.27 for a six-course lunch, after waiting six months for a table.) In 1994, together with Taillevent, a French restaurant, Robuchon opened Château Taillevent-Robuchon in Tokyo, which soon earned a reputation as one of the finest eateries in Japan.

Later Career

After more than 15 years the stress of being a chef-proprietor became too much for Robuchon, who in 1996 announced his retirement. "I didn't want to have a heart attack," he told Scott Warner. But Robuchon remained busy in the culinary world. Even after closing his second restaurant, he served as a consultant for fine restaurants internationally. His first venture as a restaurateur after closing Restaurant Joël Robuchon was the Robuchon à Galera (later renamed Robuchon au Dôme), at the Grand Lisboa Hotel in Macao, which he opened in 2001. Robuchon also appeared on a daily ten-minute cooking show, *Cuisiner Comme un Grand Chef* ("Cook Like a Great Chef"); wrote his autobiography, *Le Carnet de Route d'un Compagnon Cuisinier* (1995), as well as several cookbooks; gave celebrity endorsements to cheeses and other culinary products; and led the team that revised a new edition (2001) of *Larousse Gastronomique,* a premiere encyclopedia of food, first published in 1938. Robuchon's later television projects were *Bon appétit bien sûr* and *Planète gourmande.*

On May 7, 2003, Robuchon opened a new restaurant, L'Atelier de Joel Robuchon, located on the Left Bank in Paris, in the Hotel Pont Royal. "I'm coming back through a very small door," he told Florence Fabricant of the *New York Times* (August 21, 2002). "What I have in mind is a place with a very relaxed convivial atmosphere. That's what I think people want. There will be lots of interaction between the chef and the customers." L'Atelier is far more informal (and less expensive) than Jamin or Restaurant Joël Robuchon were and features a radical design for a fine restaurant: a large, U-shaped counter surrounding an open kitchen. Customers sit around the counter on stools and watch the chefs prepare the food. "Everything will revolve around the kitchen," Robuchon told Fabricant. "The food will depend on the best products in the market, simply prepared. It's the opposite of what I was doing before. And there's really nothing like it in Paris." In his previous restaurants, Robuchon rarely left the kitchen to interact with customers, but at L'Atelier he frequently talked with people as he prepared their meals; he attributed his inspiration for the new approach to his experience performing every day on French television. "Now [Robuchon] has something to prove," Pierre Gagnaire, another Michelin three-star chef in Paris, said, as quoted by Fabricant. "He has already personified perfection for a generation of chefs. It'll be interesting to see how he'll pull off something so simple. Expectations will be high."

L'Atelier received favorable reviews: "I'm betting on Robuchon," R. W. Apple Jr. wrote for the *New York Times* (May 21, 2003). "I think he's right in judging that most people today want real food, full of flavor but not needlessly complex, served without ceremony in a good-looking space by agreeable people. That's what he's offering here." The popular response to the new restaurant was extraordinary. "There are entire internet message boards in the US devoted to L'Atelier," Decca Aitkenhead wrote for the London *Observer* (August 10, 2003), "with fierce arguments raging about everything from the carpaccio langoustines with pink peppercorns, to the 'icy efficiency' of the service and 'weird' lunch-counter design." The Paris location was the first of several L'Ateliers: in 2003 Robuchon opened a L'Atelier restaurant in Tokyo, and there are now L'Ateliers, according to Robuchon's website, in Las Vegas, opened in 2005; London and Hong Kong, opened in 2006; Taipei, opened in 2009; and Singapore, opened in 2011. L'Ateliers were set to open in 2014 in New York City, Bangkok, and Mumbai. Robuchon told Kathleen Squires of Zagat that New York City "really is the capital of the world and I want to be there." Robuchon had opened a L'Atelier in New York City in 2006, at the Four Seasons Hotel, but he closed that location in 2012, saying that he planned to return to New York. He explained to Squires that the New York City L'Atelier was successful, but the hotel location presented certain constraints; he wanted a freestanding L'Atelier location in the city, open to the street. (Meanwhile his only restaurants in the United States were the L'Atelier and the three-Michelin-starred Joël Robuchon, at the MGM Grand Hotel in Las Vegas.) In 2014 he also planned to open a 'gastronomic' restaurant in Bordeaux.

Increasingly Robuchon focused on Asia. According to Don Mendoza in *Today* (April 17, 2014), Robuchon's "Singapore outposts at Resorts World Sentosa (RWS) — the stylishly informal L'Atelier de Joel Robuchon and Joel Robuchon, his eponymous 'gastronomic' restaurant serving the chef's award-winning interpretation of French haute cuisine—are doing well. The restaurants are also his first two in South-east Asia."

Although he has spent his career in pursuit of culinary perfection, Robuchon told Patricia Wells that "the perfect meal does not exist." He continued: "It could well be a slice of toasted bread and some melted cheese, or fondue, shared with a friend. It's a question of simplicity, spontaneity, good times with friends." In Robuchon's opinion, "it's only later, long after you've experienced a great meal, that you realize, in retrospect, how wonderful and how perfect it really was."

Robuchon claimed to have no interest in awards or rankings other than Michelin's, but his many accolades include, in addition to the Meilleur Ouvrier de France and the Pierre Taittinger Prize (1970), the Grand Award of *Wine Spectator* (2009) and the Laurent Perrier 2009 Lifetime Achievement Award of the S. Pellegrino World's 50 Best Restaurants.

Robuchon lives in Paris with his wife, Janine. They have two children, Eric and Sophie; Sophie appeared with Joël Robuchon on *Planète gourmande.*

Further Reading:

Business Insider Mar. 28, 2014

Chicago Sun-Times p8 Dec. 10, 1997, with photo

Eater website Sep. 23, 2011

Hartford Courant E p1 Dec. 25, 1991

Los Angeles Times p3 June 6, 1996

New York Times C p1 Nov. 6, 1991, with photo, F p1 Aug. 21, 2002, with photo, F p1May 21, 2003, with photo, May 30, 2012

[London] *Observer*, Aug. 10, 2003

[Singapore] *Straits-Times* Mar. 31, 2011

Today Apr. 17, 2014

USA Today D p1 Apr. 14, 1995, with photo

Zagat website Oct. 7, 2013

Selected Books:

Ma Cuisine Pour Vous, 1986

Simply French, 1991

Le Carnet de Route d'un Compagnon Cuisinier, 1995

L'Atelier de Joel Robuchon, 1996

La Cuisine de Joël Robuchon: A Seasonal Cookbook, 2001

The Complete Robuchon, 2008

Rosenfeld, Irene B.

Chairwoman and chief executive officer of Mondelēz International

---

Born: 1953, Long Island, New York, United States

On June 26, 2006 Irene B. Rosenfeld was appointed chief executive officer (CEO) of Kraft Foods Inc., a $34 billion enterprise, thus making it the largest company in the world to be headed by a woman. Nine months later Rosenfeld became the chairwoman of the firm as well. Headquartered in Northfield, Illinois, a suburb of Chicago, Kraft is the largest packaged-food company in the United States and the second-largest in the world, behind the Swiss company Nestle; it owns some of the most recognizable brands in the U.S., among them Post, Nabisco, Maxwell House, Sanka, Kool-Aid, Tang, Velveeta, Jell-O, Planters, Oreo, and Oscar Mayer. Rosenfeld joined Kraft in the 1980s, after completing a Ph.D. in marketing. In the years that followed, she rose through the company's ranks, holding such titles as executive vice president and general manager of the beverages division and president of Kraft Foods Canada. During that time she developed a reputation as an innovator and clever marketer. In 2003, after she had served for two years as president of Kraft Foods North America, dissatisfaction with the management of the company led her to quit. She spent two years as the chair and CEO of Frito-Lay Inc. before returning to Kraft as its top officer.

One of the world's most powerful businesswomen, according to Fortune, Rosenfeldis a "no-nonsense problem-solver with an almost laserlike focus on improving business," as Robert A. Eckert, a former Kraft executive, told Patricia Sellers for that magazine (October 16, 2006). Tierney Remick of the executive search firm Korn/Ferry International told Susan Chandler for the Chicago Tribune (June 27, 2006), "She brings a great balance of strategy and execution, and she truly understands the organization--where it has come from and where it needs to go. The credibility she has with the employee population, combined with her knowledge of the business and its challenges, will translate into a very fast start." Jean Spence, Kraft's executive vice president of global technology and quality, told Chandler that Rosenfeld "is really coura- geous and willing to speak up for what needs to be done. She is one of the smartest people I have ever worked with in business." In recent years Kraft has been plagued by serious problems, some of which have also affected other companies in the food industry, such as the rapidly rising costs of raw materials and energy. One of Rosenfeld's primary goals was to make Kraft "bolder, more agile, more creative and more focused," according to Robert Manor, writing in the Chicago Tribune (September 12, 2006). "I think there's an optimistic feeling at the company," Jean Spence told Adrienne Carter for BusinessWeek (June 26, 2006). "Her focus has always been on growth--growth through innovation."

"I think the opportunity to just break down barriers to enable collaboration rapidly across the different parts of the globe is the single biggest opportunity available to us…" Rosenfeld said in a 2012 Fortune ar- ticle, maintaining a consistently expansive worldview.

Education and Early Career

A native of Long Island, New York, Irene B. Rosenfeld was born on May 3, 1953. She attended Cornell University, in Ithaca, New York, graduating with a B.A. degree in psychology in 1975. She stayed on at Cornell to earn both an M.S. degree in businessin 1977, and a Ph.D. in marketing and statisticsin 1980. In 1979, while pursuing her doctorate, Rosenfeld took a job with Dancer Fitzgerald Sample Advertising (now Saatchi and Saatchi). In 1981 she joined the General Foods Corp. as an associate market-research manager. In 1989 the Philip Morris Companies (now the Altria Group, Inc.), which owned both General Foods and Kraft Foods, merged those two companies, and she became an employee of Kraft.

Early in her career with General Foods and Kraft Foods, Rosenfeld served as product manager for Country Time Lemonade. She rose on the corporate ladder to become the head of Kraft's beverage division in 1991. In that post, in which she oversaw such brands as Kool-Aid, Tang, and Maxwell House, Rosenfeld handled Kraft's acquisition of the distribution rights in North America for Capri-Sun juice drinks, which are produced by a German company. She transformed what was then a regional product in the United States into a nationally recognized brand that filled a significant void in Kraft's portfolio. Rosenfeld's success in the beverage division led to a promotion to general manager of desserts and snacks in 1994.

Later Career

In 1996 Rosenfeld was named president of Kraft's Canadian operations, a position in which she earned praise for her innovations. In one example, Rosenfeld mailed free copies of a magazine of recipes and cooking tips to one million households in Canada. The stratagem sparked increased sales for the Kraft products featured in the recipes. Its success prompted the mailing of similar material to an additional 12 million households in the United States as well as Canada. In 2000, while retaining her duties in Canada, Rosenfeld was named a Kraft Foods group vice president and president of operations, technology, and procurement. In 2001 her responsibilities grew to include the management of Kraft's information services and its activities in Mexico and Puerto Rico. Among her many accomplishments during that period, Rosenfeld led the highly successful $19 billion integration of Nabisco into the Kraft portfolio after Nabisco was acquired by Philip Morris in 2000. In 2001 Rosenfeld served on the senior executive team that handled Kraft's initial public offering in the stock market, which brought the company a profit of $9 billion.

In 2002 Rosenfeld was promoted again, this time to president of Kraft Foods North America, by far the company's largest division, with five operating groups and 15 divisions. In July 2003, with Kraft struggling to maintain its stock price, Rosenfeld unexpectedly resigned, stating, according to Susan Chandler in the Chicago Tribune (June 27, 2006), that she had grown frustrated by the slow decision-making of Kraft's co-CEOs, Betsy Holden and Roger Deromedi. By then Rosenfeld was seen by many as one of the stars in the company, and some analysts thought that Kraft should have tried harder to retain her. "I felt at the time that the wrong person [left], that it should have been Betsy," John McMillan, a senior food industry analyst with the Prudential Equity Group, a Wall Street investment firm, said, as quoted by Chandler. He added that in 2005, when Holden resigned, "people realized how badly Irene was missed."

Rosenfeld was offered a slew of jobs after she left Kraft, and for over a year she considered her options. She turned down several CEO positions, heeding the advice of her onetime boss, James M. Kilts, a longtime Kraft executive, who told her, "Always go with the super company. Don't get caught up in the title," as Kilts recalled to Patricia Sellers for Fortune (October 16, 2006). In 2004 Rosenfeld accepted the position of chair and CEO of the $10 billion Frito-Lay division of PepsiCo, Inc. Frito-Lay is composed of two main businesses, salty snacks and convenience foods, and features brands such as Lay's, Doritos, Fritos, Cheetos, Rold Gold, Tostitos, and Quaker. During her less than two years with Frito-Lay, Rosenfeld directed the addition of healthier snacks to the firm's product lines. Sales of such snacks increased by double digits in 2005, while sales of the company's traditional products grew by single-digit figures. Under the Quaker label Frito-Lay introduced a 90-calorie chewy granola bar--30 percent fewer calories than the original bar--and acquired Stacy's Pita Chips, adding to the company's appeal to increasingly nutrition-conscious consumers. In March 2006, making good on a promise for continuous innovation, Rosenfeld announced the debut of 100-calorie miniature versions of Frito-Lay's popular Doritos and Cheetos snacks. In an attempt to satisfy increasing consumer demand for spicy foods, Frito-Lay also began to offer new lines of snacks known as Lay's Sensations and Tostitos Sensations, flavored by, for example, lime and cracked black pepper and sweet chili and sour cream. Overall, Frito-Lay's net revenues rose 8 percent in 2005, Rosenfeld's first full year with the company, while operating profits (defined by investorwords.com as "a measure of a company's earning power from ongoing operations, equal to earnings before deduction of interest payments and income taxes") climbed 5.5 percent, to $2.5 billion.

> **"I think the opportunity to just break down barriers to enable collaboration rapidly across the different parts of the globe is the single biggest opportunity available to us..."**

In June 2006 Rosenfeld abruptly resigned from Frito-Lay to assume the CEO position at Kraft Foods. According to Lorene Yue in Crain's Chicago Business (June 29, 2006,), she was given a base salary of $1.3 million, guaranteed bonuses of $1.95 million and $3.2 million in 2006, and 387,230 shares of Kraft stock (equivalent to $12 million, based on the then-current stock price) as a signing bonus. Rosenfeld has said that her experiences at Frito-Lay and, by extension, PepsiCo--where she "learned the value of a relentless focus on growth," as she told Sellers--made her a stronger leader and better prepared her to manage Kraft Foods. When Rosenfeld took over the reins at Kraft, the company was suffering financially. Its stock price had not grown since its IPO, and its profits had stagnated, in part because of fierce global competition and rising commodities prices. The former CEO, Roger Deromedi, who had run the company as its sole CEO since 2003, had begun to cut costs aggressively with the goal of increasing Kraft's profits. Rosenfeld continued those cost-cutting measures. Deromedi had also shed the company of such barely profitable products as Altoids and Milk-Bones and developed several new items, the most successful being the South Beach Diet brand of frozen foods, which recorded more than $170 million in sales in its first year (2005-06). "I feel very good about a lot of things that have happened," Rosenfeld told John Schmeltzer in the Chicago Tribune (October 24, 2006). "The company is in much better shape than it was two years ago." On the other hand, Deromedi had been criticized for not using that additional capital to buy new businesses or to develop more new products. Many industry observers believed that Kraft needed a change in leadership and a more visionary business plan. "[Rosenfeld is] not a bureaucrat, and she will shake the place up," Barbara Pickens, the founder and president of the executive search firm Pickens & Co., told Stephanie Thompson for Advertising Age (July 3, 2006). Rosenfeld, Pickens continued, is "made of different material than a lot of people at Kraft--the overanalytical, super-playing-it-safe types. She is a tiger, she really is."

While Deromedi had favored a top-down leadership approach, Rosenfeld believed that empowering regional directors would necessarily give them a greater understanding of consumer preferences in their markets. She therefore spent the first 100 days on the job traveling to the company's business centers and factories around the world, meeting not only with Kraft staff but also with retailers, their employees, and their customers, in order to discern their interests and motivations. Rosenfeld learned thattoo often Kraft had relied on decision-making from those at its center of operations, in Northfield, Illinois, and often launched products globally without assessing the strength of particular brands or the prospects for particular products in individual markets. Rosenfeld said that those discussions reinforced her conviction that much decision-making should be in the hands of "the people closest to our consumers, customers and markets," as quoted by Robert Manor in the Chicago Tribune (September 12, 2006). Some analysts have expressed skepticism about that philosophy, on the grounds that Kraft's more-general business concerns may get short shrift. "More autonomy can create more chaos, less focus on brands," Laura Reis, the president of the marketing firm Reis & Reis, told Sonia Reyes for Brandweek (September 18, 2006). "It's like each military general following his own orders. This is not going to solve the problem of companies like Kraft relying on line extensions [that is, applying an existing brand name or image to new products] rather then trying to build new brands. I mean, how many Jell-O and Philadelphia Cream Cheese extensions can consumers take?"

Most business analysts agree that Rosenfeld's task of increasing profitability and growth will be difficult. They have pointed to Kraft's reliance on middle-of-the-road customers who view many food-staple brands as interchangeable and are just as likely to purchase house brands at Wal-Mart, Target, or Costco as Kraft products. At the same time, Kraft had to contend with the tendency of growing numbers of consumers to seek high-end, organically produced, or more nutritious or healthful items. The rising costs of raw materials, packaging, and energy present additional problems. Between 2003 and 2005 the amount that Kraft paid for raw materials increased by $1.7 billion. Robert Campagnino of the Prudential Equity Group wrote in a note to investors, as reported by Dave Carpenter for the Associated Press (June 26, 2006), "Kraft decided to switch jockeys. . . . Ultimately the horse matters, and unless new CEO Irene Rosenfeld can push commodity prices lower . . . Kraft is still, in our view, a somewhat troubled company."

In early 2007 the Altria Group (formerly Philip Morris), Kraft's parent company for years, announced the imminent spin-off of Kraft. In March of that year, Altria distributed 89 percent of Kraft's stock to shareholders, and Kraft was rendered an independent company. Subsequently, Louis Camilleri, the CEO of Altria, stepped down as the chairman of Kraft's board of directors, and Rosenfeld succeeded him in that post. In 2011 Kraft split into two companies and Rosenfeld heads Mondelēz International, which focuses on the huge snack market. Rosenfeld has two grown childrenand keeps a kosher home. She earned a Masters in Excellence Award from the Center for Jewish Living in 2005 and has been elected to the YWCA Academy of Women Achievers. She has served on the boards of Cornell University, the Steppenwolf Theatre Companyin Chicago, and AutoNation, Inc., and has also held leadership roles with the Grocery Manufacturers Association.

Further Reading:

Advertising Age p3 July 3, 2006
BusinessWeek June 26, 2006, Feb. 1, 2007 Chicago Tribune C p1+ June 27, 2006, Business Sep. 12, 2006, Oct. 24, 2006
Crain's Chicago Business p39+ Aug. 7, 2006
Fortune p134+ Oct. 16, 2006, Oct. 2, 2012
Who's Who in America, 2007

Rusesabagina, Paul

Rwandan humanitarian, inspiration for the film *Hotel Rwanda*

Born: 1954, Murama-Gitarama, Rwanda

A hero, Paul Rusesabagina told Bob Nesti for the *Boston-Bay State Banner* (January 13, 2005), "is not someone who performs his duties and obligations. I didn't save people, I helped people; and that's the crucial difference. I did not save. I helped people to go through. Being a hero is something different than helping people." Regardless of those sentiments, there are almost certainly at least 1,268 people who consider Rusesabagina a hero: the individuals he sheltered during the 1994 Rwandan genocide, when he was the manager of a luxury hotel in Kigali, the capital of Rwanda. The filmmaker Terry George dramatized the genocide and Rusesabagina's humanitarian response to it in a critically acclaimed motion picture, *Hotel Rwanda*, released in 2004. Largely due to the success of *Hotel Rwanda*, people around the world are now comparing Rusesabagina to Oskar Schindler, the German businessman who saved more than 1,000 Jews during the Nazi Holocaust and whose actions were immortalized in *Schindler's List* (1993), a film by Steven Spielberg. In December 2004 the organization Amnesty International, which helped to promote *Hotel Rwanda* in order to educate the public about ongoing atrocities in such regions as the Sudan and the Congo, presented Rusesabagina with its Enduring Spirit Award, one of a host of human-rights honors he has received over the last decade.

In the early 1990s the population of Rwanda, a nation in Central Africa south of Uganda, west of Tanzania, and north of Burundi, consisted mostly of ethnic Hutus; more than four out of five Rwandans were Hutus, who have traditionally been farmers. The Tutsi ethnic group, traditionally cattle herders, comprised 15 percent of the population, and about 1 percent of Rwandans were members of the Twa, a subgroup of African Pygmies. Despite their common culture and language, the Hutus and the Tutsis had long been at odds. Belgian colonists, who had arrived in the region in 1916, considered the taller, thinner, fairer Tutsis superior to the shorter, stockier, darker Hutus and issued identification cards to differentiate between the groups. The colonists' favoritism toward Tutsis on matters of power and influence bred resentment in many Hutus. In 1959, three years before Rwanda gained independence from Belgium, the Hutus rebelled, killing the Tutsi king and assuming control of the state. Over the ensuing years, thousands of Tutsis were killed or driven into exile. In 1990 a civil war began among the Hutus and a rebel Tutsi group called the Rwandan Patriotic Front (RPF). The conflict escalated after the airplane carrying the Rwandan president, Juvenal Habyarimana, a Hutu, was shot down above the Kigali airport, on April 6, 1994. The crash also killed the president of Burundi, Cyprian Ntayamira, who, with Habyarimana, had just attended a meeting of African leaders to discuss ways to allay the ethnic tensions in the region. Many observers have theorized that the plane was shot down by Hutu extremists unhappy with Habyarimana's moderate politics. Some Hutu politicians, along with people controlling a prominent local radio station, however, promptly blamed the deaths on Tutsi rebels; within hours, the Hutu militia--called the *Interahamwe*, or "those who work together"--began slaying Tutsis at a breakneck pace. They first killed Tutsis of prominence in business or politics, then turned on ordinary citizens. The militia instructed civilian Hutus to kill their Tutsi neighbors, friends, and relatives; the killers included some of Rusesabagina's best friends, among them some who resisted the Hutus' orders until they realized that many of those who refused to kill others were put to death themselves. The slaughter lasted 100 days, during which more than 800,000 Rwandans--roughly 10 percent of the nation's population--were murdered.

Education and Early Career

Not all Hutus and Tutsis had regarded one another as enemies. Indeed, many families included members of both ethnic groups. Paul Rusesabagina's was among them. Rusesabagina was born into a farming family on June 15, 1954 in Murama-Gitarama, in the south of Rwanda. He was one of nine children of a Hutu father and a Tutsi mother, and thus, according to the patrilineal system in place, was classified as a Hutu. In 1962 Rusesabagina entered the Seventh-day Adventist College of Gitwe, a primary and secondary school run by missionaries. From 1975 to 1978 he attended the Faculty of Theologyin Cameroon. In 1979 the Sabena hotel chain hired him as the manager of a newly opened hotel in the Akagera National Park. Realizing he had a talent in that field, from 1980 to 1984 he studied hotel management at Kenya Utalii Collegein Nairobi. (A portion of his coursework was done in Switzerland.) He then moved to Kigali, where he became the assistant manager of the elegant Hotel des Milles Collines, another Sabena facility. He remained there until 1993, when he was promoted to the top spot at the nearby Hotel Diplomats. Meanwhile, he had married a Tutsi woman named Tatiana and had four children with her.

One day in April 1994, Rusesabagina, Tatiana, their children, and many of their neighbors, most of them Tutsis, were rounded up by armed militants. The militants forced them out of their houses and onto a bus, where one of the militiamen handed Rusesabagina a gun. "Their leader told me to kill all the cockroaches [Tutsis]," Rusesabagina told Kyle Smith, Dietland Lerner, and Michael Fleeman for *People* (January 24, 2005). Horrified at the thought of murdering his friends and family, Rusesabagina thought quickly. "I showed [the leader] an old man and said, 'Do you really believe this old man is the enemy you are fighting against? Are you sure your enemy is that baby? Take me to the hotel, and I will give you some money. But I am the only one with a key, and if you kill me, you will not have the money." The bribe succeeded, and, after paying off the gunmen with money from the safe at the Hotel Diplomats, Rusesabagina promptly drove the group to the Hotel des Mille Collines, a five-story building that had also been left in his care by its fleeing Belgian owners.

Once Rusesabagina established the Hotel des Mille Collines as a refuge, its reputation spread quickly, attracting frightened Tutsis from across Rwanda. Though the hotel was designed to house 200 occupants, it was soon crowded with more than 1,200 people, who slept in rooms, corridors, and even the snack bar. "People came to the hotel raped, injured, bleeding," Rusesabagina told Anne-Marie O'Connor for the *Los Angeles Times* (December 28, 2004). Relief agencies dropped off orphans, some Hutu military officers brought their Tutsi wives, and a local priest, Father Wenceslas, deposited his Tutsi mother at the hotel, knowing that she would be safer there than in his own church. (Later, Rusesabagina watched helplessly from the roof of the hotel as machete-wielding Hutus attacked people hiding in the church.) Rusesabagina and his wife made a pact with each other: rather than be butchered, she would jump off the roof of the hotel with their children if the militia invaded.

Soon the militia cut off the hotel's electricity, water, and switchboard lines; Rusesabagina doled out water twice daily from the hotel pool and made use of one remaining phone line that the militia had missed. Via that one line, he made calls "like a madman," as he told O'Connor, dialing everyone he could think of who might be able to help, including employees of the French government and the White House. Few of Rusesabagina's frantic calls were fruitful. The United Nations withdrew forces after some of its peacekeepers were killed, and no one in the international community sent troops. (Both Bill Clinton, during his second term as U.S. president, and U.N. secretary-general Kofi Annan have publicly apologized for their inaction.) The militia regularly attempted to infiltrate the hotel and remove its temporary inhabitants; Rusesabagina managed to stall them repeatedly by bribing them with Scotch, cigars, and money--and by using all the connections he had made as a hotelier to call in favors from high-ranking officials. Once, his wife and children hid in a bathtub while he arranged to have the militia ordered out of the hotel. In the midst of widespread slaughter, Rusesabagina managed to protect everyone within the hotel.

"I never imagined so many people would join the killing mobs. That's why I don't trust people anymore. I know there are good people. But I'm always suspicious. I have completely changed."

Only when the approach of Tutsi guerrillas was imminent did the Hutu militia retreat, thus making it possible for Rusesabagina and the others to drive to a refugee camp near the Tanzanian border. Rusesabagina described the terrible journey to O'Connor: "There were no human beings; just dogs eating dead bodies," he recalled. "The whole country reeked. I never realized that all these people had been butchered. I felt like someone in a dream." At the refugee camp the Rusesabaginas found two nieces whose parents had been killed (along with most of Tatiana's family and some of Paul's relatives); Paul and Tatiana later adopted the girls.

After he left the camp, Rusesabagina returned to Kigali to resume his work as a hotel manager, but he found that the new Tutsi authorities viewed Hutu survivors with distrust, so he and his family moved to Belgium. He now lives in Brussels with Tatiana; their children, Lys, Diane, Roger, and Treasure (some sources spell the name "Tresor"); and their adopted nieces, Carine and Anaise (sometimes spelled "Karine" and "Anais"). He spends much of his time in Zambia (a nation southwest of Tanzania), where he runs a transport company. Rusesabagina told Anne-Marie O'Connor, "I never imagined so many people would join the killing mobs. That's why I don't trust people anymore. I know there are good people. But I'm always suspicious. I have completely changed."

Later Career

In the aftermath of the genocide, many journalists, authors, documentarians, and filmmakers interviewed Rusesabagina in the vain hope of telling his story. After the director Terry George approached him, Rusesabagina watched films that George had either written or directed, including *In the Name of the Father* (1993), about a man accused of a terrorist bombing in England, and *Some Mother's Son* (1996), about a hunger strike among members of the Irish Republican Army in a British prison. Rusesabagina liked George's sensitivity and handling of politically charged issues and agreed to collaborate on the project. In early 2002

Rusesabagina spent several days with George and the writer Kier Pearson, recounting stories for them as they mapped out the script for *Hotel Rwanda*. George wanted the actor Don Cheadle to play Rusesabagina but feared that, in order to secure funding for the film, he might be forced to recruit an actor with proven box-office appeal, such as Will Smith or Denzel Washington. Then the producer Alex Kitman Ho joined the project and independently raised the needed funds, thus giving the filmmakers the freedom to hire Cheadle. Some critics have suggested that the reason why arranging both funding and studio distribution was difficult was that few in Hollywood cared about what had happened in Africa. "Ask anybody what was happening in '94, they probably remember O.J. Simpson [and his murder trial]," Ho told Justin Chang for *Variety* (January 3-9, 2005). "That was the big headline in this country."

Cheadle spent a week with Rusesabagina while preparing for the role, and Rusesabagina traveled to Johannesburg, South Africa, where the picture was being made, to lend support and supervise, when needed, during the filming. "When I met [Rusesabagina] I was struck that he wasn't 10 feet tall, he didn't swagger. He didn't cut an amazing path when he walked," Cheadle told Anne-Marie O'Connor. "He was just a man who did an extraordinary thing in an extraordinary circumstance. . . . The script really did a great job of not making him this huge heroic figure, but making him this common man who applied everything he knew as a hotel manager to survive." Cheadle continued, "He had to know how to talk to people, how to persuade, how to cajole, when to be forceful and when to back off. He applied that to save those lives, thinking every day was going to be his last day on Earth."

Ho told Justin Chang that the filmmakers "made a conscious effort to keep the slaughter [depicted on-screen] minimal." George explained further:"This has to be one of the most savage wars in a hundred years--just the enormity of the physical violence . . . people macheted to death. There's no way [to convey that] unless you use horror film tactics and prosthetics and all that stuff, and I didn't want to." Because of its relative lack of on-screen carnage, the movie secured a PG-13 rating. *Hotel Rwanda* premiered at the 2004 Toronto Film Festival. Although Rusesabagina has expressed his satisfaction at the depiction of his experiences, he found the film difficult to watch, as he still has nightmares about the genocide. Tatiana cried the first time she watched the picture, and some of their children have yet to see it. After the release of *Hotel Rwanda*, Rusesabagina and his wife decided that it was time to tell their nieces that they were adopted. (The girls were too young at the time of the genocide to comprehend or remember what had occurred.) "We did not want our children to learn their history from other people," he told O'Connor.

Hotel Rwanda was nominated for several Golden Globe Awards, and Cheadle was nominated for an Academy Award as best actor. Such acclaim was important to Rusesabagina only to the extent that it has brought the film and its message to the public. "The message of our movie is to say--look, this happened in Rwanda 10 years ago," he told a writer for *CollegeNews.org* (February 10, 2005). "The people of the world were not informed. Now today you are informed and again it is happening--are you not going to take action? Please do take action because it is happening in Sudan. It has been happening in the Congo for the last eight years--about [three and a half] million people have been killed. The world does not start and end in America and Europe. It goes beyond." He added, "The politicians keep saying, 'Never again, never again.' Those two words are the most abused words in the world."

Rusesabagina has won, among other honors, the Peace Abbey Courage of Conscience Award (shared with his wife) and the Immortal Chaplains Foundation Prize for Humanity. He launched the Rusesabagina Foundation to aid survivors of the Rwandan genocide. He has spoken at the White House and continues to give talks frequently in many other places around the world.

Further Reading:

Amnesty International Web site

Boston-Bay State Banner Jan. 13, 2005

Los Angeles Times E p1 Dec. 28, 2004

People p113 Jan. 24, 2005

Variety p12 Jan. 3-9, 2005

Film:

Hotel Rwanda, 2004

Selected Works:

Rusesabagina, Paul, and Tom Zoellner, *An Ordinary Man: An Autobiography*. New York: Viking, 2006.

Steves, Rick

Travel expert, writer, radio and television host, entrepreneur

---

Born: 1955, Washington State, United States

Rick Steves's travel guidebooks have been praised for their upbeat tone and their emphasis on tourism that is economical, focused on out-of-the-way places, and aimed at learning rather than self-indulgence. Steves's advice to travelers, as he explained to Sara Corbett for the *New York Times*(July 4, 2004), is, "Stow your camera and be there. Pick grapes. Go to church. Buy something at the [local] market." He told Becky Emmons for the *South Bend* (Indiana) *Tribune* (December 11, 2005), "A lot of people's idea of travel is eating five meals a day and seeing if you can snorkel when you get into port. Don't call that travel. Call it hedonism."

Steves, who also hosts a long-running PBS travel program, *Rick Steves' Europe,* as well as the syndicated radio show *Travel with Rick Steves*, is perhaps best known for his quirky, personality-driven *Europe Through the Back Door* guide, first published in 1980. He told Corbett that the majority of his competitors in the guidebook market are "so dry they make your lips chap." His work, on the other hand, has inspired such devotion that his fans are often referred to in the travel industry as "Rickniks."

Steves sees travel as more than mere recreation. He explained to Emmons, "Travel paints a human face on our globe [and] helps us celebrate differences and overcome misunderstandings between people." After the March 11, 2004 train bombings in Madrid, Spain, Steves said that the attacks, rather than discouraging people from traveling, should be viewed as a lesson in the importance of exploring other cultures. He told Harry Shattuck in the *Houston Chronicle* (March 21, 2004), "Tourism can be a vital force for peace. If we stop traveling, there will be more terrorism. I wish every American could travel before they voted. Our country would be smart to give every young person a stipend to travel."

Education and Early Career

Richard "Rick" Steves was born in Edmonds, Washington, on May 10, 1955. His mother was a homemaker and his father ran a thriving piano-importing business. When he was 14 years old, Steves visited Europe for the first time, accompanying his parents on a trip to tour piano factories. He told Norma Libman in the *Chicago Tribune* (April 23, 1995), "I remember thinking, this is stupid, I haven't even seen my own country, I don't speak those people's languages, I'd rather be with my friends. But when I was at the airport in Oslo and I saw mothers taking care of their little children, it hit me like a bombshell that the world is filled with five billion equally precious people. This was a real enlightening sort of thing." Visiting such places as Ede, a town near Amsterdam, in the Netherlands, helped shape Steves's fascination with offbeat destinations, and after traveling to Europe with his father again at age 16, he decided to return there on his own. He recalled to Libman, "I was looking at a train schedule and all the backpackers at the Copenhagen train station, and suddenly it hit me: I could go to sleep on this train and wake up on the Rhine River or Amsterdam or Berlin or Stockholm. And I don't need my parents to do this."

In 1973, the day after he graduated from high school, Steves embarked on a backpacking trip across Europe with his best friend, Gene Openshaw. During the 10-week trip, which they have referred to as "Europe through the gutter," the two traveled with little money and were occasionally forced to sneak away without paying their hotel charges. Upon their return home, Steves studied European history and business at Seattle's University of Washington, graduating in 1978.

Steves had worked as a piano teacher to help pay his college tuition; recognizing the improbability of getting reluctant students to practice during the summer months, he spent each of his school breaks in Europe. After graduating and beginning to teach piano full-time, he maintained his summer ritual. He recalled to Kristin Jackson in the *Seattle Times* (February 11, 1996), "Each trip I made got so much easier. I was learning from what I did wrong." Citing as major influences Arthur Frommer's seminal *Europe on Five Dollars a Day* series and the guidebooks *The Art and Adventure of Traveling Cheaply* by Rick Bergand *Turn Right at the Fountain,* by George W. Oates, Steves made it his mission to behave and eat as much like a local as possible.

Once, in preparation for an overland trip from Europe to India, Steves signed up for a course called "Istanbul to Katmandu: An Independent Traveler's Guide" at the University of Washington's Experimental College. He recalled in his memoir, 1999's *Postcards from Europe*: ("When I signed up, I considered the class a godsend. But the teacher was unprepared, lazy, and disorganized. The room was filled with vagabonds about to embark on the trip of their lives. And the teacher didn't care. While he had the information we needed, he insulted us with pointless chatter. I learned nothing about travel to Katmandu, but the class taught me something far more important: I learned the value of well-presented travel information. And I realized that I could teach European travel."

In the late 1970s, Steves, who had developed the habit of taking detailed notes during his travels, began offering an eight-week course, "European Travel--Cheap," at the Experimental College. Although he expected, at most, a few dozen college students to sign up, the first course, which cost $8 per person, attracted 100 middle-aged adults seeking his advice. Steves realized that he had discovered a business niche. He wrote in his memoir, "At first I was happy to earn enough to pay for my annual plane ticket. But as enrollment grew, I began making more teaching travel than I did teaching piano."

In 1980 Steves rented an IBM Selectric typewriter and talked his girlfriend into typing a 256-page manuscript that he had written. Titled, at his father's suggestion, *Europe Through the Back Door,* the volume included illustrations by his college roommate. Steves used $3,000 to self-publish 2,500 copies of the book. He recalled in his memoir, "As if to sabotage my own work, I forgot to put on an ISBN number, which made it difficult for retailers to order the book. The first cover of the book was so basic that people in the media mistook it for a pre-publication edition."

That year Steves also organized his first tour, guiding seven women around Europe for three weeks and charging them only $350 each. Steves, who sometimes had to borrow money from his clients, took the women to places unknown to most tourists, including a tent at the Munich Botanical Gardensin Germany, in which people were allowed to sleep for 50 cents a night. The trip, which Steves recalled to Corbett as "a cross between Woodstock and a slumber party," was a huge success. Once word had spread about the women's adventures, Steves led numerous similar tour groups throughout the 1980s Steves received his big break after the travel editor of the *Seattle Post-Intelligencer* decided to serialize *Europe Through the*

Back Door soon after its publication. The first edition of the book started selling in local stores, and Steves peddled the remaining copies through his travel classes. In 1981 he polished the prose for a second edition, which was published by Pacific Pipeline and distributed to bookstores throughout the Northwest. A third edition, even more polished than its predecessor, was professionally typeset but, Steves wrote on his Web site, "still looked so simple and amateurish that reviewers and talk show hosts repeatedly mistook it for a pre-publication edition."

"A lot of people's idea of travel is eating five meals a day and seeing if you can snorkel when you get into port. Don't call that travel. Call it hedonism."

By 1982 Steves had abandoned piano lessons altogether in order to focus on his travel business. In 1983 Carl Franz, who had written the highly acclaimed *People's Guide to Mexico,* helped Steves land a deal with John Muir Publications, which had been looking for other books similar to Franz's. The fourth edition of *Europe Through the Back Door,* published by Muir, quickly won a wide readership for its budget-conscious approach to travel and for its emphasis on unusual destinations. Other guidebooks of the time tended to concentrate on such mainstream attractions as the Roman Colosseum and the Tower of London. "You have to be more engaged--you have to figure out how to drive in a town, how to order a meal, how to use a phone booth," Steves explained to Joanne Blain for the Canwest News Service (May 10, 2008).

In 1984 Steves teamed up with his friend Gene Openshaw to write and self-publish the book *Europe 101: History and Art for Travelers,* which was aimed, according to Steves's Web site, at "smart people who slept through their art and history classes before they knew they were going to Europe." Steves and Openshaw followed up that volume in 1988 with *Mona Winks: Self-Guided Tours of Europe's Top Museums,* which covered such famed venues as the Louvre in Paris, London's Tate Gallery, i; and the Uffizi Gallery in Florence, Italy.

In the mid-1980s Steves wrote a rudimentary handbook to accompany his popular "Europe in 22 Days" tours. He displayed a sample of the book at his storefront business as a way to lure prospective travelers, but, as he noted on his Web site, the book started "driving decent people to theft. It needed to be available for sale." He self-published an expanded edition of the manual, which sold well and provided independent travelers with a blueprint for an efficient, economical 22-day tour. Muir subsequently expanded the guide into a series, each book detailing itineraries for two- to 22-day trips to Great Britain, Germany, Austria, Switzerland, Spain, Portugal, France, Scandinavia, and Italy. Steves told Blain, "I honestly wanted to put the information in my books so that I could drive myself out of business as a tour organizer. It didn't work, in a way, but I really wanted people to do the tours without me." (Muir has since been acquired by Avalon Travel Publishing, which continues to work with Steves.)

Later Career

In 1990 Steves launched his own public-television program, *Travels in Europe* with Rick Steves, which aired across the country. Produced with his own funding and provided to public-television stations for free, the shows helped Steves become a nationally known figure. Thanks to the media exposure, his travel business, which had employed just five people until the show debuted, quickly became one of the leading private travel firms in the country. (Rick Steves' Europe now has approximately 80 staff members.

In 1993 Steves, who speaks no language other than English, began publishing phrase books; containing translations by native speakers, they are designed specifically for the independent budget traveler. The books have been lauded for their practicality and humor. Steves commented on his Web site, "Berlitz knew his languages but he never slept in a hotel where he had to ask 'At what time is the water hot?'" By the mid-1990s Steves had some 20 books in print, many co-authored by Openshaw or another friend, Steve Smith. (Dave Hoerlein, an associate of Steves's and an architect by training, provided sketch-like, user-friendly maps for the volumes requiring them.) During the mid-1990s Steves also launched ricksteves.com, which quickly became one of the most popular European travel Web sites.

While Steves made his name in the travel world by focusing on little-known destinations, treasured for their picturesque surroundings and lack of commercialism, he has been accused of single-handedly spoiling some of those locales, which are now visited by tens of thousands of tourists per year. One of the destinations he brought to prominence was Gimmelwald, a small village in the Swiss Alps accessible only by gondola or foot. Home to 140 dairy farmers, it had been known as one of the poorest places in Switzerland. While backpacking through the village during the late 1970s, Steves had become enamored with its quaint character and serene setting and featured it in the first edition of *Europe Through the Back Door*.

Gimmelwald now draws an average of 20,000 visitors per year, and many of the town's farmers moonlight as innkeepers. The town of Rothenburg, Germany, has also undergone a major transformation since it was highlighted in Steves's guidebook. Steves wrote in his memoir, "Twenty years ago, I fell in love with a Rothenburg in the rough. At that time, the town still fed a few farm animals within its medieval walls. Today Rothenburg's barns are hotels and its livestock are tourists. Once the premier stop on a medieval trading route, Germany's best-preserved walled town survives today as a popular stop along the tourist trail called the Romantic Road. The English and German signs that long marked the entire route have been replaced by new ones--still bilingual, but in English and Japanese. And Mr. 'Off the Beaten Path' is right here with the camera-toting masses." The Rue Cler, a cobblestone pedestrian street in Paris known for its eclectic mix of cafes and markets, suffered a similar fate, after Steves called it the most Parisian of all Paris streets. (Parisians now jokingly refer to it as Rue Rick Steves.) Steves defended such changes to Blaine Greteman in *Time*(June 16, 2003): "Sure, there are places like Gimmelwald, or Cinque Terre in Italy, that I've promoted heavily and really had an impact on. They're now touristy, admittedly. And it's my fault, admittedly. But when I get back there, I check in with the locals and the tourists, and everybody's happy. The locals might be renting rooms and cooking nice meals instead of making wine--but they're also making money."

In contrast to other travel writers, who typically e-mail restaurants and hotels in order to update their guidebooks, Steves continues to travel for at least four months each year to discover new sights and attractions. While in the U.S., Steves tours the country, lecturing not only on travel but on other issues of importance to him. Along with the actor Woody Harrelson, he is one of the nation's most outspoken advocates for the legalization of marijuana; he currently serves on the advisory board of the National Organization for the Reform of Marijuana Laws (NORML). As noted by a writer for the *Contra Costa* (California) *Times* (April 10, 2008), Steves told the talk-show host Dave Ross, "The more I travel in Europe the more I realize how outdated and foolish our laws criminalizing marijuana are in this country." He added, "Prohibition didn't work, and neither does this." He has also been outspoken in his opposition to the war in Iraq and about other foreign-policy issues, and has blogged from the Middle East.

His travel empire currently includes a variety of guidebooks, videos, downloadable audio tours, and a weekly public-radio program called *Travel with Rick Steves*, which features interviews with guest travel experts and listener call-in segments. His seminal book, *Europe Through the Back Door*, has expanded to almost 700 pages and is the number-one best-selling budget guidebook in the U.S. In January 2009 Steves appeared in an hourlong television special, *Rick Steves' Iran: Yesterday and Today*, which aired on public television stations. In that documentary, filmed during an 11-day visit to Iran in 2008, Steves addressed the country's reputation as a haven for terrorist organizations. Steves's book, *Travel as a Political Act* (2009), includes field reports from Europe, Central America, Asia, and the Middle East.

Steves lives in Edmonds, Washington.He is divorced and has a son, Andy, and daughter, Jackie. Steves has donated much of his multimillion-dollar fortune to various charities, and in 2005 he and his then wife, Anne, founded Trinity Place, a 24-unit apartment complex in Lynwood, Washington, which provides housing and other social services to homeless mothers and their children. In 2007 he spent $80,000 to plant trees, in an attempt to counteract--to a small degree--the air pollution caused by his European flights. Steves, a devout Lutheran, gives $30,000 a year to the Christian collective Bread for the World and is an avid supporter of the Mercy Corps, an organization that offers international assistance to refugees and those in need. "I don't just want to leave a scrapbook of smiling faces and barbecues when I leave this planet," he told Christy Karras in the *Salt Lake Tribune* (October 31, 2004).

Further Reading:

Chicago Tribune C p1+ Apr. 23, 1995

Houston Chronicle T p2 Mar. 21, 2004

New York Times p20+ July 4, 2004

Publishers Weekly Jan. 30, 2006

Seattle Post-Intelligencer A p1+ Apr. 23, 2005, D p1 Aug. 17, 2007

Seattle Times K p1+ Feb. 11, 1996, F p8 Apr. 9, 2008

South Bend (Indiana) *Tribune*D p12 Dec. 11, 2005

Time p50+ June 16, 2003

Selected Books:

Europe Through the Back Door,1980

Europe 101: History and Art for Travelers (with Gene Openshaw), 1984

Europe in 22 Days, 1985 *Mona Winks: Self-Guided Tours of Europe's Top Museums* (with Gene Openshaw), 1988

Rick Steves' Europe Through the Back Door, 1995

Postcards from Europe, 1999

Travel as a Political Act, 2009

Selected Television Shows:

Travels in Europe with Rick Steves (1990-98)

Rick Steves' Europe (1999-)

Rick Steves' Iran: Yesterday and Today (2009)

Waters, Alice

Restaurateur, chef, cookbook author, activist

Born: 1944, Chatham, New Jersey, United States

Since she founded Chez Panisse, in Berkeley, California, more than four decades ago, Alice Waters has revolutionized restaurant cooking and how people think about food in the United States. Waters is credited with launching the farm-to-table movement that has swept the country in recent years—several decades after Chez Panisse pioneered what came to be called New American cuisine. "More than any other single figure, Miss Waters has been instrumental in developing the exciting and imaginative style that has been labeled New American cuisine," Marian Burros wrote for the *New York Times* (September 26, 1984). "Its trademarks … are an adventurous, often improvised use of the finest American ingredients and an exquisitely simple and straightforward approach to their preparation." Before Waters's arrival on the culinary scene, prepackaged, chemical-laden convenience foods constituted a large part of the American diet, and gourmet dining was virtually synonymous with French cuisine. Owing largely to Waters and Chez Panisse, American cuisine became as widely respected as French cuisine and a fixture of fine dining establishments everywhere. Moreover, Americans are now more likely than ever before to purchase and prepare locally grown fruits and vegetables. As the online magazine *California Monthly* noted, "Anyone who has been to a local farmer's market, bought organic produce, or eaten a cafe-baked pizzetta has been touched by Waters' gentle, discriminating hand."

Waters wanted Chez Panisse to do more than bring people pleasure; she hoped it would help to initiate a social revolution. She believes that people who eat food grown or produced by local farmers will be more likely make it a priority to take care of one another and the environment. Waters is a staunch proponent of the Slow Food Movement, whose founders deplore the fast-food industry's effects on cultures and environments. (She has served as one of Slow Food International's three vice presidents since 2003.) The movement stresses the importance of sustainable agriculture and of eating as a family-centered act. Sustainable agriculture, according to the website of the Alliance for Sustainable Agriculture, means "ecologically sound, economically viable, socially just and humane" agricultural practices. Waters has set up a number of school-based community-garden and nutrition projects, with the goal of showing youngsters the rewards of eating home-grown fruits and vegetables. "We need to wake up and pay attention and educate ourselves about what we are eating and what the consequences are," she said to AgBiotech Buzz (July 29, 2002), an online newspaper funded by the Pew Initiative on Food and Biotechnology. "I call it a rather delicious revolution. It isn't hard to do. This isn't like a diet. This is the ultimate diet. You eat delicious things and it makes you feel better and it changes how you relate to people. You become part of a community." "Alice rolled the dice and created the demand for sustainability," claims David Prior, then a Chez Panisse spokesperson, as reported by

Robin Wilkey in the Huffington Post (August 26, 2011). Chez Panisse spawned dozens of imitators, many protégés, and numerous cookbooks, most of them co-written by Waters.

Education and Early Career

The second of the four daughters of Pat Waters, an accountant and business-psychology consultant, and Margaret Waters, a social worker, Alice Louise Waters was born in Chatham, New Jersey, on April 28, 1944. During World War II, her mother and father, responding to an appeal from the federal government, grew a so-called victory garden—as did millions of other people—as a way of decreasing the country's dependence on imported products. After the war ended, her parents continued to maintain their garden. Waters told *California Monthly* that her mother always served healthful, nutritious meals, but she "really wasn't a very good cook. We never had anything especially fancy … but we always had dinner together, at the table, at the same time, and we always had to sit there and do that every night." At the New Hampshire lake where the family spent summers, the neighboring families would gather for huge picnics featuring seasonal New England food: blueberries, clams, corn on the cob, tomatoes. When Waters's parents entertained at home in New Jersey, young Alice insisted on playing hostess by setting the table and making flower arrangements and name tags. Pat Waters recalled for Linda Witt of the *New York Times* (May 11, 1986), "Two things emerged rapidly in Alice's personality. She was a great socializer. If she wanted a party, she had a party. Even if she had to ask the boy and then go over and get his suit pressed for him, if she wanted to go to a school dance, you could bet she'd find a boy. And that's the second thing—she was determined. If Alice wanted to do something … Well, Margaret and I finally figured out the only way to handle the situation was to say to ourselves, 'Okay now, how do we help her?'" As a child, according to Dean Riddle at Waitrose.com (November 1998), Waters once won a costume contest outfitted as the "Queen of the Garden."

After leaving New Jersey and living for several years in Chicago, the Waters family settled in Van Nuys, California, in 1962. The following year Waters and several of her friends enrolled at the University of California at Santa Barbara. To their dismay, they found that campus life revolved around sororities, fraternities, and beach games rather than academics. They also discovered that their burgeoning left-wing political consciousness put them at odds with many of their fellow students. In the spring of 1964, they transferred to the University of California at Berkeley; the following fall the Free Speech Movement swept the campus. The movement began when student activists staged a two-day protest sparked when school administrators declared off-limits to political activities parts of the campus traditionally used for such purposes. "We came at the right moment," Waters told Witt. "It was a great time. The Free Speech Movement immediately focused one's energies. It was impossible to be left out of the rage at what was happening here on campus and in society." Waters subsequently became involved with local politics, working for the journalist and peace activist Robert Scheer during his unsuccessful campaign for a seat in Congress.

At age 19 Waters spent a year in France. "I lived at the bottom of a market street"—a street on which farmers sold their produce—"and took it all in by osmosis, and I hung out in a lot of great French kitchens," she told Dean Riddle. Referring to the nearly ubiquitous farmers' markets in France, she recalled for AgBiotech Buzz, "People wouldn't think of having food several days old. There was a kind of life to everything I ate, a kind of beauty about it. I just had never experienced those tastes." A dinner she ate in a small inn in the Brittany region made an especially strong impression on Waters. The chef, a woman, served cured ham with melon from her garden, trout caught a few hours earlier from a nearby stream, and small tarts made with fresh raspberries. "It was a wonderful experience for [Alice]," Pat Waters recalled to Linda Witt. "When everyone gave the chef a standing ovation, she said, 'Ah that's it. A way to entertain my friends and have a wonderful time.'"

After she graduated from Berkeley, in 1967, with a bachelor's degree in French cultural studies, Waters spent a year in London, studying the Montessori method of early-childhood education. Back in Berkeley she got a job as a teacher in a Montessori school and moved in with the illustrator David Lance Goines, who would later design and illustrate a number of Chez Panisse cookbooks and posters. In her leisure time she prepared meals for friends, following the recipes in Elizabeth David's classic book *French Country Cooking.* The home she and Goines shared soon became a place to meet and eat for people seen by themselves or others as political radicals. Goines told Leslie Crawford for Salon.com (November 16, 1999), "Alice wanted to have her friends to dinner every night. The only way to do that was to open a restaurant." In addition, as Eleanor Bertino, one of Waters's college roommates, told Witt, Waters and her friends saw themselves as "part of a community, part of a greater world. Alice's first fantasies about a restaurant came out of that. It would have one fixed price. Friends cooking. It would be a replacement for the family. This was 1968 or 1969. We didn't see ourselves getting married or having children. We saw ourselves in this greater community of peers."

Later Career

In 1971 Waters, Paul Aratow, and several friends opened a small restaurant on Shattuck Street near the Berkeley campus. They funded their venture with a $10,000 loan from Waters's father, who had agreed to mortgage the family house to help them. The restaurant was designed to resemble the sorts of bistros that Waters had seen in Provence, in southern France. She named it after a character (an elderly sail maker) in the films *Marius, Fanny,* and *César* (known as the Marseilles Trilogy), which the French writer Marcel Pagnol adapted from his own plays. At that time many fine restaurants in the United States, inspired by their counterparts in France, served rich, heavily sauced dishes made with imported products. American cuisine— macaroni-and-cheese and meatloaf, for example—was widely ridiculed by chefs and gourmands. Familiar with the abundant resources of the area surrounding her restaurant, Waters decided to serve the same simple meal for all patrons on any particular day, using the freshest food available from local markets. "The food began with very much a French country overtone, simple and uncomplicated," Goines told Crawford. "You served a fresh fish and left it alone. You didn't tart it up with all sorts of sauces. This basic philosophy matured over the years into Alice's search for pure, fresh ingredients."

Waters's first few years as a restaurateur proved exceedingly difficult. Her workload was exhausting: in addition to taking care of the administrative aspects of the business, she cooked almost every night. As Tom Luddy, a film producer with Francis Ford Coppola's Zoetrope Studios who became romantically involved with Waters, recalled to Witt, "Many, many times I'd pick her up from the restaurant after an 18- or 20-hour day, walk her to the door, put the key in the lock, and she'd faint. She'd just pass out, and I'd have to carry her in and I'd put her to bed. The next morning at 7 she would come awake like a shot, saying, 'I have to call about the chickens.' I'd literally have to hold her down and tell her to 'slowly count to ten. Then you can use the phone.'" In the beginning, and for some time afterwards, the restaurant lost money, in part because organic ingredients were far costlier than others, and the food required more extensive preparation than meals served elsewhere. (Apparently, the prices Waters charged were not high enough to cover her costs.)

As word spread about the culinary revolution being waged at the California eatery and its extraordinary menu, "foodies" began to flock to eat there, along with superstars and power brokers from many fields. At the same time glowing reviews of Chez Panisse started to appear in the media. Through the years the restaurant continued to draw high praise. In 1992 the James Beard Foundation (named for one of the nation's most celebrated cooks) chose Chez Panisse as the best restaurant in the United States; in 2001 *Gourmet* magazine honored it with the same encomium. Waters cooked at Chez Panisse full time until her daughter, Fanny, was born in 1983. A year later Waters opened Café Fanny, a diminutive, Parisian-style cafe located a few miles away from Chez Panisse. The café served breakfast and lunch. (It closed in 2012.)

At Chez Panisse the menus change daily, depending on the availability of fresh ingredients sold by local farmers and other providers. Currently, the restaurant has two facilities: a formal dining room upstairs and a more casual eatery, called the Cafe at Chez Panisse, downstairs. Chez Panisse takes reservations up to one month in advance. A Thursday night dinner menu at Chez Panisse might include Frisée and roasted apricot salad with Padrón peppers, squab liver crostini, and sherry vinaigrette; King salmon in saffron brodetto with Black Prince tomatoes and basil; Grilled Wolfe Ranch quail with Romano beans, sweet corn frittelle and fennel agrodolce; and Île flottante with peaches and strawberries. Prices for a three-course meal are $65 on Monday, typically a more rustic menu; $85 Tuesday through Thursday; and $100 on Friday and Saturday. The café offers a moderately priced à la carte menu for lunch and dinner. Chez Panisse is closed on Sunday. Some 75 farmers, ranchers, fishermen, cheese makers, vintners, and florists in the Berkeley area provide Chez Panisse with produce, poultry, fish, meat, cheese, wine, and flowers. Waters employs a "forager," who scours local markets and farms for the best ingredients.

Chez Panisse was nearly destroyed in a devastating fire in 1982. In March 2013 an electrical fire that began under the restaurant's porch caused extensive damage. After repairs and something of a facelift, the restaurant opened again the following June. Commenting for *Bon Appétit* (June 24, 2013) on Waters's response to the fire, David Prior, a former restaurant spokesperson still associated with Waters, said that, "Despite her public image as a softly spoken dreamer, when it comes to the restaurant Alice is a fearless leader, never more motivated than when faced with adversity and doubt." Waters, Prior said, "has a management style that can only be described as 'very Berkeley,' but that approach has meant the staff feels immense loyalty to the restaurant and to one another, whether they choose to devote their entire working life to the restaurant—or move on to other jobs." At Chez Panisse, according to Julia Moskin, writing in the *New York Times* (January 21, 2014, Waters "instituted job-sharing programs between parents, instituted a six-months-off furlough system for head chefs and put time and money into building a deep bench of cooks, which allows employees to move in and out of her kitchens as their lives change."

Waters's work at Chez Panisse can be seen as a continuation of the radical politics she espoused as a college student. In Waters's view, eating is a political act. As such, it may benefit farmers who practice sustainable agriculture and those who distribute their products; or it may support large corporations that care more about profit margins than public health. "Good healthy eating is simply not compatible with processed food," she told *California Monthly*. "When you eat together, and eat a meal you cook yourselves, such meals honor the materials from which they are made; they honor the art by which they are done; they honor the people who make them, and those who share them. I believe food is a medium for us all to do more meaningful work in our own lives. And, more than that, I believe we have an ethical obligation to do this work, for the sake of humanity—better lives for each other and for the generations who come after us." In her books and interviews, Waters has urged people to shop at their local farmers' markets and abstain from buying food that has been genetically modified. "I like to buy my food from people who have integrity and honesty about what they are doing, people who care about nourishment and that's their primary purpose," she told

AgBiotech more than a decade ago. "They take care of the land for the future and think about consequences for the next generation. … I'm very happy eating tomatoes three months out of the year. I don't want them all year long."

Waters urges a succession of U.S. presidents to plant a garden at the White House in order to lend visibility and support to the sustainable food movement and to make the connection between good food and good health in a very direct, public way. According to Kate Pickert, writing in *Time* magazine (March 25, 2009), "When Michelle Obama broke ground on the new White House vegetable garden, there was probably no one in America more elated than Alice Waters." In a question-and-answer session with Pickert, Waters observed, "We know the five big companies that run this country in terms of food are vulnerable in so many ways, like food safety. We're not just talking about this product that doesn't have herbicides and pesticides. We're talking about farm workers and the conditions under which they produce that food. We're talking about a kind of biodiversity of the land. We're talking about a care for the land beyond the superficial. Food isn't like anything else. It's something precious. It's not a commodity."

Food isn't like anything else. It's something precious. It's not a commodity."

In 1996, to celebrate the twenty-fifth anniversary of the restaurant, Waters established the Chez Panisse Foundation, with the aim of "transforming public education by using food traditions and rituals to teach, nurture, and empower young people." The foundation donates money to nonprofit organizations that promote sustainable agriculture. One of its main recipients is the Edible Schoolyard at Berkeley's Martin Luther King Jr. Middle School. Students in the project plant vegetables and fruits on an acre of school property and then harvest, cook, and serve them for lunch. In honor of the restaurant's fortieth anniversary, the name of the foundation was changed to the Edible Schoolyard. In 2003 Waters initiated a pilot program at Yale University, in New Haven, Connecticut, called the sustainable food project, whereby one of the school's 12 dining halls serves food prepared from locally grown products. "The essence of it is to integrate food into the curriculum at Yale," Waters told Marc Santora of the *New York Times* (August 16, 2003). "When one out of every three kids is likely to be obese, I think the importance of what we eat is hitting home in a shocking way."

Waters's many honors include the Restaurant and Business Leadership Award from Restaurants and Institutions magazine, the Excellence in Education Award given by U.S. senator Barbara Boxer of California, the Rachel Carson Environmental Award from the National Nutritional Foods Association, and the Lifetime Achievement Award from *Bon Appétit* magazine. The James Beard Foundation named her the best chef in America in 1992. Waters became a knight of the French Legion of Honor in 2010, one of only three Americans to awarded that honor (Julia Child and Thomas Keller are the other two). In 2004 Dartmouth College, in Hanover, New Hampshire, awarded her an honorary doctor of arts degree. In a signal honor, the Louvre, in Paris, France, in 1998 invited Waters to open a restaurant in the museum. After she realized that museum officials wanted simply an eatery and had no interest in her suggestions of making it a place to educate the public about food as well, Waters withdrew from the project.

Waters inevitably attracted a certain amount of criticism, mostly for what restaurant critic Todd Kliman called on a NPR blog (January 29, 2009) her "inflexible brand of gastronomical correctness." "Shopping is not cooking," Kliman continued. Kim Severson in the *New York Times* (September 19, 2007) quotes Ruth Reichl (then the editor of *Gourmet*) as saying that the "remarkable thing about Alice Waters is that she simply doesn't stop: 'She's relentless in that way revolutionaries are.'"

In the early 1970s Waters was briefly married to Jean-Pierre Gorin, a French filmmaker. Waters married Stephen Singer, an olive-oil and wine merchant and painter, in 1985. The couple divorced in 1997. They have a daughter, Fanny, born in 1983, who is named for another of the characters in the Marseilles Trilogy. Fanny at age eight is the supposed narrator of the first part of *Fanny at Chez Panisse: A Child's Restaurant with 46 Recipes,* introducing readers to some of the people who work at the restaurant, provision it, or patronize it. According to Crawford, Waters "lives her own life with as little pretension and as much simplicity as she demands of her food."

Further Reading:

AgBioTech Buzz Jul. 29, 2002

Bon Appétit June 24, 2013

California Monthly Dec. 1999

Chicago Tribune C p10+ May 11, 1986, with photos

Huffington Post June 24, 2013

New York Times Sep. 19, 2007 pF1; Jan. 21, 2014

The Observer Jun. 11, 2005

Salon.com Nov. 16, 1999

San Francisco Chronicle (SFGate) Jun. 24, 2013

Selected Books:

Waters, Alice, Patricia Curtan, and Martine Labro, *Chez Panisse Pasta, Pizza, and Calzone,* 1984

Waters, Alice, with Bob Carrau and Patricia Curtan, *Fanny at Chez Panisse,* 1992

Waters, Alice, and the Cooks of Chez Panisse, *Chez Panisse Vegetables,* 1996

Bertolli, Paul, and Alice Waters, *Chez Panisse Cooking,* 1996

Waters, Alice, with Linda Guenzel, *Chez Panisse Menu Cookbook,* 1999

Waters, Alice, and the Cooks of Chez Panisse with David Tanis and Fritz Streiff, *Chez Panisse Café Cookbook,* 1999

Waters, Alice, and the Cooks of Chez Panisse, with Allan Tangren and Fritz Streiff, *Chez Panisse Fruit,* 2002

Waters, Alice, with Patricia Curtan, Kelsie Kerr & Fritz Streiff, *The Art of Simple Food: Notes, Lessons, and Recipes from a Delicious Revolution,* 2007

Waters, Alice, with Daniel Duana, *Edible Schoolyard: A Universal Idea,* 2008

Waters, Alice, *In the Green Kitchen: Techniques to Learn by Heart,* 2010

Waters, Alice, *40 Years of Chez Panisse: The Power of Gathering,* 2011

The Art of Simple Food II, 2013

Wheeler, Tony

British-born co-founder of Lonely Planet, author

Born: 1946, Bournemouth, England, United Kingdom

Philip Shenon, writing for the *New York Times* (June 30, 1996), once described Tony Wheeler as "the trail-blazing patron saint of the world's backpackers and adventure travelers." Wheeler was the co-founder (along with his wife, Maureen) of Lonely Planet, the world's largest independent travel-guide publisher. In 1973 Wheeler and his wife published their first guidebook, a 94-page pamphlet titled *Across Asia on the Cheap*, which Wheeler wrote at the couple's kitchen table in Sydney, Australia, where they had arrived after completing a lengthy journey across Asia. Although the couple hadn't planned on writing a book when they initially set off from London, *Across Asia on the Cheap* became an almost overnight success. Realizing that there was a strong market for low-budget travel guides, the Wheelers embarked on subsequent adventures and published their findings in a series of Lonely Planet guidebooks, including *South-East Asia on a Shoe-string* (1975), *Trekking in the Nepal Himalaya* (1976), and the very popular *Lonely Planet India* (1981). Featuring a distinctively direct and plucky style, these early Lonely Planet titles helped bring into existence "a floating fourth world of people who travelled full time," according to the travel writer Pico Iyer, as quoted by Tad Friend for *The New Yorker* (April 18, 2005). "The guides encouraged a counter-Victorian way of life, in that they exactly reversed the old imperial assumptions. Now the other cultures are seen as the wise place, and we are taught to defer to them." For many of the scores of adventurous independent travelers that set off to visit distant lands in the late 1970s and the decades that followed, the Wheelers' guidebooks have been essential reading. Lonely Planet sells millions of guidebooks annually.

Education and Early Career

Tony Wheeler was born in Bournemouth, England in 1946. Wheeler's father was an airport manager for the British Overseas Airways Corporation (the forerunner to British Airways); because of his changing job assignments, the Wheeler family moved frequently. "When I was about a year old the whole family moved to Karachi, Pakistan, where we lived for the next 5 years," Wheeler recalled in an interview with Rolf Potts for the *Vagabonding* Web site (August 2003). "There was a short interlude in England when I lived with my grandparents, then the whole family upped and moved to the Bahamas. Another short spell followed in England, and then we moved to the U.S., where I spent the next 6 years, nearly all of my high school years. So I finally arrived permanently in England when I was 16." Wheeler enjoyed making maps of his surroundings in his youth, and when he was 10 years old, he asked his parents for a globe and a filing cabinet as a Christmas gift so he could plot all the countries in the world he would some day visit. "I don't think I was particularly close to either of my parents," Wheeler told Friend. "There was an English coolness there—though I did love going to the airport with my father."

Wheeler studied engineering at the University of Warwick in England; he was distracted from his studies, however, by an avid interest in journalism and writing. "I almost failed my first year at university because I was spending so much time working on the university newspaper instead of going to classes," he told a writer for the *Young Pioneers* Web site (spring 2004). After he graduated from Warwickin 1969with a degree in engineering, he accepted a position designing cars for the Chrysler Corporation, where he worked for almost two years. At that time, Britain's economy was in turmoil and the country's manufacturing base was being dismantled. "It was an eye-opening couple of years there [at Chrysler]," Wheeler told Linda Anderson in the *Financial Times* (September 8, 2003). "The total decline of British industry. I saw everything that was going on. It was fascinating, but I could see being an engineer there as a dead end, and also that I would not be terribly good at it." Having enjoyed an undergraduate business course he had taken at Warwick, Wheeler decided to apply to business schools in both the U.S. and England. Several U.S. schools accepted his application, but Wheeler opted for the London Business School, where he began a two-year MBA program. Finding the coursework more satisfying than his undergraduate studies, he graduated with an MBA in 1972.

"To research a big guidebook, you need some people who live in the country, but you also need some parachute artists, someone who can drop into a place and quickly assimilate, who can write about anywhere. I'm a parachute artist."

Although the Ford Motor Company offered him a job, Wheeler decided to postpone accepting and embarked instead on a prolonged honeymoon with his new wife, Maureen. Wheeler had met Maureen, a native of Belfast, Ireland, on a bench in London's Regent's Park, while Wheeler was a student at the London Business School. They married a year later, agreeing to go on a journey together before beginning their careers. Taking off in a weathered minivan, the couple ventured east from Europe into Asia--a jaunt that, as it grew in popularity in the 1960s and 1970s, came to be known as the "hippie trail," after the numerous backpackers and hitchhikers who set out to broaden their horizons by exploring the region. The route generally wound its way through Turkey, the Middle East, and the Indian subcontinent, often ending in Goa, India, or Kathmandu, Nepal.

"I remember crossing the Bosporus into the Asian side of Turkey, and suddenly everything changed," Maureen recalled to Shenon. "It was like nothing I had ever seen in my life--wandering into little villages, with camels by the side of the road. Suddenly I was in this place I had no reference points for. I loved it." From Turkey the Wheelers passed into Iran, then Afghanistan, Pakistan, India, and on into Southeast Asia before they helped crew a yacht that brought them from the island nation of Bali to Australia. Making landfall in Western Australia, the Wheelers then crossed the expansive Nullabor Plain, ending their journey in Sydney on the day after Christmas in 1972. "Even now, that six-month trek, that half-year of restlessness, is hard-wired in my mind like a read-only file," Tony Wheeler told Alasdair Riley for the *London Times* (January 6, 2001). "Every day seems crystal clear, every step cut into stone."

The Wheelers settled in Sydney without much money. (Wheeler reportedly pawned a camera in order to buy food.) Wheeler began collecting his and Maureen's reflections of their overland journey, of which they each had kept meticulous notes (in some cases on cigarette packs, notepads, and bus tickets). Using his wife's typewriter, Wheeler began writing what would become a basic travel-advice guide, *Across Asia on the Cheap.* The small pamphlet was written, hand-collated, and stapled at the Wheelers' kitchen table in Sydney. The couple originally printed 1,500 copies, pitching the book themselves to nearby bookstores. The book sold out quickly (in a matter of days, according to some reports), so the Wheelers printed another 1,500 copies, which sold at an equally rapid rate. "No one realized how big the underground travel market was," Maureen told Shenon. "No one realized how many thousands of people were on the so-called hippie trail."

The book's straightforward style appealed to readers. As Tad Friend observed, "With its buccaneering opinions on the textures of daily life--'The inertial effect of religion is nowhere more clearly seen than with India's sacred cows, they spread disease, clutter already overcrowded towns, consume scarce food (and waste paper) and provide nothing'--the book hearkened back to the confident sweep of the great European guides of a century before." *Across Asia on the Cheap* offered advice not only on what to see and do, but on such offbeat subjects as whether to take advantage of the cheap narcotics that were made available to young tourists. On whether to purchase food from Asian street vendors, for example, the authors wrote, as quoted by Shenon: "If he looks as if he's about to drop dead, eat elsewhere!"

The success of the first book encouraged the Wheelers to do a follow-up. "The second trip, 12 months around Southeast Asia on a motorcycle, was much more planned," Wheeler explained to Rolf Potts. "We definitely had the book in mind all the way through." Again the priority was on living cheaply. The outcome, *South-East Asia on a Shoestring*, was written by Wheeler in 1975, during a three-month period in which the couple lodged at an inexpensive Singapore hotel. The book, with its yolk-colored cover, was an even greater success than its precursor; it became known as the "yellow bible," much loved by independent travelers and backpackers for its distinctive attitude and coverage, which included in-depth discussions of local history and economics. According to Friend, that book and those that followed "read like engineering reports, with topics such as 'History,' 'Climate,' and 'Fauna & Flora' before you got to the actual sights. This eat-your-vegetables earnestness made reading the books feel like taking up a vocation." *South-East Asia on a Shoestring* remains one of the most popular guidebooks ever published--it has sold more than a million copies--and opened the door for subsequent Lonely Planet efforts, including *Trekking in the Nepal Himalaya* in 1976 and a series of books in 1977 on such regions as Australia, Europe, Africa, and New Zealand. In 1980, with a staff of 10, the Wheelers published *Lonely Planet India*, which promptly sold more than 100,000 copies. A winner of both critical praise and commercial success, *Lonely Planet India* brought the Wheelers financial security, changing Lonely Planet from a fledgling company into a stable operation.

Later Career

During the 1980s Lonely Planet outpaced its competitors by staying true to its reputation as an alternative travel guide. Catering mostly to young people from Australia, Britain, and North America trying to get around on a limited budget, Lonely Planet brought scores of adventure travelers into low-cost tourist areas. As Friend, who relied upon Lonely Planet during his own youthful wanderings, wrote, "The guides didn't tell me [everything]. . . . But they did teach me, as they taught a whole generation, how to move through the world alone and with confidence." Many have pointed out that the deregulation of commercial aviation, which made airline tickets more affordable, has nurtured the independent travel market, and Lonely Planet has capitalized on that.

Over the years the company has garnered its share of critics, some of whom accuse Lonely Planet of inspiring young travelers to prematurely wander across the globe. Using her own children as an example,

Maureen Wheeler defended Lonely Planet to Sam Wollaston for the *London Guardian* (July 7, 1998): "My children have travelled all over the world so they're aware of a lot of things. It helps you grow up a lot, just knowing how other people live and what happens in their countries. It's a huge improvement on growing up in the suburbs and never knowing anything else. Secondly, being on your own, having to make your way from one place to the next and work out how you do that, gives you a self-sufficiency that I think is very important." Lonely Planet garnered criticism for publishing a guide to Myanmar (formerly known as Burma) despite the fact that the country was controlled by a military junta, and the Nobel Peace Prize-winning dissident Aung San Suu Kyi had previously urged travelers to boycott the country. "People were dumping books in front of our offices, [and] there was a deluge of letters for a short while," Wheeler told Linda Anderson. "I found it all very unpleasant." The guidebook included a section acknowledging the objections but asserted that travel "is the type of communication that in the long term can change lives and unseat undemocratic governments," as quoted by Friend. The experience, Wheeler told Anderson, "has been an education. I have learned what thick skins politicians must have. It affected me personally."

Lonely Planet (the "Publications" was eventually dropped from the name)has experienced significant growth, both in the size of its workforce and in the number of countries it spotlights. The company currently has offices in Australia, the U.S., and the U.K. Wheeler and his wife eventually abdicated control of Lonely Planet to a management team that favored marketing to more mainstream, bourgeois travelers and tourists. In 2004 each Lonely Planet series was reissued to fit the needs of the company's new target audience, a strategy that displeased some longtime customers. Wheeler admitted that the need to market to a broader audience might have taken away from Lonely Planet's trademark characteristics. "Those vivid colors of the early books, once they get blended with so many other authors and editors and concerns about what the customer wants," Wheeler told Friend, "they inevitably become gray and bland. It's entropy." Lonely Planet publishes more than 600 guidebooks in English and also offers guidebooks in such languages as French, Italian, Spanish, Korean, and Japanese, enjoying sales of more than six million guidebooks annually, or approximately one quarter of all the English-language guidebooks sold worldwide. The name of the company comes from a lyric in the song "Space Captain," by Joe Cocker and Leon Russell; the words are actually "lovely planet" but Wheeler misheard them as "lonely planet."

Friend described Wheeler as "a slight, graying man . . . who goes to the office every day in subfusc clothing." In 2000 Wheeler received the award for outstanding contribution to travel journalism at the Travelex Travel Writer's Awards, and in 2002 he won the British Guild of Travel Writer's lifetime achievement award. As Wheeler told Friend: "To research a big guidebook, you need some people who live in the country, but you also need some parachute artists, someone who can drop into a place and quickly assimilate, who can write about anywhere. I'm a parachute artist."

Tony and Maureen Wheeler no longer live by humble means; their home in Melbourne, Australia, overlooks the Yarra River, and Tony has been known to keep a red Ferrari in the garage. The Wheelers have two grown children, Tashi and Kieran, both of whom spent many of their childhood days traveling with their parents. Observers often identify Maureen Wheeler as a savvy business professional and a major factor in Lonely Planet's success; back in the 1990s, when the couple was still involved in managing the company, Maureen explained that her husband tended to leave the business matters in her hands. "But that's because Tony really can't be bothered," she explained to Wollaston. "It's not that he hasn't got a really good business mind or come up with really good ideas, it's just that he can't be bothered. So someone has to pay attention, and that tends to be me."

"Writing guidebooks is like a combination of search-and-find and making a jigsaw puzzle," Wheeler told Rolf Potts. "You've got to find all the pieces and then put them all together to make [a] picture. Some of the pieces may be hard to find, some of them may be hard to assemble." The biggest reward, he told Potts, is "the weird alleys guidebooks can lead you down. . . . [There's a] real satisfaction in doing books to unusual places and covering something you know nobody else has done. And you get a real kick when people enjoy using your books and you lead them to places they wouldn't otherwise have got to."

The Wheelers sold Lonely Planet to the BBC in 2007. Subsequently, as Emily Brennan reported in the *New York Times* (June 7, 2013): "Mr. Wheeler has devoted his time to the Planet Wheeler Foundation, which finances educational and health projects in the developing world…." He has also authored two books, 2010's *Tony Wheeler's Bad Lands*, a travel guide to such improbable tourist destinations such as Iran and North Korea, and *Tony Wheeler's Dark Lands* in 2013.

Further Reading:

Lonely Planet Web site

New York Times VI p34 June 30, 1996, with photos, June 7, 2013, with photos

The New Yorker p78+ Apr. 18, 2005

Vagabonding Web site

Selected Books:

Across Asia on the Cheap, 1973

South-East Asia on a Shoestring, 1975

Trekking in the Nepal Himalaya, 1976

Chasing Rickshaws, 1998

Tony Wheeler's Bad Lands, 2010

Tony Wheeler's Dark Lands, 2013

Wynn, Stephen

Casino and hotel magnate

Born: 1942, New Haven, Connecticut, United States

"I am infected with an incurable malady called developer's disease," Steve Wynn told Pam Lambert for *People* magazine (December 6, 1993). "What I do for a living and what keeps me young and happy is creating places where people go, 'Wow!'" Wynn's Mirage, Treasure Island, and Bellagio hotel-casinos have, indeed, inspired awe in millions of gamblers and nongamblers alike. Not only are the immense structures on Las Vegas's famous Strip three of the largest and most successful casinos in the world, they have markedly changed the popular conception of gambling, which has been long frowned upon in the United States.

In 1989, with the grand opening of the Mirage, which re-created the atmosphere of a lush, tropical jungle in arid Las Vegas, Wynn began the trend in the entertainment and tourism industries to combine gambling with family-style fun. As Priscilla Painton of *Time* (May 3, 1993) noted, Wynn was the first developer ever to "apply to gambling the Disney formula for class-crossing, universal family leisure: cleanliness, measured frivolity, and a sense of architectural detail." As a result, family vacationers, many of whom had never before considered spending time at a hotel-casino, comprised the majority of guests at the Mirage--and, since its opening in 1993, at Wynn's second resort, Treasure Island.

Wynn has expanded the appeal of the casino even further, by attracting travelers who would usually spend their vacations enjoying the culture and art of Europe. In October 1998 he opened his Bellagio resort, which had a softer, more romantic atmosphere, and featured an art gallery with works by van Gogh, Matisse, and Picasso.

Education and Early Life

Born on January 27, 1942 in New Haven, Connecticut, Stephen Wynn grew up in Utica, New York. His father, Michael Weinberg, changed the family name to Wynn, because, as a Jew, he feared employment discrimination. As Michael Wynn, he managed bingo parlors throughout the Northeast. When Stephen was 11, his father took him on a trip to Las Vegas, where Michael intended to open another, larger bingo operation. According to Lambert, Steve was mesmerized by the bright lights and excitement of the Glitter Gulch section of the city. "When I grow up, I'm going to be a casino boss," the boy told his father.

Although Michael Wynn was a compulsive gambler who was frequently in debt, young Steve rarely felt the financial strain that often burdened his family. He spent summers waterskiing on a lake in the Adirondack Mountains of New York, and during the school year, he attended the Manlius Military Academy, which prepared its students for the U.S. Military Academy at West Point. After graduating from high school, Wynn attended the University of Pennsylvania and on weekends worked at his father's bingo hall in a suburb of

Washington, D.C. Although he originally intended to study medicine, Wynn changed his major to English and he took several additional courses at the university's prestigious Wharton School of Business.

Three weeks before his college graduation in 1963, Wynn's father, aged 46, died while having open-heart surgery. Several of Michael Wynn's substantial gambling debts (by some accounts, as much as $200,000) were left unpaid, and Steve was suddenly faced with the responsibility of paying them. Wynn took over his father's business with his wife, Elaine Pascal, to whom he had been married for less than a year, and his mother, and because he did not himself gamble, he was able to improve the business's overall profitability. "The only way to make money in a casino is to own one," he has been known to say. He also "[made] bingo a social recreational experience," as Wynn told Mark Seal for the book *The Players: The Men Who Made Las Vegas*, so that it attracted more area residents. After several years of hard work, his father's debts were paid in full. "I'd give up anything for fifteen minutes with my father," Painton quoted Wynn as saying, "to have him walk through [my] hotel and see what happened."

"The only way to make money in a casino is to own one."

In 1967, at the age of 25, Wynn, Elaine, and their newborn daughter, Kevyn, moved from their home in Maryland to Las Vegas. With $45,000 that he had saved from his work in the bingo parlor, Wynn was able to buy a 3 percent stake in Las Vegas's Frontier hotel, and took a job as a slot manager at the hotel's small casino. But shortly after establishing himself in that position, an investigation of the hotel was conducted, and it was discovered that a majority of the hotel's shares were owned by Detroit mobsters. Denying that he knew anything about the hotel's connection to organized crime, Wynn immediately sold his interest in the company. Through this mishap, however, Wynn met E. Parry Thomas, the founder and owner of the Valley Bank, which was later to merge with the Bank of America. Thomas helped Wynn to start up a liquor importing company, which Wynn ran until 1972, when Thomas once again helped him by financing the purchase of a strategically located plot of land, owned by Howard Hughes, for $1.1 million. Although Wynn planned to build a casino there, 11 months later he sold the land to Caesars Palace for $2.25 million.

Since he had moved west, Wynn had gradually accumulated shares in a somewhat run-down old casino called the Golden Nugget. Although his keen interest in the moderately profitable company may have seemed strange to some onlookers, in 1972, with his profits of $766,000 from the land sale to Caesars Palace and some capital from his liquor business, Wynn increased his holdings in Golden Nugget to 5.5 percent, and gained a seat on the company's board of directors. Because he had become well informed about the activities in the city's many casinos through his work in the liquor business, Wynn knew that many of the employees of the Golden Nugget were stealing from the company. After gathering evidence, he convinced the establishment's director to resign. Wynn was elected president of Golden Nugget Inc. at an emergency board meeting on August 1, 1973, and at 31 years of age, became the youngest person ever to head a casino. He immediately fired the majority of the casino's staff and called on his only sibling, Kenneth, who is 10 years his junior, to be his assistant. Throughout the mid-1970s, Wynn transformed the dingy Golden Nugget, located just across the street from the building where his father had attempted to open a bingo parlor, into a brighter and more elegant establishment that was frequented mostly by high rollers--individuals who gambled at extremely high stakes and, thus, helped to generate higher profits for the casino.

In 1978, Wynn visited Atlantic City, New Jersey, which had recently legalized gambling, but had long been out of fashion as a vacation spot. Hearing that the city was about to undergo an enormous comeback, Wynn bought an old hotel called the Strand for $8.5 million. Two years later, using the financial strategies of his friend Michael Milken, a pioneer in the use of high risk-high yield bonds to finance new businesses, Wynn demolished the old building and created a new Golden Nugget hotel-casino in its place. Although the 506-room hotel-casino was small by today's standards, within months of opening its income exceeded expectations by 50 percent, and it became the most successful casino-hotel in Atlantic City. During the following years, Wynn displayed his great talent for marketing and advertising by stealing such coveted performers as Diana Ross and Frank Sinatra from neighboring casinos, and convincing them to sign exclusive contracts for hotel-casino appearances with Golden Nugget. A series of television commercials for the Atlantic City Golden Nugget that were said to have been written by Wynn featured Sinatra, who had previously refused to appear in any commercials, pressing money into Wynn's palm and saying, "Make sure I get enough towels." From the time of Wynn's takeover of Golden Nugget Inc., in 1973until 1984, the company's annual revenues grew from $19 million to $385 million.

In 1987, Wynn sold the thriving Atlantic City Golden Nugget to the Bally Entertainment Corp. for $440 million, making a $250 million profit. The success of this sale not only enabled Wynn to begin planning the construction of his 3,044-room chef d'oeuvre--the Mirage--it also prevented the well-known developer Donald Trump from taking over the Bally Entertainment Corp., because of a law that limited the number of Atlantic City casinos that could be owned by a single party. With the addition of the Golden Nugget, the acquisition of Bally's holdings on Atlantic City's Boardwalk would have put Trump over the legal limit. The two developers have been rivals ever since.

Later Career

While building the Mirage, Wynn carefully oversaw every detail of the hotel's design, including the decor, lighting, and seating in each of the restaurants and guest rooms. Wynn's hard work and financial risks paid off, however, when the hotel opened in November 1989. By 1991, it had become the most successful casino in history, grossing $201 million that year. Golden Nugget Inc., of which Wynn by now held the majority of shares, was renamed Mirage Resorts Inc.

Famous throughout the world, the Mirage hotel-casino had many extravagant features, including a man-made volcano that erupted every 15 minutes, a glass tank full of sharks that stared out at guests from behind the registration desk, a pool full of dolphins, an exotic habitat populated by white tigers (an endangered species), an indoor rainforest with almost $100 million-worth of exotic flowering plants from around the world, 10 acres of outdoor gardens complete with waterfalls and ponds, an 18-hole golf course with pine trees imported from northern California, and a specially designed theater where the world-famous illusionists Siegfried and Roy performed. Wynn described the Mirage to Lambert as "what God would have done if he'd had the money." The hotel-casino was said to have sparked the $5 billion building boom that followed its opening and made Las Vegas the fastest-growing city in the U.S. Since the success of the Mirage, many such family-oriented hotel-casinosthrive on the Las Vegas Strip—making Wynn, as Julie Creswell wrote in the *New York Times*, "the man credited with changing the landscape of the Strip and bringing a semblance of class to Sin City." (August 3, 2008) Wynn constructed an 1,800-room, $600 million resort in Biloxi, Mississippi, called Beau Rivage, which opened in 1999. The hotel-casino suffered damage during Hurricane Katrina and was subsequently renovated.

As early as 1971, when he was just 29 years old, Wynn was diagnosed with retinitis pigmentosa, an incurable, inherited disease that causes its victims to gradually lose their sight. "I can't see my own hand underneath my nose. And I can't see if you stick your hand out to shake with me, but my central vision is perfect," Wynn has said. Since being diagnosed with the disease, the developer has established, in his father's memory, the Michael M. Wynn Center for Inherited Retinal Diseases at the John Moran Eye Center at the University of Utah.

Wynn donates generously to the political campaigns of both Democrats and Republicans. A biography, *Running Scared: The Dangerous Life and Treacherous Times of Las Vegas Casino King Steve Wynn*, was written by John L. Smith and published by a small publisher, Barricade Books, in 1996. After reading a description of the book that mentioned a Scotland Yard investigation into Wynn's connections to organized crime, the casino owner sued the publisherand won $3 million in damages. While it is true that several Mirage executives have been investigated, and that such investigations have been a favorite subject with journalists, Wynn, who has never had a problem renewing his licenses with the Nevada or the New Jersey gaming commissions, told David Cay Johnston for the *New York Times* (June 27, 1995), "None of us have any relationship with any nefarious characters, except as customers. . . . It's time to put all this childish stuff about organized crime to rest."

Wynn divorced his wife, Elaine, in 1986, but neither he nor his wife moved out, and Elaine remained one of the directors of Mirage Resorts Inc. In 1991, they remarried. "The divorce just didn't work out," he jokingly told Lambert. (The couple subsequently divorced again and Wynn has remarried.) The Wynns have two adult daughters, Kevyn and Gillian; Kevyn was kindnapped and briefly held for ransom in 1993. She remained, thankfully, unharmed and the kidnappers were later apprehended.

Stephen Wynn is around six feet tall and has a big, white-toothed smile. He is also described as having a strong personality and being difficult to work with. "I am a self-made brat," he told Painton. "I'm like everybody else: I want to get away with it if I can. . . . I'm harsh because I'm frightened that in my isolation as a chairman who doesn't see everything . . . that basically I don't really know what's going on."

He is no stranger to controversy, notably—as Keith Bradsher reported in the *New York Times* (March 2, 2012)— his recent gambling ventures in Macao, the Chinese-controlled seaport resort and former Portuguese colony. Wynn and his then business partner went through a bitter litigation process. The stakes were crucial. Macao, "where annual gambling revenue is four times that of the Las Vegas Strip," was the entire source of Wynn holdings' "$613.4 million profit." Wynn has also taken strong, often contradictory, stances on the fast-growing world of online gambling (Steve Ruddock, *NJ*.com, February 10, 2014).

He is almost equally renowned for his extensive painting collection and passion for collecting art, although some of the renown was probably unwelcome: In 2006 Wynn accidentally punctured one of his Picassos, valued at over $100 million (and since restored).

Further Reading:

Las Vegas Review Journal Jan. 21, 1998, Feb. 14, 1998

The New Yorker, Oct. 23, 2006

New York Times D p1 June 27, 1995, with photos, III p1 July 6, 1997, with photo; Aug. 3, 2008, with photos, March 2, 2012, with photos

NJ.com, Feb. 10, 2014

People p75+ Dec 6, 1993, with photos s

Time p52+ May 3, 1993, with photos

Wall Street Journal A p14 June 7, 1996

Zagat, Tim

Publishers, business executives, lawyers

Born: 1940, New York City, New York, United States

Zagat, Nina

Born: 1942, New York City, New York, United States

At a dinner party in 1979, Nina and Tim Zagat and their 20 fellow diners had a discussion about reviews of New York City restaurants. They all agreed that the majority were poorly written, often leaving readers baffled about the types and quality of the food served in particular establishments. By the end of the meal, Tim Zagat had developed a restaurant questionnaire with a 30-point scale in four categories: decor, food, service, and cost. The hosts of the dinner and their guests then assessed a total of 75 of their favorite restaurants and rated various features of each on legal-size paper. Each person received a photocopy of the evaluations, free of charge. That egalitarian approach to restaurant recommendations appealed to the Zagats, who had tried it years before, during a two-year stay in Paris, France; as they told Bob Weinstein of *Entrepreneur* (August 1996), "A group of people are more likely to be accurate about a restaurant than one person."

The people at the party then surveyed some of their friends about New York City restaurants; that second set of reviewers then queried others, who did the same in turn. By 1982 the survey, conducted annually by the Zagats for fun, had grown to include 300 restaurants critiqued by approximately 600 people, who came to be known as Zagateers. Also by that time, as Nina Zagat has said on many occasions, their hobby was costing them nearly $12,000 a year and had become very time-consuming, too. She and her husband decided to charge a fee for their survey and have it published professionally. But none of the publishers whom they contacted expressed a willingness to take on their project. Even an uncle of Tim Zagat's who owned a publishing company was wary. "My uncle said his company had printed a guidebook by eminent *New York Times* food critic Craig Claiborne," Tim Zagat told Weinstein. "And it never sold more than 30,000 copies a year."

The Zagats resolved to publish the book themselves, a decision they regard as perhaps the best—and luckiest—of any they have ever made: once the survey gained in popularity and became a profitable business, they collected all the proceeds, instead of the small standard percent they would have received from a publisher. In 1983 Zagat Survey, as their company is called, sold 7,500 copies of their guide. In 2007, according to Andrew Ross Sorkin in the *New York Times* (January 14, 2008), they sold 5.5 million guides in 100 countries. In addition to *New York City Restaurants,* Zagat Survey publishes guides that review restaurants in 100 other cities worldwide. Other Zagat guides assess golf courses; nightclubs and other nightlife venues; international hotels, spas, and resorts; New York City theaters; New York City shops; movies ("the 1,000 top films of all time"); and music ("1,000 top albums of all time"). At the turn of the 21st century, Zagat Survey went online. Zagat has a restaurant-and-nightlife software application on the social-networking website facebook.com.

In January 2008 the Zagat family began seeking a buyer for their company. Within six months, however, they ended their search, having decided to keep the company independent—temporarily, at least. In September 2011, Google purchased Zagat Survey. The Zagats remained with the company.

Residents of New York, Tim and Nina Zagat use their guides when they visit other cities, but they never participate in their surveys, because they believe that doing so would result in a conflict of interest and might introduce an element of unfairness into their work. At the same time they have acknowledged that, although they have learned to recognize and weed out responses that seem suspicious, malicious, or dishonest in some other way, such assessments undoubtedly have slipped by them. As celebrities in the New York City restaurant scene, the Zagats have received many offers of free meals from eager-to-please chefs, but they have always turned them down.

While the accuracy and legitimacy of the Zagat surveys have been questioned, restaurateurs recognize their importance to many customers. Alan Stillman, the owner of the New York City restaurants Smith & Wollensky and Park Avenue Cafe, told Paul Frumkin of *Nation's Restaurant News* (January 1995), "I know people who own five Zagat guides. They have one at home, one in the car, one in their office. It is the most influential guide. It has more impact on sales than the *New York Times* guide to dining." "What we have done is empowered hundreds of thousands of people to think that their voice counts, too. It's not just the critic who counts," Tim Zagat told David Leonhardt of the *New York Times* (November 23, 2003). He said to Samantha Miller and Bob Meadows of *People* (September 6, 1999), "We came along at the right time. Wouldn't you rather have 3,000 opinions on whether a place is good than just one?" According to Julia Lawlor, writing in the *New York Times* (October 9, 2008), Tim Zagat "likes to call the Zagat survey an 'expression of consumer democracy.'"

Education and Early Career

Tim Zagat was born Eugene H. Zagat Jr. on June 13, 1940, to Eugene H. Zagat Sr. and the former Cornelia Ernst. He grew up with his sister, Cornelia, in New York City, where he attended the Riverdale Country School, a private prep school in the borough of the Bronx. He then enrolled at Harvard University, in Cambridge, Massachusetts, and received a B.A. degree cum laude in 1961. After his graduation, during the administration of President John F. Kennedy, he worked in Washington, District of Columbia, as a senior staff member of the newly formed Peace Corps; his title was book coordinator, with responsibility for publishing textbooks and organizing, reading, and writing training materials.

Nina Zagat was born Nina Irene Safronoff on August 12, 1942 to Samuel Safronoff and his wife, Lily. With her brother, Peter, she grew up in Merrick, Long Island, New York. She attended Vassar College, in Poughkeepsie, New York, and received a B.A. degree cum laude in 1963. The Zagats met while attending law school at Yale University, in New Haven, Connecticut, Nina with the support of the Helen Dwight Reid fellowship for study in international relations and international law. Tim and Nina were married in 1965.

During that period Tim Zagat worked for NBC News, for which he conducted political surveys connected with the 1964 presidential campaigns of the incumbent, Democrat Lyndon B. Johnson, and his Republican opponent, Senator Barry Goldwater of Arizona. Immediately after completing their law degrees, in 1966, the Zagats moved to Paris to work in the offices of the law firms they had joined: Hughes, Hubbard & Reed (Tim) and Sterling and Sterling (Nina). During the next two years, Nina Zagat took classes at the renowned Paris culinary school Le Cordon Bleu. The idea of surveying people about which restaurants they preferred, instead of relying on critics for evaluations, came to the Zagats in Paris. Consisting of a single page and titled the *Guide de Guides,* the survey was copied for their friends but never gained wider popularity.

In 1970 the Zagats left Paris to work in the New York City offices of their respective law firms. Six years later Tim joined another firm, Pomerantz, Levy, Haudek & Block. In 1979 the Zagats co-founded Zagat Survey (the name is a registered trademark as well as their company name). For the next few years, their research remained avocational; the couple regarded it simply as a way for them and their friends to gain as much knowledge as possible about the growing number of New York City restaurants. The first professionally published Zagat Survey was printed in 1983. Serving as their own salespeople, the Zagats would drive from one New York bookstore to another in attempts to persuade the owners or managers to carry their guides. Then, in 1986, less than a year after a few cover articles and stories about the survey appeared in newspapers and magazines, sales increased exponentially, to more than 100,000 copies. At the end of 1986, the Zagats hired their first full-time employee. The next year Tim Zagat quit his job—he had been chief litigation counsel for Gulf & Western Industries since 1980—to devote himself to the survey full-time. (Nina Zagat continued working as a lawyer until 1990.)

Later Career

The success of the New York City restaurant survey led the Zagats, in 1988, to provide similar surveys for restaurants in other cities (among them Washington; Los Angeles and San Francisco, California; and Chicago) and for hotels, resorts, and spas. Two years later they produced surveys of airlines and car-rental agencies. The year 1992 saw the publication of two nationwide Zagat surveys: *America's 1,000 Top Restaurants* and *America's Best Value Restaurants.*

In the months leading up to the 1992 Democratic National Convention, held that year in New York City, Tim Zagat and other local businesspeople created NY'92—a promotion that enabled the 5,000 delegates and 15,000 members of the press who attended the convention to buy meals at a discount at many of the city's finest restaurants. Zagat persuaded some of the participating restaurants to serve lunches for $19.92—a high price relative to the costs of lunches at most places in the city and elsewhere but substantially less than what those restaurants would normally have charged. NY'92 proved to be a boon to the local economy; its success led to similar promotions in 1993 and 1994. "Tim is an extraordinary asset for New York City and the restaurant community," Joe Baum told Frumkin. "He is willing to put his time and effort on the line to stimulate New York as a major attraction. He fights for what he thinks is right. He's the best kind of leader—he provides solutions for different problems."

In 1999 the Zagats sold one-third of their business for $31 million to General Atlantic, a private equity firm, to raise capital for a new effort: the posting of surveys online. Visitors can vote at the site, and with a paid subscription, subscribers can access many of the same services offered by the guides, plus regularly updated lists of restaurants and other attractions. Citing one example, the Zagats told Pamela Parseghian of *Nation's Restaurant News* (October 4, 2004), "We can produce—in five minutes or less—the French restaurants on the East Side [of Manhattan] that have fireplaces and are romantic and cost less than $50."

During the summer of 1999, the Zagats hosted a gathering of restaurateurs and other industry professionals to discuss their proposal for a nine-point "diner's bill of rights." No one disputed the inclusion of courteous service, sanitary facilities, and smoke- and cellular-phone- free environments, but some items, among them the rights of diners to bring their own wine to restaurants, complain to managers, and refrain from tipping in some circumstances, sparked controversy. The assumption of such rights, some restaurateurs complained, would give diners a sense of privilege and perhaps even the expectation of compensation. Drew Nieporent, a New York City restaurant owner, told Frank DiGiacomo of the *New York Observer* (July 19, 1999): "[The Zagat guide] has been an invaluable tool to the restaurant industry. However, what we don't need are people to come into our restaurants looking for problems. The experience should be one of relaxation and civility, not one of what's wrong with this place? Those rights are implicit. They don't need to be written down." By contrast, another restaurateur, who requested anonymity, declared, "There's nothing better than empowering the common people. You'll never get more people on your side than telling a complete idiot that his opinion counts." The restaurateur Danny Meyer told DiGiacomo that he considered the bill of rights "a conversation piece that at its best could foster a better understanding of dining out and could promote dining out."

"What we have done is empowered hundreds of thousands of people to think that their voice counts, too."

In June 2008 the Zagat family ended its six-month search for a buyer. Instead, the company would be allowed to continue its "organic growth," as Tim and Nina Zagat stated in a June 5, 2008, press release. Rejecting some observers' belief that the company's $200 million price tag was too high to attract buyers, the Zagats maintained that the weak economy was a major reason for their failure to sell their company. Increasingly, however, the Zagat guides faced online competition, notably from the website Yelp—which, like the Zagat surveys, offered user-generated content. In September 2011, however, the company was acquired by Google for a reported $151 million. At the time of the sale, Tim Zagat told "Dealbook" columnists Michael J. De La Merced, Ron Leiber, and Claire Cain Miller of the *New York Times* (September 8, 2011) that the "print books were 'very profitable.'" According to their article, Melissa Mayer, then Google's vice president for local, maps and location services, announced that "Google planned to expand Zagat's team, which now includes sales staff, fact-checkers, hundreds of contractors who conduct the surveys and, most important, the hundreds of thousands of reviewers in more than 100 cities." The Zagats remained with the company as co-chairs; Tim Zagat is its chief executive officer. Zagat offers full integration with Google Maps and Search.

Tim Zagat has served on many boards and committees. He is currently a board member of the Partnership for NYC, the World Travel & Tourism Council (WTTC), and NYC & Company, the official marketing, promotion and tourism arm of New York City, which he chaired twice. He also received the Ordre national du Mérite from the French government. Nina Zagat has served on the White House Conference on Travel and Tourism. In 2000 Harvard College named her Entrepreneur of the Year; in 2001 the Star Group named her one of the Leading Women Entrepreneurs of the World, and she was listed among Crain's Top Tech 100, a survey of New York City's most influential people in technology. The Zagat Survey biography page recounts that in 2000 both Ernst & Young and Harvard Business School named the Zagats Entrepreneurs of the Year. In 2001 they were inducted into New York University's Entrepreneurship Hall of Fame, and in

2004 *Nation's Restaurant News* named them Innovators of the Year. They are also inductees of the Hospitality Industry Hall of Honor and the James Beard Who's Who in Food & Beverage, are fellows of the Culinary Institute of America, and have served on the White House Conference on Travel and Tourism.

In addition to an apartment overlooking Central Park, in Manhattan, Tim and Nina Zagat own a 160-acre estate two hours north of the city by car. The couple have two sons: Ted, who was the president of Zagat Survey for several years (he left in 2007 to join Univision as a vice president) and John. In 2000 Ted, then 25, completed a survey of nightlife in New York City.

Further Reading:

Entrepreneur p120+ Aug. 1996

Nation's Restaurant News p223+ Jan. 1995, p136+ Oct. 4, 2004

New York Times p1+ Nov. 23, 2003, Dec. 17, 2006 C p1+, Jan. 14, 2008, Oct. 9, 2009, Sep. 8, 2011

People p117+ Sep. 6, 1999

States News Service Feb. 28, 2007

Zagat Survey website

Zhang, Xin

Business executive, real estate developer

Born: 1965, Beijing, China

Beijing, the northern Chinese city formerly known as Peking, is marked by great architectural variety. Structures built in the ornate traditional style of Imperial China coexist with those built from the 1950s through the 1970s in the boxy, somewhat nondescript style known as Sino-Soviet. There has also been a major boom—particularly in the wake of the announcement that the city would be hosting the 2008 Olympics—in innovative, modern buildings, often designed by foreign architects. "You are in a city like no other on Earth," Lu Xiaojing and Jeremy Goldkorn wrote for *China Daily* (May 8, 2004). "Beijing is not the New York of China, nor the London of northeast Asia, nor the Mexico City of the Orient. Within a few years it may resemble the set of [the science fiction film] *Blade Runner* or [the director] Fritz Lang's [futuristic 1927 film] *Metropolis* more than any of those places." "The urbanization of Beijing is unique," Zhang told John Ridding of the *Financial Times* (March 20, 2004). "Even in cities like Delhi or Paris, you have [separate] old parts and new parts. But here it is all together. Chaos and mix are the defining characteristics of Beijing."

SOHO China, an architectural development firm, is at the forefront of this trend toward modernization. Zhang Xin, who was named one of the top global leaders under the age of 40 by the World Economic Forum, co-heads the company with her husband, Pan Shiyi. Together they have overseen the design and construction of such cutting-edge projects as SOHO New Town, the Commune by the Great Wall, and Jianwai SOHO, all of which combine residential, retail, and office space. Recently the company has worked with the renowned Iraqi-born architect Zaha Hadid on several projects in Beijing and Shanghai.

Education and Early Career

Zhang Xin was born in 1965 in Beijing, the capital city of China. Her family, of Chinese ancestry, had owned confectionary businesses in Burma, but returned to their homeland in the 1950s, when anti-Chinese sentiment began surfacing in Southeast Asia. Zhang's parents were assigned work as translators at the Bureau of Foreign Languages in the early 1960s. In 1966, however, with the advent of the decade of radical social and economic reform known as the Cultural Revolution, an ideological and political rift opened between Zhang's mother and father. The couple separated, and in 1970 Zhang and her mother left Beijing for a Communist-run camp in Henan Province, in central China. They returned to Beijing in 1972. Struggling to survive financially, Zhang's mother worked at various menial jobs, while Zhang was shuffled among the homes of any relatives able to take her. She attended at least seven elementary schools as a child.

When Zhang was 14 years old, she and her mother relocated to Hong Kong. There Zhang worked in a garment factory and later, on the assembly lines of various manufacturing plants. "I don't remember it being miserable; I do remember it feeling very different. In China there was always a government out there to provide. You never felt like you were left alone. But in Hong Kong, if you don't wake up and go to work, who was going to give you food?" Zhang explained to John Ridding. She soon grew frustrated with the drudgery of her jobs and the monotony of her environment. "They were giant buildings. Over 20 floors high, with hundreds of assembly lines inside, each line a small plant. The workers had no sense of belonging. They switched jobs—maybe just to the plant across the hallway—over the smallest pay raise," she told Jianying Zha for the *New Yorker* (July 11, 2005).

In 1984 a friend of Zhang's who had attended a university in the United States persuaded her to consider going to college herself. "[He] turned my whole world upside down," Zhang told Zha. Zhang moved to England and worked at a secretarial school in Oxford, where she practiced her English; in 1987 she enrolled at the University of Sussex, known for its student activism and its cadre of leftist British intellectuals. Zhang grew enamored with the romanticized Marxist ideals of her classmates and professors. She told Zha, "The Chinese talked endlessly about Cultural Revolution sufferings, while thinking about how to get their 'eight big pieces' home. [The term *eight big pieces* refers to electronics and consumer goods that were then scarce in China.] I also experienced the life of Hong Kong assembly lines. Communism was complex for me." The 1960s-era campus architecture—although it has attracted numerous detractors, including, most famously, Charles, Prince of Wales—left an indelible impression on Zhang. "The Sussex architecture is beautiful. Every piece of architecture represents the era in which it was built. We can't expect a Sixties building to look like 18th-century architecture. ... That's why Cambridge is Cambridge, Oxford is Oxford and Sussex is Sussex," Zhang told Yuan Wang for the University of Sussex website.

After completing a thesis on the dangers of privatization in China, Zhang graduated, in 1991. She stayed in the United Kingdom to attend the University of Cambridge, completing a master's program in development economics. While at Cambridge, Zhang was recruited by the Hong Kong branch of the Barings Bank, a British institution, which hired her to analyze privatization trends in mainland China. Although she had hoped to return to her native country, Zhang relocated to New York City, to work on Wall Street, after Barings was acquired by the investment firm Goldman Sachs. "On Wall Street, all values seemed upside down. People spoke crassly, treated others badly, looked down on the poor and adored the rich. They'd do anything to get promoted. Whoever made the most profit was a hero, and everyone was fighting everyone else," she told Zha. "[On a Hong Kong assembly line] the competition turns everyone into short-sighted mice, whereas on Wall Street it turns them into wolves and tigers."

Zhang eventually left Goldman Sachs and endured a brief stint as an investment banker at the Travelers Group (which merged with Citigroup in 1998). A Cambridge classmate, knowing that Zhang still longed to return to China, sent her a prospectus, in 1994, from a new Chinese company called the Vantone Industry. Vantone's mission—to develop and construct new commercial and residential real estate in a rapidly privatizing Beijing economy—awoke Zhang's lingering sense of idealism. "It got me so excited! The way these young intellectuals wanted to contribute to their country, their grand ideas about building enterprises—suddenly I found ... kindred spirits in all my romantic longings," she told Zha.

Later Career

Zhang immediately arranged to meet with Vantone's executives, including its ambitious co-founder, Pan Shiyi, the son of peasant farmers from Gansu Province. Within days, Pan proposed marriage. (Zhang quipped to Zha, "He's extremely sensitive to opportunities.") The pair married in October 1994, and their ideological differences immediately threatened to derail their honeymoon trip to the Great Barrier Reef.

(Zhang, to Pan's distress, still held to the romantic view of Marxism she had developed in college, and she seemed to him to be dismissive of the suffering the Cultural Revolution had caused.) Still, the pair decided to leave their respective jobs and embark on their own real-estate venture, which they named Hongshi (or, in English, Redstone). They set their sights on developing property for Beijing's rapidly emerging middle-class and decided to market a hybrid form of commercial and residential unit they called SOHO (Small Office, Home Office), which was inspired by a thriving architectural format in Japan. They soon changed the company name to SOHO China to reflect that focus. By 2005, according to William Mellor, writing in *Bloomberg News* (August 11, 2010), SOHO China had become the largest property developer in central Beijing. Mellor estimated the worth of Zhang's ownership stake at about $2.2 billion.

"Communism was complex for me."

The business partnership proved stressful; Zhang was considered too Westernized by many of the couple's employees, and she, in turn, was frustrated by what she considered shoddy standards on their part. Zhang and Pan bickered over such issues as attracting investors and buying land, and the pair separated for a time, with Zhang flying to England to stay with friends, and Pan going to Japan to regroup. Ultimately, they decided that both the marriage and the business partnership—given a strict division of labor—were worth salvaging. They returned to Beijing, where Pan began handling the company's financial and contractual affairs, and Zhang focused on architectural design and aesthetic.

Their first major project, SOHO New Town, was a group of sleek, minimalist buildings totally unlike the stodgy Sino-Soviet apartment units elsewhere in Beijing. Zhang had employed several noted Chinese architects, including Zhu Xiaodi, the head of the Beijing Institute of Architectural Design. As Zha described them in the *New Yorker,* "The apartments [in SOHO New Town] had large living rooms, but small bedrooms and no balconies—the opposite of traditional Beijing apartments. They had floor-to-ceiling windows, which traditionalists considered unsafe, and fine-finish woodwork, rather than the usual unfinished 'white box' surfaces. Instead of the traditional gray, the color scheme was vibrant; red, yellow, green, and purple were used on the facade of every tower. … Some apartments had sliding walls, so that they could easily be adapted as office spaces." SOHO New Town generated a loud buzz among Beijing's commercial tenants, who faced long waiting lists to secure a unit. Commenting on the huge demand, Zhang told Sue Herera for CEO Wire (November 3, 2004), "What [people] need is a very efficient space where they can work and they may work for 24 hours and so they can live there, … and then dance there and if there is a restaurant they can eat. So that's the kind of thing that we have created."

Zhang and Pan went on to develop several more such projects, including Jianwai SOHO, a complex designed by Riken Yamamoto, a well-regarded Japanese architect, consisting of 20 high-rise towers with rooftop gardens, 300 stores, and more than a dozen walking paths; SOHO Shang Du, a 1.8 million square foot complex located in the city's central business district (CBD); and Chaowai SOHO, designed by the Korean architect Seung H. Sang and also located in the heart of the CBD.

In addition to such mixed-use developments, Zhang and Pan are well known in China for an innovative architectural experiment near the historic Great Wall. The Commune, as it is known, contains a dozen avant-garde homes available for rental; a boutique hotel; and a clubhouse. Envisioned as a sort of museum of modern architecture, as well as an exclusive enclave for Beijing's wealthy, the Commune boasts the designs of such architects as Gary Chang, who created what is known as the Suitecase House, a long, narrow structure in which the rooms are tucked into compartments under the floor; Shigeru Ban, whose design called for extensive use of laminated bamboo; Yung Ho Chang, whose house is made of tightly packed earth; and Antonio Ochoa, who dealt with the steep slope of the building site by constructing a massive, dramatic staircase. "To write almost anything about the Commune by the Great Wall … is to feel complicit in a well-orchestrated and seductive public-relations campaign. But that is exactly what the 'Commune' is about: a sophisticated real-estate operation with significant cultural content that places contemporary Asian architecture at the centre of a global stage," Ricky Burdett wrote for *Domus* (January 28, 2003). "The Commune is all about the real world, albeit a version of that world that blurs the edges between economic and social emancipation, cultural identity and architectural innovation. In a country that produces millions of cubic metres of vulgar postmodern buildings in the name of 'progress' and continues to pursue an aggressive policy of forced urban repopulation with the systematic destruction of traditional neighborhoods, the Commune represents more than a breath of fresh air. It is a mature and confident statement that reconciles the needs of art and commerce."

In 2007 Zhang and Pan decided to take their company public in Hong Kong. According to William Mellor, "The timing of the initial public offering on October 8, 2007, was exquisite. Less than a month later, global markets began to tumble in the early days of the credit crisis. They raised $1.9 billion—the biggest IPO by a property company in Hong Kong that year." In 2009 the company expanded into Shanghai with Exchange-SOHO, a 50-story building on Nanjing Road purchased from Morgan Stanley. According to the company website, SOHO China "completed its extension into Shanghai's prime commercial districts including Nanjing West Road, the Bund, Hongqiao Transportation Hub, XuJiaHui, and Pudong" in 2011–2012. Several SOHO projects were designed by the Pritzker Prize–winning architect Zaha Hadid, most recently the Galaxy SOHO in Beijing.

Zhang also made some real estate purchases in New York City. In 2011 she bought a 49 percent stake in the Park Avenue Plaza, a midtown skyscraper, and in May 2013 Zhang's family and the Safra family of Brazil jointly bought a 40 percent stake in the General Motors building on Central Park South. The following November Zhang purchased a townhouse on East 74th Street in Manhattan.

The Commune earned Zhang her first major international award, the Special Prize at the 2002 Venice Biennale. She also received the Mont Blanc Arts Patronage Award, in 2004, for her contributions to contemporary Asian architecture. In August 2011 Zhang Xin was listed as number 48 among the World's 100 Most Powerful Women by *Forbes* magazine, and the following month 2011 Zhang was selected as one of the 50 Most Powerful Women in Business by *Fortune* magazine, at number 24. In 2013 she received an honorary Doctor of Law degree from the University of Sussex. Zhang served as a Trustee to the China Institute in America (2005–2010).

William Mellor of *Bloomberg News* commented that Zhang was outspoken about government control of the Chinese economy: "Unlike most of her rich Chinese peers, who keep a low profile to stay on good terms with officials, Zhang has been very public in her criticism of government policies. 'The market should be making the decision to buy or not to buy, not be told by the government,' says Zhang."

Zhang and Pan live in Beijing and have two children. Their apartment is said to be outfitted with simple, modernist furnishings, and Zhang works from a sparsely decorated space carved out of SOHO China's showroom. "I can't stand antique this and antique that," Zhang told Shai Oster for *Asia Week* (June 29, 2001). "To me, it's total pretension. I like things simple, straightforward."

Further Reading:

Architectural Record p40 Oct. 1, 2004

Asia Week Jun. 29, 2001

BusinessWeek p143 Aug. 21, 2006

Bloomberg News Aug. 11, 2010

CEO Wire Nov. 3, 2004

Chicago Tribune p13 Aug. 8, 2004

Domus Jan. 28, 2003

Financial Times p14 Mar. 20, 2004

New York Times Jun. 3, 2013, Jun. 25, 2013, Nov. 15, 2013

New Yorker p72 July 11, 2005

SOHO China website

Appendixes

Historical Biographies

James Beard

American chef, food writer, educator

James Beard vastly expanded the American palate through his cookbooks, television shows, and his teaching and outreach. He stands as the first true celebrity chef.

Areas of achievement: Culinary arts, writing, education

Born: May 5, 1903; Portland, Oregon, United States

Died: January 21, 1985; New York City, United States

Early Life

James Beard was born in Portland, Oregon in 1903, and the Pacific Northwest remained a crucial reference point for his entire life. His childhood fascination with the speed and skill of short-order cooks and love for basic, small-town cuisine stayed with him always, and as a chef and cookbook author, he goal was to expand the traditional American palate—not reject it.

As a young man, Beard was smitten with the desire for stardom. He joined up with a theatrical troupe, tried to make it as an opera singer, and spent time in Paris and London before eventually finding his way to New York City. Show-business fame, though, did not beckon, and he shifted his focus to catering. "Food," as he stated, "is very much about theater," and Beard's natural flamboyance quickly garnered attention, as did his physical appearance: At six-foot-three with fluctuating weight that eventually led to a 300-pound frame, Beard favored conspicuous plaid suits and brightly colored bow ties.

On August 30, 1946, Beard's fifteen-minute show, *I Love to Eat*, debuted on the new, limited medium of television. The show came and went, but occupies the distinction as the first cooking show in TV history.

Life's Work

I Love to Eat failed to make much of an impression, but Beard had accurately gauged the culinary mood of the country. The Second World War was over and a new, much more comfortable postwar America had emerged.

This newfound comfort came an onslaught of mass-produced food: TV dinners, frozen foods, and the multi-million-selling Betty Crocker cookbook, with its recipes for—among other items-- baked prune whip.

The United States in the 1950s was a culinary disaster. "Why is it that each year," James Beard inquired, "our bread gets less and less palatable, more and more flabby and tasteless?"

Yet at the same time, Americans began to travel as they never had before. Television, record albums, and radio brought in more and more of the outside world. "By the fifties," Beard stated, "…people were taking time to cook complex dishes, international dishes… it was only now that the general public began to realize the varieties and possibilities of food…. No longer was eating simply a necessity; it became a pleasure."

Sophisticated palates had long given up on American cuisine and looked elsewhere, mostly to France. James Beard, though, went against the tide. "We have a rich and fascinating food heritage that occasionally reaches greatness in its own melting pot way." Beard's feeling was that cooking was an art form, and with that in mind he strove to create a sophisticated, national cuisine that owed more to his Oregon roots than the latest innovations from Paris.

Beard disseminated his ideas via magazine writing in *House & Garden*, *Gourmet*, and the mainstream *Reader's Digest,* and then began a lengthy series of highly popular cookbooks. He established the idea that American cooking didn't have to be synonymous with a provincial palate, utilizing the wide array of cuisine that developed in the United States: New England clam chowder, layer cakes, muffins, and fruit pies. Beard also took the idea of the melting pot seriously and his repertoire included Jewish kreplach, Turkish stuffed eggplant, Spanish paella, and food from the Arab world.

James Beard was a showman, with an outsized, flamboyant personality and physique to match (although he suffered serious health issues as a result of his obesity). In total he wrote 22 books, a syndicated column, and launched his own successful TV show in the 1960s.

He also stayed in the public eye with the ethically questionable practice of endorsements. Beard promoted Green Giant products, did commercials for Heckers Flour, and served as pitchman for Omaha Steaks, shippers of filet mignon and other meats. The practice, along with raising his visibility, also raised eyebrows.

Beginning in 1955, Beard's Greenwich Village apartment became the site of his cooking school, which eventually became the focal point of New York's food world. Beard anticipated Julia Child and the whole notion of chef-as-star: He can be considered the grandfather of the Food Network.

James Beard, despite being plagued by serious, debilitating health issues, remained active right up until his death in 1985. Ultimately, it is Beard's innovative cooking that is his true legacy. "I don't like gourmet cooking or 'this' cooking or 'that' cooking. I like good cooking."

Significance

James Beard was the first superstar chef, but his influence runs even deeper. In the 1970s, he and others in the New York culinary world—horrified by the city's poverty and deprivation—founded Citymeals-on-Wheels, a service bringing food to those in need and housebound; an invaluable resource still very much in operation today.

Beard occupied an ambiguous niche as a gay man in the pre-Stonewall era. While certainly not open about his homosexuality, he didn't keep it a total secret, and his legacy is an important one to the gay community.

The James Beard Foundation, which still maintains his Greenwich Village apartment and conducts classes and workshops, is a huge, prestigious force in the culinary world, bestowing awards for noteworthy chefs, restaurants, food writing, and in many other categories as well.

Craig Claiborne

American gastronomist, journalist, *New York Times* food editor

Craig Claiborne introduced millions of Americans to the world of fine cuisine and international dining. As food editor of the *New York Times* from 1957 to 1986, he shaped restaurant writing into a creative, respected form of critical expression.

Areas of Achievement: Culinary arts, journalism

Born: September 4, 1920; Sunflower, Mississippi, United States

Died: January 22, 2000; New York City, United States

Early Life

Craig Claiborne was born in the tiny Mississippi Delta town of Sunflower on September 4, 1920. The family later moved to nearby Indianola, Mississippi and his mother established a boardinghouse. It was her expert Southern cooking—and the solace of the kitchen-- that spurred Claiborne's lifelong passion for food.

He joined the navy in World War II and after the war did PR work in Chicago and then New York City. A good portion of the job involved wining and dining clients, which exposed him to the array of top-notch restaurants. But much of what he sampled was, in Craig Claiborne's eyes, ultimately lacking. "I decided that if I wanted to eat good food, I'd have to cook it myself. The more I tried, the more hooked I became, and it's never worn off."

That passion led to a period of study at Ecole Hoteliere de la Societe Suisse des Hoteliers, the renowned culinary institute near Lausanne, Switzerland, and upon his return to the United States he began food writing in earnest, eventually becoming an editor at *Gourmet* magazine.

Life's Work

Craig Claiborne became food editor of the *New York Times* in 1957. Food writing was not held in high regard. It often seemed more akin to advertising or PR, or was dull, aimed at homemakers. The intended audience was female, and that was enough, in the Eisenhower era, to relegate food coverage to a very low rung.

Claiborne, the first man to hold the position as the *Times*'s food editor, essentially invented serious culinary reportage by applying journalistic strictures. The review template that we take for granted today was Claiborne's brainchild. He and a little group of friends would visit a restaurant multiple times, all the better to accurately glean the full extent of its offerings. The visits would be anonymous, avoiding any conflict of interest (and also ensuring the restaurant wouldn't be picking up the tab). There would be a rating system: 1 to 4 stars.

Along with his rigorous standards and format, Claiborne was a creative writer and had a broad range of interests. He modeled his food writing on drama or painting criticism--and turned restaurant reviewing into its own art form.

Cooking itself held a stigma: it was a laborious chore and something that men weren't supposed to do. Nor was it a proper subject for discussion around the dinner table. Claiborne also changed this notion. Cooking could be fun and it could be communal, and men could also be full-fledged participants. And it could be discussed—all things we take for granted today.

Claiborne idolized French cuisine, just as the United States was becoming more engaged with the outside world. There was a certain snobbishness to this, but he was also an ardent advocate of ethnic cuisine, urging New Yorkers to branch out and try the huge, eclectic array of food and produce readily available—sometimes just a subway ride away.

Claiborne wrote *The New York Times Cookbook*, published in 1961 and eventually selling some 3 million copies. His output was enormous; eventually he wrote around 20 cookbooks (many in collaboration with the chef Pierre Franey) as well as a syndicated column.

As the *Times* critic, he enjoyed a prominence and power that is difficult to imagine today. A rave review was a godsend to a restaurant; the opposite could be a catastrophe.

He was an extraordinarily generous friend and mentor to a whole generation of chefs, but was also a massive drinker and a turbulent, unhappy person. In the mid-1970s he was the unexpected winner of a charity auction. The prize was dinner at a restaurant of one's choosing, and Claiborne and Pierre Franey dined at Chez Denis--one of the most exclusive restaurants in Paris—consuming 31 courses for a price of $4000 (equivalent to much, much more by today's standards). Claiborne's conspicuous consumption in an era of economic hardship generated a huge backlash.

Craig Claiborne died on January 22, 2000.

Significance

Claiborne, because of his prestigious position at the *New York Times* and his immensely successful writing (including his 1982 memoir, *A Feast Made for Laughter*), held enormous power in the culinary world. A good deal of his power, though, came from being anonymous. He was rarely photographed, allergic to television appearances, and certainly did not have anything close to the visibility of food personalities Julia Child or James Beard.

The immense authority he wielded is very much a thing of the past: No one person has the vast power to boost or doom a restaurant's chances. For these reasons, his fame has gradually faded over the years.

Craig Claiborne's influence, though, is felt in many, many ways. The restaurant review has taken on a codified, recognizable form, and the availability of international cuisine has spread to the mainstream in such a way that Claiborne could not have possibly envisioned it: imported cheeses, cappuccino, pastas, and countless other items are available in almost every corner of the country.

Walt Disney

American animator and entrepreneur

Disney was only an average artist, but he was a great storyteller and showman who established one of the major media and entertainment corporations of the twentieth and twenty-first centuries.

Areas of Achievement: Cartooning, animation, motion pictures, theme parks

Born: December 5, 1901; Chicago, Illinois, United States

Died: December 15, 1966; Los Angeles, California, United States

---

Early Life

Walt Disney, the son of Elias and Flora Call Disney, was born in Chicago in 1901. While growing up, Disney and his family lived in Chicago, on a farm in Missouri, and in Kansas City. He drew cartoons for his high school newspaper, and his formal training in art came from classes at the Kansas City and Chicago art institutes. Disney tried to join the U.S. Navy during World War I but was rejected because he was underage. He dropped out of high school in 1918 to join the American Red Cross and was sent to France to drive an ambulance.

He returned to the United States in 1919, settling in Kansas City to begin a career as a commercial artist. After reading a book on animation, he decided to go into the animated cartoon business and made a deal with a local movie theater chain to show his earliest cartoons.

Disney's Laugh-O-Grams became so popular in the Kansas City area that he was able to expand his studio and hire additional animators. However, he was an inexperienced businessman, and his first studio eventually went bankrupt.

Life's Work

Disney moved to Los Angeles in 1923 with only a suitcase and $40. He tried to get a job with one of the film studios, but after no one hired him he set up his own. He started his studio in a garage and later moved into a building on Hyperion Avenue in the Silver Lake district of Los Angeles. The studio remained there until 1939, when Disney opened a larger facility in Burbank.

His cartoon series *Alice Comedies* (1924-1927), based on Lewis Carroll's book *Alice's Adventures in Wonderland*, was moderately successful, and in 1927, Universal Pictures contracted with him for a new series. These cartoons, featuring Oswald the Rabbit, were so successful that Disney expanded his studio and hired more animators. In February 1928, Disney was prepared to renew his contract, but Charlie Mintz, his distributor, wanted to reduce Disney's fee for each cartoon. Disney also discovered that Universal, not

Disney, owned the rights to Oswald, and that Mintz believed he could make the cartoons without Disney by hiring away most of Disney's staff. Disney walked away from the deal and from that time on became aggressively vigilant about protecting his intellectual properties.

To replace Oswald, Disney based a new character on a mouse he had adopted as a pet while living in Kansas City. The character's name was originally Mortimer, but was later changed to Mickey Mouse by Disney's wife Lillian, who did not like the name Mortimer. Disney failed to find a distributor for the first two cartoons starring Mickey, both of which were silent films. The third Mickey Mouse cartoon, 1928's *Steamboat Willie*, added synchronized sound—a first for an animated film. *Steamboat Willie* was an instant success, and all future Disney cartoons were released with sound tracks.

In 1929, Disney began a series of musical shorts called *Silly Symphonies. Flowers and Trees* (1932) was the first cartoon filmed in Technicolor, and it was so successful that Disney, who had an exclusive five-year license for the Technicolor process, switched all his cartoons from black-and-white to color.

Disney began developing full-length, animated features, and in February 1938 released *Snow White and the Seven Dwarfs*, the year's most commercially successful motion picture. *Fantasia*, released in 1940, is considered a milestone in the development of animated film as a significant art form.

After World War II ended in 1945, Disney returned to work on full-length animated features. During this period, he further developed the concept of feature-length films that combined live action and animation, such as *Song of the South* (1946) and *So Dear to My Heart* (1949). He revived the concept more than a decade later when he made *Mary Poppins*. Released in 1964, it became the most successful Disney film of the decade and was also the most technically advanced film to that point in its combination of animation and live action.

While Disney's two daughters were growing up, he and his wife had difficulty finding places to take them on weekends. He got the idea for a children's theme park after visiting Children's Fairyland in Oakland, California, in the late 1940s. This idea eventually developed into a concept for a larger park that became Disneyland, which opened on July 17, 1955 in Anaheim, California, and was immediately successful, drawing visitors from around the world.

In 1959, Walt Disney began looking for land for a second theme park to build on the success of Disneyland. Marketing surveys showed that only 2 percent of Disneyland's visitors came from east of the Mississippi River, where 75 percent of the United States's population then lived. Disney also disliked the businesses that had grown up around Disneyland and wanted control of a much larger area of land for his next major enterprise.

Disney flew over the site southwest of Orlando, Florida, where Walt Disney World eventually was built. One of the advantages of the Orlando site was the well-developed network of roads in the area. Three interstate highways and the Florida Turnpike connected Orlando with the rest of Florida, the East Coast, and areas north and west of the state. McCoy Air Force Base (later renamed the Orlando International Airport) was located east of the site.

Disney died in 1966. Construction of the theme park began the following year, and Walt Disney World opened on October 1, 1971, consisting of the Magic Kingdom theme park and two hotels, the Contemporary and the Polynesian. Disney World later added three theme parks: Epcot, Disney's Hollywood Studios, and Disney's Animal Kingdom. By 2009, Disney World was the most visited and largest recreational resort in the world, and contained two water parks, Typhoon Lagoon and Blizzard Beach; thirty-two hotels; five golf courses; a bus service; a monorail train system; and numerous shopping, dining, and entertainment facilities, including Walt Disney World Village Marketplace and Pleasure Island. The recreation complex employed sixty-six thousand people with an annual payroll of $1.2 billion, making it the largest single-site employer in the United States. At its peak, the resort owned roughly thirty thousand acres, which is about the size of San Francisco, or about twice the size of Manhattan Island. Portions of the original property were sold off, including the land later occupied by Celebration, Florida, a town built by the Disney corporation.

Significance

Walt Disney helped create the twentieth-century entertainment industry. He and his studio elevated the art of animation, raising the standards of animated films and using this medium, which initially focused on short subjects, to produce full-length features. His studio also produced successful live-action films and innovative television programs. Disneyland and its successor theme parks offered the public new attractions where families could spend their leisure time.

The Walt Disney Company of the twenty-first century owns theme parks in California, Florida, France, and Japan; vacation resorts; water parks; hotels; cruise ships; motion-picture and television studios(such as Pixar), Internet sites; record labels; publishing houses; cable television networks; and the American Broadcasting Corporation (ABC).

Dorothy Draper

American interior designer, marketing innovator, real estate stylist

In the 1930s Dorothy Draper broke with the prevailing style of interior decoration, advocating for, as she herself put it, "masses of beautiful color, a sense of balance and scale, and an awareness and love of smart accessories."

Areas of Achievement: Interior design, marketing, real estate styling

Born: November 22, 1889; Tuxedo Park, New York, United States

Died: March 10, 1969; Cleveland, Ohio, United States

Early Life

The success story behind the interior design firm Dorothy Draper Inc. was not at all the feminine version of the Horatio Alger pattern. Dorothy Tuckerman was born on November 22, 1889, in Tuxedo Park, New York, into a family long regarded as one of New England's most aristocratic. Her paternal great-great-great grandfather was Oliver Wolcott, one of the signers of the Declaration of Independence. Her parents were Paul Tuckerman and Susan (Minturn) Tuckerman. Dorothy was listed in the Social Register, and she started her career from the ballrooms of Newport and Tuxedo Park. In a report for the CBS television program *Sunday Morning* (October 1, 2006), Caitlin Johnson noted that she even was drawn by American portraitist John Singer Sargent. She grew up in New York and Newport, and had, as she put it, "no schooling to speak of, except that I was brought up where I had the privilege of being constantly in touch with surroundings of pleasant good taste." She did not study art or decorating in school, but extensive travels in Europe augmented and enriched her own background and natural good taste. Draper claimed that "All that anyone needs to become a good decorator is a sense of beauty, a sense of fun, and some common sense."

Following her marriage in 1912 to Dr. George Draper—a specialist in psychosomatic medicine who later studied with Carl Jung and became Franklin Delano Roosevelt's personal doctor after Roosevelt contracted polio—Dorothy Draper lived as a glamorous young society matron. By one account "tall, statuesque, always beautifully dressed and meticulously groomed," she wrought such magic in her own houses that friends and acquaintances began urging her to "do" their houses or apartments for them. News of what she accomplished in decorative design got around to architects and real estate professionals. In 1923 she opened a shop in her house on East 64th Street in Manhattan; according to Carleton Varney, her assistant and successor at Dorothy Draper, Inc., it was the first interior decoration firm.

Draper and her husband had three children together before divorcing in 1929. After her divorce Draper remarked, "American women are divided into two classes, the happily married and the decorators."

Life's Work

Despite her success with her friends' homes, Draper much preferred larger-scale, commercial projects. Her own professional career began in earnest in 1930, when Douglas Elliman, one of New York's best-known real estate brokers, gave her the Hotel Carlyle to decorate. Draper consolidated her fame with the decorating of the five-story River Club in 1933. It was she who proposed that the lower floors of the River House, on East 52d Street in New York City, which had been deemed unsuitable for apartments, be used for a club. The same year she attracted attention for a distinctly different venture: remodeling tenements on Sutton Place between 55th and 56th Streets in New York City for the Phipps Estate. With her characteristic confidence, Draper painted the outside of the buildings black with white trim—an instant mark of chic—and then painted each door a different bright color. Under the Draper rejuvenation an average of $15,000 was spent on each of the 11 buildings. The results were 100 percent occupancy with a comfortable waiting list of well-heeled tenants; increase of rental amounts from $25 to an average of $100; return of property to an income-paying basis in addition to amortization of improvement costs; and general betterment of the neighborhood." Draper performed face-lifting operations on older buildings and pulled many an anemic property out of the red. In decorating circles the term "Draperized" came to be shorthand for her particular and individual technique. In 1934 Draper was chosen as sole representative in decoration by the National Federation of Business and Professional Women.

In 1937 Draper was chosen to handle the redesigning and furnishing of New York's famous Hampshire House apartment hotel on Central Park South. At the time this was the largest decorating commission ever to be awarded to a woman. Always pragmatic, Draper negotiated a contract clause allowing her and her children to live in a suite at Hampshire House at a reduced rate. She belonged to the River and Tuxedo clubs (two of New York's most exclusive), and entertained the "best" people in her beautiful tower apartment in Hampshire House. Her success with this project is said to have revived the real estate market on the West Side. (Draper later lived at another hotel she had decorated, the Carlyle.) Among her numerous other commissions were the Terrace Club of the World's Fair; Hollywood's Arrowhead Springs Hotel; the Camellia House restaurant at the Drake Hotel in Chicago; the Delnor Hospital, St. Charles, Illinois; New York's Maison Coty; and the Mayflower Hotel in Washington, District of Columbia.

Draper reached a wide popular audience in the United States through her articles in magazines such as *Vogue* and *House and Garden.* Her extension course "Learn to Live" grew out of the countless letters on decorating and entertaining problems she received from women in many countries. Early questions ranged from "I have red hair, but do you think I can do my bedroom in pink?" to "Will a new dining room rug help me hold my husband?" It soon became apparent to Draper that often women's whole lives needed refurbishing, not just their interiors; the course became as much concerned with such matters as "Understanding Yourself" and "How To Love and Be Loved" as with home styling. The course nevertheless proved to be a financial failure.

Draper extended her influence with *Decorating Is Fun! How To Be Your Own Decorator* (1939) and *Entertaining Is Fun! How To Be a Popular Hostess* (1941). *Decorating Is Fun!* encouraged women to express their own tastes in decorating their homes and offered advice on how to do so at little expense. A practical book of design, it answered "a huge variety of questions with a blithe spirit as well as with professional competence." In *Entertaining Is Fun!*, Draper advocated "intelligent planning, daring and originality," also emphasizing the art of enjoying oneself as hostess. The book covers everything from a buffet supper to a weekend, and, redolent of its day, it includes a chapter on how to entertain one's husband.

Draper called herself a "stylist and designer." She managed to convince realty owners that "low-cost but intelligently-applied cheerfulness has boosted rentals." She combated drabness in buildings by selling principally "imagination and paint-and-color jobs." In 1944 she finished decorating the Palácio Quitandinha in Petrópolis (state of Rio de Janeiro, Brazil), where her devotion to bright color, bold fabric prints, over-sized mirrors, and neo-Baroque moldings and other features was fully displayed in a fusion of international Art Déco and Brazilian Baroque styles with tropical vegetative motifs. Inspired by her sojourn in Brazil, Draper, in 1947, designed the Brazilliance fabric and wallpaper collection for F. Schumacher and Company. The packaging of Dorothy Gray Cosmetics's In the Pink line was designed by Draper, and in the 1950s she also designed car interiors and even jet interiors. Among her projects was the cafeteria (1954) at the Metropolitan Museum of Art; the "Roman Court" was informally known thereafter as the Dorotheum. For the World's Fair of 1964, Draper designed and furnished the Dorothy Draper Westinghouse Dream Home in the fair's Better Living Center, using only furnishings and lighting readily available to ordinary consumers. The house's fanlike layout did not meet with universal approbation, but it drew many fairgoers for multiple visits.

Dorothy Draper retired in 1960. She died in on March 11, 1969. Her assistant, Carleton Varney, bought and continued Dorothy Draper and Company, Incorporated. Varney, who says that "Dorothy Draper was to decorating what Chanel was to fashion," wrote *The Draper Touch; The High Life and High Style of Dorothy Draper,* a biography (1988) and *In the Pink; Dorothy Draper, America's Most Fabulous Decorator* (2006). In 2006 Draper was given the first retrospective exhibition ever accorded an interior designer by the Museum of the City of New York, called "The High Style of Dorothy Draper." Its curator, Donald Albrecht, focused on what he described to Caitlin Johnson as Draper's "eclectic, theatrical style." Showing Johnson a sofa Draper designed for the Dorotheum, he told her, "That's the Draper style, the Draper touch. It makes you want to laugh." In a 1957 TV appearance, Dorothy Draper told Edward R. Murrow, "We always say in our organization that if it looks right, it is right."

Significance

Draper's work survives at a number of her project sites, most notably at the Greenbrier Hotel resort in White Sulphur Springs, West Virginia. The Greenbrier has been selected as the location of the Dorothy Draper Museum, intended to "house the whole Dorothy Draper archive, just as Taliesin is the archive of Frank Lloyd Wright," according to Carleton Varney, who has faithfully maintained Draper's vision. The website of the Museum of the City of New York on its 2006 exhibition comments that Draper was "thoroughly modern in that she approached design as entertainment—a themed experience that ranged from a room's architecture to its furnishings, menus, and matchbooks." This attention to accessorizing down to the matchbooks led Caitlin Johnson to observe that "Draper was her own brand"—another respect in which Draper was ahead of her time. Among the growing number of contemporary young designers drawn to her work is Kelly Wearstler, who explained, "The sense of play in her interiors is infectious." According to Carleton Varney, Draper "made interior decoration a profession."

Henry M. Flagler

American entrepreneur, industrialist, and philanthropist

Flagler used a fortune acquired in the oil industry to build railroads and luxury hotels in Florida, thus establishing that state as a prime destination for tourists and enabling his heirs to pursue numerous philanthropic endeavors.

Areas of Achievement: Oil, railroads, real estate, tourism

Born: January 2, 1830; Hopewell, New York, United States

Died: May 20, 1913; Palm Beach, Florida, United States

Early Life

Henry Morrison Flagler was born into the family of a Presbyterian minister in Hopewell, New York, on January 2, 1830. His father, the Reverend Isaac Flagler, married Elizabeth Caldwell Morrison Harkness after the death of her first husband, providing a family connection that would give young Flagler his start in business. Flagler left school after the eighth grade and moved to Bellevue, Ohio, where he worked in his cousin's grain business, L. G. Harkness and Company, for $5 a month plus room and board. By the time he left this company in 1849, Flagler had demonstrated his worth as a salesman, increasing his salary to $400 a month. In 1852, he joined another family business, D. M. Harkness and Company, and soon married Mary Harkness. Their first child, Jennie Louise, was born on March18, 1855, and their second child, Carrie (who would die at the age of three), on June 18, 1858. On December 2, 1870, Mary gave birth to Henry's only son, Harry Harkness Flagler, who would later become an important philanthropist in his own right.

Flagler's entry into the salt business failed with the declining price for salt that followed the Civil War. His small fortune eliminated, Flagler returned to another Harkness family business, where he met John D. Rockefeller, who was working at that time for a firm that sold grain and other produce on commission. When Rockefeller left the grain business to enter the emerging petroleum industry, he approached Flagler for a loan to support his new venture. Stephen Vanderburgh Harkness agreed to become a silent partner in Rockefeller's company only if Rockefeller gave Flagler a position as partner. In 1870, the chemist Samuel Andrews joined with Rockefeller, Harkness, and Flagler to create the company that would soon be known as Standard Oil Company.

Within two years, Standard Oil had purchased or merged with all other oil companies in Cleveland and embarked on a plan to become a major national industry. The company's headquarters was relocated to New York City, and by 1879 Standard Oil had captured 90 percent of the American oil market. By producing only the amount of oil needed to maintain a consistently high price, the original partners in the company all became extremely wealthy. Flagler and his wife purchased a spacious home on Fifth Avenue, but because of Mary's poor health the couple also spent part of each year in Florida on the advice of her doctor. Through their winters in the Jacksonville area, Flagler became convinced that the region had potential for development and began formulating plans that would eventually introduce him to yet another source of wealth.

Mary died on May 18, 1881, the year before the Standard Oil Trust was formed. This trust pioneered a new concept in business: Rather than functioning as the property of any individual owner, Standard Oil would be owned in common by a group of stockholders, with major decisions rendered by a board of trustees. Instead of receiving profits directly from the company's operations, Rockefeller, Flagler, and the other partners received their incomes from trust certificates, which became more valuable as the business continued to expand. On June 5, 1883, Flagler married Ida Alice Shourds, who had cared for Mary in her final illness. Because of Flagler's familiarity with Florida, the couple honeymooned in St. Augustine, which Flagler found distressingly lacking in convenient hotel accommodations.

Life's Work

With the trust now in charge of Standard Oil's day-to-day operations, Flagler began building a hotel worthy of St. Augustine's history and charm. Named the Hotel Ponce de Leon, Flagler's 540-room resort started the trend of making Florida a tourist destination for America's elite. Realizing that a major hotel would prosper only if it were easy to reach, Flagler purchased and extended local railroad lines, eventually forming the Florida East Coast Railway. The almost instantaneous success of the Ponce de Leon after it opened in 1888 caused Flagler to continue expanding his tourist empire. He proceeded south to Daytona with the Hotel Ormond in 1890 and extended his railroad to West Palm Beach in 1894, which he initially believed would be the southernmost point to which tourists would travel. Flagler's Royal Poinciana Hotel, on the shores of Lake Worth, boasted 1,150 rooms, and in 1896 he opened the Palm Beach Inn (renamed the Breakers in 1901) on a pristine stretch of Atlantic coastline.

In addition to the Ponce de Leon, Flagler operated two other hotels in St. Augustine: the Alcazar Hotel, which later became the Lightner Museum, and the Casa Monica Cordova, which had been built by Franklin Smith in 1888 and originally named the Casa Monica (the name it was given once again following its 1997 restoration). Flagler's hotels were innovative for their features and luxurious appointments. At one time, the Cordova had the largest indoor heated pool anywhere; the Alcazar was one of the earliest examples of poured concrete construction in the United States; and the Royal Poinciana Hotel once boasted that it was the largest wooden structure in the world. Flagler's guests would frequently arrive at his hotels in private railcars, attended by a sizable household staff and equipped with numerous trunks of clothing. Guests would often change their clothing for each meal and wear the latest fashions for the numerous parties, balls, and social gatherings held in the hotels and at nearby estates.

Flagler's hotels originally remained open only from mid-December through late February, since Florida summers proved too hot for the elite clientele from Philadelphia, Boston, and New York. However, when cold winters hampered business in 1894 and 1895, Flagler decided to extend his railroad south to Biscayne Bay country, a site that avoided the frigid conditions farther north. Julia Tuttle, a local citrus grower, offered Flagler a substantial land grant in order to develop the area, and by 1896 Flagler had provided the infrastructure necessary for a city to thrive. When it was proposed that the new town be called Flagler, the industrialist demurred, preferring the name Miami, after the tribe of Indians that had given their name to a local river. It was thus in the new city of Miami that Flagler opened his Royal Palm Hotel in 1897.

For several years, Ida Alice's mental health grew increasingly unstable, and in 1901 Flagler took advantage of a new law that allowed him to divorce her on the grounds of insanity. On August 24 of the same year, Flagler married Mary Lily Kenan, the sister of the philanthropist William Rand Kenan, Jr. As a wedding present, Flagler built Mary Lily a lavish estate, which she named Whitehall, not far from the Palm Beach Inn-- later renamed the Breakers in honor of the waves that continually lapped its sandy beaches.

Whitehall is today regarded as a leading example of Gilded Age architecture. When construction of the palatial residence was completed in 1902, the *New York Herald* described Whitehall as more wonderful than any palace in Europe, grander and more magnificent than any other private dwelling in the world.

Whitehall's design featured an entry hall where guests would be met by a marble image of the emperor Augustus (based on the marble statue *Augustus of the Prima Porta*, now in the Vatican), an ornate clock by the cabinetmaker Franois Linke, and a full-length portrait of Flagler by Raimundo de Madrazo y Garreta. Overhead, the domed ceiling was adorned with a massive painting depicting the Oracle of Delphi surrounded by a number of mythological and allegorical figures. This juxtaposition of styles from various periods reflected the tendency of Gilded Age patrons to combine symbols of luxury irrespective of their divergent styles. Elegant spaces for formal and casual dining, individually designed guest bedrooms, more than twenty bathrooms, and central heating suggest the house's primary role in receiving and entertaining Flagler's friends. Whitehall's technological features included telephones and electric lighting, making the mansion highly advanced for its time.

Flagler then spent seven years extending his railroad to Key West. He and his wife also became central figures in the Palm Beach social scene and helped inaugurate what became known as the season, an annual period when the wealthy would migrate from the north to Flagler's luxurious hotels along the eastern coast of Florida. In 1913, Flagler suffered a severe fall at Whitehall and died on May 20. He was buried in St. Augustine in a plot that he shares with his first wife and his eldest child, Jennie Louise.

After the death of Flagler's widow in 1917, Whitehall became the property of her niece, Louise Clisby Wise Lewis, who later sold the property to investors. The new owners transformed the property into a hotel, and once Palm Beach became a popular tourist destination they built a three-hundred-room hotel annex at the back of the building. This additional structure was demolished in 1963, and the mansion was restored to its original state, becoming the Flagler Museum. The building is listed on the National Register of Historic Places.

Significance

Henry Morrison Flagler's influence on Florida was substantial. He helped transform what had been a largely uninhabited region into a major tourist destination, established a standard for luxury in the hotel industry that would be imitated by many successors, and helped create the city of Miami. Flagler's wealth also became the basis for numerous philanthropic enterprises through the efforts of his third wife and his son. The William R. Kenan, Jr., Charitable Trust, named for the brother of Mary Lily Kenan Flagler, has funded numerous educational and cultural endeavors. In 1968, another of Flagler's heirsfounded Flagler College, using the former Hotel Ponce de Leon as its central building. The fortune developed by Henry Morrison Flagler through his enterprises in oil, railroads, and the hotel industry thus continues to benefit the educational and cultural activities throughout the region that Flagler once called home.

Ernest Gallo

American business executive and philanthropist

The son of Italian immigrants, Ernest Gallo was the driving force and business genius behind the wine company that he founded with his brother Julio. From the cheap Thunderbird to wine coolers to expensive imports, the E. & J. Gallo Winery shaped wine tastes in America.

Areas of Achievement: Business, philanthrophy

Born: March 18, 1909; Jackson, California, United States

Died: March 6, 2007; Modesto, California, United States

Early Life

Ernest Gallo (GAL-loh) was born on March 18, 1909 in Jackson, California, the first of three sons of Italian immigrants Giuseppe "Joe" Gallo and Assunta "Susie" Bianco Gallo, whose parents ran a family winery. After a five-year separation provoked by Joe's violence, Susie and Joe reconciled and the family moved to Oakland, where Joe ran a small wine company, a retail liquor business, a saloon, and a hotel. When Prohibition neared, Joe sold his businesses and bought vineyard property in Antioch, California, anticipating that raising and selling wine grapes would remain a legal activity. Ernest and his younger brother Julio were forced to work from sunrise to after dark in the vineyards, attending public schools in the middle of the day. During Prohibition, Joe became involved in various bootlegging schemes with his brother, Michelo (Mike), a flamboyant hustler who served several prison sentences.

In 1925, after purchasing 40 acres in Modesto, California, which would become the enduring home base of the Gallo family, Joe went into the grape shipping business. Ernest accompanied his father and the wine shipments to the Chicago exchange. The teenager immediately plunged into selling and demonstrated his abilities as a shrewd businessman. He returned to high school, graduated with honors, and enrolled in agricultural courses at Modesto Junior College. In 1927 Ernest went to Chicago alone, delighted with his new responsibilities and independence, for his father still bullied him at home.

In 1929 Joe built underground tanks to save his harvest, essentially starting a winery, which was illegal. He shipped wine under the legal juice label. Ernest wanted to partner with his father but was rejected. Another source of tension was Joe's treatment of his youngest son. Born in 1919, Joe, Jr., was his father's favorite and suffered none of the abuse leveled at the two older boys.

In 1930 Ernest announced his plans to enter the wine business after Prohibition was repealed and to marry Amelia Franzia, the daughter of a wealthy winery owner. The couple spent their honeymoon at the 1931 grape market in Chicago. Anticipating the repeal of Prohibition, in December 1933 Ernest filed an application to open a bonded wine storeroom, but the petition was denied because he did not own a bonded winery.

Prohibition had ended, but the Great Depression was under way. Heavily in debt, Joe and Susie Gallo suddenly, and secretly, moved to a run-down farmhouse in Fresno. On June 21, 1933, in the farmhouse kitchen, Joseph Gallo evidently shot and killed his wife and then himself. Officially the deaths were recorded as murder-suicide. Nevertheless, there was speculation then and later that the Gallos had been ordered killed by the syndicate. The older brothers became guardians of young Joe Jr., and Ernest imposed a code of silence on the family regarding the shocking deaths.

Twenty-four-year-old Ernest was granted permission to continue his father's business. He and his brother Julio formed a partnership, the E. & J. Gallo Winery, excluding Joe, Jr. With a craving for respectability and a knack for revisionist history, Ernest moved forward with his grandiose plans to build Gallo into the largest winery in the state and then the nation.

Life's Work

By 1935 the Gallo winery was producing an annual yield of 350,000 gallons. Ernest sometimes traveled five months at a time, working grueling hours and expecting others to do likewise. In the winter of 1936, he was hospitalized for exhaustion; his six-month hospital stay became one of many Gallo secrets. After his convalescence, Ernest returned with his typical vigor, adding a distillery, expanding production to a full array of sweet, fortified wines and table wines, and purchasing a distribution company in New Orleans, making it the first Gallo-controlled distributor. The entrepreneur was determined to learn how to build, market, and sell a brand. He spent the winter of 1940–1941 interviewing businessmen; from these contacts Ernest devised an intensive and carefully structured sales program that broke new ground in marketing strategies. In March 1942 Ernest applied for the first trademark Gallo name, claiming it had been used continuously by his family since 1909. Company restructuring papers filed in 1944 listed the winery's capital stock at $500,000, with the home and vineyards valued at $760,000. A division of labor had been set, with Ernest in charge of sales and marketing and Julio supervising the vineyards, the laboratory, and wine production. Their oft-repeated boasts that Julio "would make all the wine you can sell" and Ernest would "sell all the wine you can make" made the arrangement public.

After World War II, the brothers developed lighter wines sold with aluminum screw-tops to ensure consistent taste. In the 1950s and 1960s, the Gallos used a huge blending vat to create a uniform blend, making the wine's vintage irrelevant. By the early 1950s, the Gallo winery was the largest winemaking facility in the United States. A light, mellow, red table wine called Vino Paisano di Gallo, sold in a rounded jug bottle, was Gallo's signature product. A bottling plant built in Modesto added to the company's vertically integrated business model.

A micromanager, Ernest demanded full loyalty from his employees, and all middle management reported directly to him. The so-called three Rs of Gallo salesmanship, described by one writer as rigorousness, relentlessness, and ruthlessness, summarized Ernest's approach. In the summer of 1957, Gallo introduced a flavored, fortified wine called Thunderbird that sold for 60 cents a quart. It became an instant hit, especially in poor, urban neighborhoods, and its success pushed production levels to 32 million gallons that year. Several years later, Gallo developed Ripple, another low-end product popular with college students.

Although hugely profitable, these street wines undercut Ernest's ambition to be seen as a respectable, discerning vintner. He launched a Beautiful Wines campaign, featuring Gallo's first champagne, Eden Roc, in 1966, as well as Gallo's Gourmet Trio: Hearty Burgundy, Chablis Blanc, and Pink Chablis. Delighted to be featured with his brother on the cover of Time in 1972, Ernest was nevertheless dismayed by the story's emphasis on Gallo's low-end wines. In an effort to change the company's image, Ernest began hiring executives with master's degrees in business administration and experience in consumer sales.

The 1970s began with enormous expansion and a stream of successful new products. The company suffered, however, from the national boycott against Gallo wine that César Chávez, leader of the United Farm Workers, began in 1973 because of Gallo's support of the International Brotherhood of Teamsters. In February 1974, a hundred thousand people marched on the Gallo home in Modesto to protest the company's policies. Chávez finally terminated the boycott in 1978. During this same period the winery was investigated by the Federal Trade Commission (FTC) for alleged intrusion into distributors' business and alleged illegal practices by its sales force. The FTC ordered monthly inspections of Gallo records in order to monitor company activities. Sales leveled during the tumultuous 1970s, but by 1981 Gallo led nationally in wine sales, shipping 131 million gallons.

During 1989 and 1990, the Gallo family contributed more to candidates for federal political office ($294,110) than any other American family. While his sons attended Notre Dame and Stanford universities, Ernest gave large gifts to each school. He also provided a $3 million endowment to establish a clinic and research center in his name at the University of California at San Francisco. The facility was founded to investigate the effects of alcohol on the brain and to conduct research in other aspects of neuroscience.

In 1983 Ernest and Julio's younger brother, rancher Joe Gallo Jr., launched Joseph Gallo Cheese Company. After a series of unresolved negotiations regarding the use of the Gallo name on these cheese products, Ernest and Julio filed a complaint against Joe and his son Mark, who was co-owner of the company. Joe and Mark countersued to obtain one-third of the winery's ownership, which was valued at more than $200 million. Litigation continued for several years until a final injunction barred Joe and Mark from using the Gallo name as a trademark. The brothers remained estranged for the rest of their lives.

In the early 1990s, the winery expanded its vineyard properties, which would eventually encompass ten thousand acres, and continued its pattern of buying grapes from independent growers. New Gallo vintage-dated varietals and premium wines were introduced, increasing the Gallo share of the premium market. The company ranked number one in sales, with an estimated 4.3 million cases sold in 1991, but the majority of Gallo profit continued to come from street wines. Over the next decade the company shifted its emphasis, importing wine and also exporting millions of cases of wine to scores of countries each year.

Julio Gallo died in an automobile accident in May 1993, and Amelia Gallo died the following December. In 2006 *Forbes* magazine estimated Ernest's net worth at $1.2 billion. The next year Ernest died at his home in Modesto, just days before his ninety-eighth birthday.

Significance

During seven decades, along with his brother Julio, Ernest Gallo created a wine empire. Known for his somber dedication to work and his often ruthless practices, Ernest was a skilled entrepreneur and a master of marketing strategies. By the time of his death, his company produced 80 million cases of wine a year and sold one of every four bottles of wine that Americans drank.

Ray Kroc

American fast-food magnate

Starting in his fifties, Kroc built an international, multibillion-dollar fast-food company, McDonald's Corporation. The company took advantage of social changes in American life and grew so large that the company altered the nation's diet.

Area of Achievement: Fast food, restaurants

Born: October 5, 1902; Oak Park, Illinois, United States

Died: January 14, 1984; San Diego, California, United States

Early Life

Raymond Albert Kroc (*krahk*) was born on October 5, 1902, in Oak Park, Illinois. He dropped out of high school to embark on a sales career in the food-service industry. His career was marked by consistent success, coupled with a burning desire to take on new challenges.

As a young man, Kroc sold paper cups to restaurants and drugstores in the Midwest. He encountered resistance from store owners who had invested in glassware. In order to win them over, Kroc had to show them that paper cups were much more cost-effective in the long run. This began his fascination with cost analysis, which would be his major contribution to the fast-food industry. He then went to work for a manufacturer of multi-mixproducts used to make several milk shakes at a time. He was such a successful salesman that he eventually bought the multi-mixer company.

Life's Work

By 1954, Kroc saw that the market for multi-mixers was in steady decline. His primary market, drugstore soda fountains, was quickly disappearing as the pace of American life changed. Independent drugstores had been fixtures in cities and small towns, but post-World War II growth was occurring in American suburbs. Kroc constantly monitored his sales and noticed an unusual demand for his mixers from a fast-food operation in San Bernardino, California. Kroc visited this restaurant, which was run by two brothers, Dick and Mac McDonald., Kroc became convinced that their type of fast-food restaurant had unlimited nationwide potential. He entered into negotiations with the McDonalds, whose efforts to expand had failed. Kroc opened a McDonald's restaurant in Des Plaines, Illinois in 1955.

The early years were fraught with obstacles and setbacks. The McDonald brothers did not share Kroc's expansive vision and were careless about the legal intricacies of franchising. Kroc was a master salesperson, but he lacked the financial acumen needed for rapid growth. In a few years, Kroc had set up a leadership team headed by Harry Sonnenborn and June Martino, and steady growth began at the cost of major sacrifices by Kroc, including the end of his first marriage.

Kroc formulated the core values of the McDonald's restaurant chain: The chain would provide inexpensive food in a family-friendly atmosphere, with high standards of service and food quality. His sales background prompted him to offer extensive support to his franchises, unlike most chains, which viewed franchises simply as a source of revenue. Kroc never hesitated to terminate suppliers who cut corners on quality. He was also intensely loyal to cooperating suppliers. Some of them, like Interstate Bakery and J. R. Simplot Company, an agribusiness that supplied Kroc with potatoes, grew into major corporations in their own right as a result of their associations with McDonald's.

Along with product quality, Kroc made product innovation a key to McDonald's success. The chain's original hamburger, fries, and shake were joined by the Big Mac, Quarter Pounder, and fish sandwich. Kroc's major product introduction was the launch of a national breakfast menu in 1977. Since then, millions of Americans have made a morning trip to McDonald's to purchase the chain's breakfast items. Not all the new products caught on, and Kroc was personally responsible for some of the flops, such as strawberry shortcake and pound cake. However, his insistence that innovation was the key to success became part of the McDonald's corporate culture.

After 1969, Kroc reduced his role in the corporation's day-to-day operations but never truly retired. He would watch a nearby franchise through binoculars, and his observations led the company to add a second drive-through window at the stores. He lectured frequently and embarked on charity work in the areas of diabetes and arthritis research. Well into his eighties, he was living an active life until two strokes finally slowed him down before his death in 1984.

Significance

Ray Kroc established a model for the fast-food business that has been widely copied. For most of his adult life, his McDonald's Corporation was the face of fast food in America. The consistent growth of his restaurant chain continued after his death.

Pundits and historians will argue endlessly about the impact of Kroc's innovations on American lifestyle and diet. On the plus side, McDonald's provides inexpensive food and consistent quality. Although it was not a Kroc innovation, the Ronald McDonald House Charities, which began in Philadelphia in 1974, are a model of corporate service to the community. On the negative side, however, the nutritional value of fast food and attendant rampant level of obesity in the United States has drawn increasing scrutiny over the years, prompting the company to add healthier menu items and to work to change its image in the twenty-first century.

John Willard Marriott

American entrepreneur, business executive, philanthropist

Marriott, who began his career with a nine-stool root-beer stand, built a $3 billion empire of food and lodging enterprises. A philanthropist, Marriott donated generously to Brigham Young University, the University of Utah, and the Church of Jesus Christ of Latter-day Saints.

Areas of Achievement: Business, philanthrophy

Born: 1900; Marriott Settlement, Utah, United States

Died: August 13, 1985; New Hampshire, United States

Early Life

John Willard Marriott (MEHR-ee-ot), the second of eight children born to Ellen Morris Marriott and Hyrum Willard Marriott, was born in Marriott Settlement, Utah, in 1900. Both of his grandfathers had immigrated to the United States from England and were converts to the Church of Jesus Christ of Latter-day Saints (LDS), more commonly known as the Mormon Church.

Young Marriott was a good student, but he never completed high school. He worked on the family farm and served the LDS church. From 1918 through 1920, he traveled as an LDS missionary to New York and New England. Upon his return to Utah, he found his father deep in debt. Marriott determined to get an education and to help his family. Despite his lack of a high school diploma, he attended Weber College and later the University of Utah, working his way through both schools. During his last year at the University of Utah, he met Alice Sheets, who would become his wife.

Marriott and Hugh Colton bought one of the first A&W Root Beer franchises in Washington, D.C., opening their nine-stool stand on May 10, 1927. This proved to be a good day for opening the business because it coincided with street celebrations for Charles A. Lindbergh's successful completion of the first nonstop transatlantic flight. Marriott returned to Utah to marry Alice on June 9, 1927, and they moved to Washington.The young couple bought out Colton's interest in the root-beer stand when Colten returned to Utah to practice law. With $2,500 in savings and loans, the couple later bought another stand.

Concerned about winter sales, Marriott received permission from A&W to add food to the menu. He later renamed his operation the Hot Shoppe, and it was one of the first establishments in the Northeast to offer Mexican food and drive-in service, with Marriott being the first person to obtain special approval for off-street parking in Washington, D.C. His wife was the bookkeeper and chief cook, while Marriott waited on customers.

The couple personally counted cars at intersections to determine where to set up new establishments, and they tried such innovative techniques as hiring people to pass out coupons for their restaurants on the streets. By 1932, they had seven establishments in Washington, D.C., and were expanding into Baltimore and Philadelphia.

In 1934, however, Marriott received a diagnosis of Hodgkins disease and a prognosis of six months to live. He called on his family for help. Two LDS leaders gave him a priesthood blessing, and by the end of the year, he was free of the disease.

When Marriott observed that passengers at a Washington, D.C., airport were carrying food from a local Hot Shoppe on board the planes, he began negotiations with Eddie Rickenbacker, the head of Eastern Transport Company (later Eastern Airlines), to provide meals for passengers, beginning in 1937. Using the name In Flight Catering Division of Hot Shoppes, Marriott's company began to serve Eastern, American, and Capital Airlines and became the world's largest airline catering service. With a 1939 contract, Marriott was also able to cater meals to the U.S. Treasury building. During World War II, Marriott operated lunch-wagon canteens and opened cafeterias. In 1945, he began to provide food service at the Miami International Airport.

Life's Work

Marriott participated in many professional, church, and community activities. In 1948, he was president of the National Restaurant Association, and from 1948 until 1958 he was president of the LDS's Washington, D.C., stake (an organizational unit comparable to a diocese of the Roman Catholic Church). Marriott later served as an Aaronic priesthood adviser and Sunday school teacher for LDS.

The yearly sales of the Hot Shoppes averaged $20 million in the early 1950s. By then, these restaurants were operating in twelve states, as well as in the District of Columbia. Hot Shoppes, Inc., later renamed the Marriott Corporation, began selling its stock publicly in 1952; the first stock offering sold out in two hours.

Marriott found time in 1950 to serve on the committee that installed the statue of LDS leader Brigham Young in the rotunda of the Capitol Building, and he also helped restore the buildings in Nauvoo, Illinois, from which the Mormons fled in 1846. As an active Mormon, he continued to contribute 10 percent of his income to the church, and he gave generously to the University of Utah and Brigham Young University. He and Alice also supported the Republican Party's causes and candidates, with Marriott chairing both inaugural committees for President Richard M. Nixon.

In 1957 Marriott and his family began building the Twin Bridges Motor Hotel, his first hotel. His son, John Willard Marriott, Jr., conceived the idea of building the facility; the elder Marriott initially was reluctant because he remembered the failure of hotels during the Great Depression. The 365-room motor hotel, located near a bridge and close to the Washington National Airport (now the Ronald Reagan Washington National Airport) in Arlington, Virginia, opened for business in 1959. The Twin Bridges competed with older, downtown hotels; it catered to business travelers, which is why it was logical to locate it near the airport and to offer conference facilities. Hygiene was a priority at the new hotel. The housekeeping staff received special training in how to complete a set of sixty-six tasks for each room in only thirty minutes. Father and son made surprise visits to their hotels and checked for cleanliness, and the name Marriott eventually became synonymous with quality lodging. In 1958 the firm launched a multimillion-dollar effort to open additional motor hotels, and Marriott hotels could eventually be found in many American cities, including Dallas, Philadelphia, and Atlanta. In addition, the Marriott Corporation obtained the Fairfield Inns, enabling the company to make lower-priced facilities available to guests.

By the 1950s, Marriott's sons were beginning to assume more responsibilities in the family's business. In 1972, John Willard Marriott, Jr., became chief executive officer of the Marriott Corporation and began to diversify its operations. The firm began offering time-sharing facilities in resort areas, provided medium-priced lodgings under the name Courtyard by Marriott, operated facilities for extended-stay travelers, and managed living accommodations for senior citizens.

John Willard Marriott's health eventually began to decline. He had hepatitis, survived an aneurism in the brain, and suffered four heart attacks from late 1975 through early 1976. Despite his poor health, he continued to serve others. He donated $1 million to the University of Utah in order to construct a library and contributed a similar amount to Brigham Young University for a basketball activities center. He chaired the 1970 Independence Day celebration in Washington, D.C., and the U.S. Bicentennial celebration in 1976.

Marriott suffered a heart attack at his family's summer home in New Hampshire and died on August 13, 1985. He was buried in Parklawn Memorial Park in Rockville, Maryland. President Ronald Reagan eulogized Marriott as a man who exemplified the American dream. By the time of his death, the Marriott Corporation maintained operations and franchises in all fifty states and in twenty-seven countries and was valued at more than $3 billion. The Hot Shoppes founded by Marriott and his wife remained popular in the Northeast for several decades; the last one closed in 1999, By that time, however, neither the Hot Shoppes nor Marriott's original airline catering operation was owned by the Marriott Corporation.

Significance

J. Willard Marriott changed the face of the American lodging industry. Cleanliness, efficiency, and service were his bywords. He treated his employees with respect and secured a place for the disabled in his corporation. Marriott gave generously of his time and wealth, and he served his nation by organizing events such as the Bicentennial celebration in Washington, D.C. The papers of John Willard Marriott and Alice Sheets Marriott from 1924 to 1984 are housed at the J. Willard Marriott Library, which Marriott had funded at the University of Utah in Salt Lake City. The university also maintains a collection of Marriott family photographs from 1890 to 1980.

André Michelin

French business executive, tourism promoter, marketing innovator, publisher

In amassing his wealth, Michelin made a significant contribution to the acceptance of the automobile as a reliable and utilitarian means of travel. He also promoted tourism and created one of the world's most famous advertising and cultural icons: the Michelin tire man.

Areas of Achievement: Business, tourism, marketing

Born: January 16, 1853; Paris, France

Died: April 4, 1931; Paris, France

Early Life

André Jules Michelin (meesh-LEHN) was born in Paris on January 16, 1853. He was the son of Adèle Barbier and Jules Michelin, an artist. Adèle was the daughter of Aristide Barbier, who with his cousin Édouard Daubrée had established a successful factory producing various kinds of machinery and a wide variety of rubber items. Michelin's younger brother, Édouard Etienne Michelin, was born on June 23, 1859. In 1877 André Michelin graduated from the École Centrale Paris with a degree in engineering. He then enrolled in the Paris School of Art to study architecture, and his brother Édouard studied art there.

After working for five years in the cartography department of the Ministry of the Interior, André Michelin opened a metal framework factory in Paris. By 1886 the company founded by his grandfather Aristide Barbier was in serious financial trouble and about to fail. Michelin was asked to go to Clermont-Ferrand and take over the company. After considerable deliberation, he agreed to do so. Michelin kept his framework business in Paris, however, and he soon found that he often needed to return to Paris to attend to his business there. Consequently, he and the rest of the family convinced his brother Édouard to join him in the effort to save the family business. Édouard agreed to abandon his art career and go to Clermont-Ferrand.

Life's Work

In 1889 both of the Michelin brothers went to Clermont-Ferrand, where they rebuilt the family's rubber products firm. A bicyclist who had a flat tire arrived at their shop and asked them to fix it; the Dunlop pneumatic tire was glued to the bicycle's rim. The brothers managed to fix the tire but spent some three hours detaching, repairing, and regluing it. Based on this experience, the brothers realized there was a need for a pneumatic tire that could be repaired or changed more quickly and easily. They began experimenting and in 1891 introduced a pneumatic tire for bicycles that could be repaired in approximately 15 minutes.

On August 14, 1891, the Michelin brothers sponsored Charles Terront, a renowned racer, in the Paris-Brest-Paris bicycle race, equipping his bicycle with their pneumatic tires. The race turned out to be a true proving ground for the tires. One of the tires was punctured during the competition, but Terront repaired it and still won the race. The Michelins had such confidence in their tires that they were announcing the victory before Terront had actually crossed the finish line. After additional work, Édouard developed a tire that could be changed in about two minutes. In 1892 André set up another race, this time over a course littered with nails, to demonstrate the ease of fixing the Michelin tire. The promotional campaign resulted in the sale of almost ten thousand sets of tires to bicyclists.

Their success with the pneumatic bicycle tire inspired the brothers to develop pneumatic tires for carriages. By this time, André was in Paris devoting himself to advertising and promoting the company's products, while Édouard stayed in Clermont-Ferrand and directed the research and development of the tires. In 1893 André presented his case for pneumatic tires to the Paris Society of Civil Engineers. Most of his listeners were skeptical, but André insisted that the tires could handle nails, glass, and other road hazards and if punctured were quickly repairable. Although there were very few automobiles in France at the time, the Michelins also began developing a pneumatic tire for these vehicles. By 1895 the company had produced a pneumatic automobile tire. André advertised the tire by entering three cars with Michelin tires in a 750-mile race. The Michelin brothers drove one of the cars, L'Éclair, which finished ninth.

The Michelins were not the only ones producing pneumatic tires in France. In view of this increasing competition, André saw the need to draw the public's attention to his company's tires. In 1894, at the Lyon Fair, Édouard, looking at a stack of tires, had remarked that it almost looked like a person. André took this idea and envisioned what was to become the Michelin Man. In 1898 he hired the French artist Marius Roussillon to draw a man made of tires. André had already described the Michelin tires as gobbling up obstacles, so a poster was created depicting a man made of tires raising a champagne glass filled with nails and glass. The poster's caption was the Latin phrase *Nunc est bibendum* ("time for a drink"). André's promotional tactic was extraordinarily successful. The tire man, referred to as Bibendum, became a folk hero throughout Europe and eventually throughout the world. In addition to the posters, at the 1898 Paris Bicycle Show, there was a large cardboard Bibendum figure, behind which André had stationed a comedian, so visitors to the show were able to talk to Bibendum.

André Michelin also realized the need to promote increased use of the automobile for tourism. Greater use of cars meant more tire sales; therefore, in August 1900, he began publishing *Le Guide Michelin* (the Michelin Guide) to aid tourists traveling in automobiles by providing useful information about restaurants, hotels, service stations, and mechanics. The early guides were blue, and they were free. Michelin's first guide contained maps, as well as information about hotels, restaurants, service stations, tires, their repair, and where to find mechanics. The first guide was approximately four hundred pages long, and thirty-five thousand copies were printed and made available free of charge. The famous pictographs giving pertinent information about hotels and restaurants were already a feature of the guide. By 1904, Michelin was publishing his first guide for tourists traveling outside France, the Michelin Belgium Guide. In 1908 he added another service for travelers: the company opened a bureau of itineraries in its Paris office, where, in addition to the guide, a tourist traveling by automobile could obtain a free travel itinerary. In 1910 the company began publishing road maps. During World War I (1914–1918), however, no guides were published.

In 1920 the guide's color was changed from blue to red and a list of Parisian hotels was added. The guides, however, were no longer free. It is believed that Michelin began charging for the guide after he found a stack of them being used to support a workbench at a tire merchant's store. Michelin published an additional guide that year, the *Illustrated Michelin Guide to the Battlefields, 1914–1918,* with photographs of the areas damaged in World War I.

The restaurant feature of the guides was extremely popular, and in 1920, André began having anonymous inspectors make repeated visits to restaurants before including them in the guide. In 1926 Michelin introduced the use of one star to indicate a good restaurant; three years later, a satisfaction questionnaire was included in the guide; and in 1931 Michelin initiated a three-star system for rating restaurants in the French provinces. (After Michelin's death in 1931, the company continued to add features to the guide and eventually published other guides, and from 1933 Paris restaurants were also evaluated by the three-star system.)

André Michelin soon found additional ways to increase the visibility of the Michelin name and to encourage automobile travel. In 1908, he began funding a program to erect road signs. Michelin's enameled signs gave automobile travelers pertinent information, and all carried the Michelin name. He continued to improve the signs. In 1918 he erected the first *bornes d'angle,* signs grouped together on one pole providing all the information the traveler needed. With his brother Édouard, André continued to head the Michelin company until his death, in Paris, on April 4, 1931.

Significance

André Michelin was a creative and astute entrepreneur who engineered the success of one of the major tire manufacturing companies in the world. Michelin's marketing techniques made significant contributions to the development of France's tourist industry. His original Michelin Guide provided a new concept of traveling. People were encouraged to explore France in their automobiles with guidebook in hand. As Michelin used his wealth to expand the family business, he also significantly enriched the daily life of French people, using his products to promote the French countryside, cuisine, culture, and history.

Jay A. Pritzker

American hotel magnate and conglomerate owner

Pritzker used his professional training in law and accounting to acquire a diverse group of small companies and build them into an enormous business empire. His most notable success was the creation of the Hyatt Hotels Corporation, which not only made him a personal fortune, but also revolutionized the business travel industry.

Areas of Achievement: Real estate, tourism, philanthropy

Born: August 26, 1922; Chicago, Illinois, United States

Died: January 23, 1999; Chicago, Illinois, United States

Early Life

Jay Arthur Pritzker (PRIHTZ-kehr) was born in Chicago, Illinois, on August 26, 1922, the son of Fanny Doppelt and Abram Nicholas Pritzker. Jay was the oldest of three sons, and he and his brothers Robert and Donald would later create a family financial dynasty. His father, Abram, was the son of a Russian-Jewish immigrant who knew the importance of hard work, education, savings, and secure investments. Jay's grandfather, Nicholas Pritzker, laid the foundation for the future financial empire by establishing the law firm of Pritzker & Pritzker and by investing the firm's profits in real estate. After graduating from Harvard Law School, Abram joined the family law firm.

Clearly, family tradition and mutual support played an important role in the success of the Pritzker family, and these values had a positive effect on Jay's developing personality and character. Growing up in Chicago in the 1920s also played a pivotal role in his early development. In this Roaring Twenties era, Chicago was experiencing rapid economic growth, notorious gangland violence, corrupt politics, and an ever-increasing immigrant population from Eastern Europe. The city was ripe for individual fortunes to be made, and Jay did not waste any time in pursuing his dreams. He finished high school at age fourteen and then attended Northwestern University in Evanston, Illinois, receiving his undergraduate degree in 1941 and his law degree in 1947. During World War II, Pritzker was a naval aviator. As a young man entering into the business world, he relied upon what he called the Pritzker work ethic to achieve success, as well as the belief that everyone should contribute to the family's wealth and not live off the money earned by others.

Pritzker, whose academic training was in law and accounting, spent the early years of his career gaining valuable experience through his involvement in his family's businesses. By age twenty-nine, he had taken the first steps toward making his personal mark on the business world. He initially bought up small, relatively inexpensive companies and turned them into highly profitable entities. Never content with success, Pritzker was always looking for ways to increase his holdings through additional acquisitions and new ventures.

Pritzker's early success was partly owed to the business opportunities that arose at the end of World War II, a period that brought many changes in the American lifestyle. During the war, women in the workplace not only filled the void left by the men who were drafted into military service, but also represented new business markets. In the postwar era, there was a great demand for manufactured goods, automobiles, housing, luxury items, and vacation travel. The travel industry flourished, creating a great demand for better means of transportation and affordable accommodations. Businessmen who were regularly away from home demanded a higher-quality accommodation that would make their stay more comfortable, but still be suitable for conducting business.

Life's Work

This desire became apparent to Pritzker in 1957, while he was waiting for a flight at Los Angeles International Airport. Always looking for a good investment opportunity, Pritzker noticed that the airport coffee shop, Fat Eddie's, was doing an unusually good business. He also learned that the airport hotel was usually booked to capacity, and he was impressed by the fact that this was the only first-class hotel he had ever seen at an airport. As luck would have it, both the coffee shop and the Hyatt von Dehn hotel were for sale. Acting upon his instincts, Pritzker immediately made an offer of $2.2 million to buy both, and the offer was accepted. Pritzker was betting that business executives like himself would be willing to pay a higher price for the convenience of staying at a quality hotel close to the airport.

His gamble paid off, and the purchase of the Hyatt hotel in Los Angeles quickly led to construction of another Hyatt hotel located near the San Francisco International Airport. With the success of a second Hyatt hotel, Pritzker and his brothers expanded their operations by acquiring additional hotel properties at several major airports across the United States. These acquisitions would eventually evolve into the multibillion-dollar international Hyatt Hotels Corporation that served as the flagship of the Pritzker family's investments.

One of Pritzker's early acquisitions was the Colson Corporation, a financially troubled manufacturer of wheelchairs and bicycles. He and his brother Robert were able to turn the company into a financial success. Similar acquisitions over the years led to the formation of the Marmon Group, a Chicago-based manufacturing conglomerate of more than one hundred companies with a diversity of industrial and service products. In 1967, Pritzker bought a half-finished Atlanta hotel and turned it into the elegant Hyatt Regency with what would become a trademark giant atrium. The success of the Hyatt Regency Atlanta led to similarly designed hotels being built in many other major markets.

However, Pritzker's investment interests extended far beyond the hotel business. Throughout the years, his family's holdings combined into a vast, multibillion-dollar empire protected by more than one thousand trust funds. A diversity of businesses, land holdings, and interests in natural resources all increased the family's wealth. In addition to Global Hyatt and the Marmon Group, the group also owned the Royal Caribbean International cruise ship line; the TransUnion credit bureau; Triton Holdings, an operator of marine cargo container ships; and the Conwood Company, a manufacturer of snuff and chewing tobacco. The Pritzker family also purchased Braniff Airlines and was involved in a famous takeover battle for RJR Nabisco. The Pritzkers had varied and extensive interests, including AmeriSuites, a chain of more than 140 mid-priced hotels. This structured diversification of business interests and investments enabled the Pritzker family fortune to continue to grow and made many of the family members billionaires.

Often cited as the creator of the Pritzker family's great wealth, Jay Pritzker had a vision of how this money should be used and maintained. It was his wish that the immense family fortune would be protected in perpetuity for the benefit of all family members in a manner respective of their individual ages and status within the family. His vision began to change in 1995, when he designated his son, Thomas, as his direct successor and placed him in control of the family businesses. Pritzker assumed that under Tom's leadership, business would continue as usual, but he was wrong. Tom had a different idea of how the family wealth should be distributed and believed that the greatest rewards should go to those family members who made the most significant contributions to the family's financial success.

Shortly after Jay Pritzker's death in 1999, his principal heirs decided to divide the Pritzker family fortune into eleven equal shares, each worth close to $1.4 billion. These arrangements would have remained outside of public scrutiny had it not been for an inheritance-dispute lawsuit filed by Robert Pritzker's children, Liesel and Matthew. They alleged that their trust funds had been compromised and they wanted their fair share of the inheritance, as well as punitive damages totaling almost $6 billion. A settlement was eventually reached, but not before turning the Pritzkers' private family business into a public spectacle, which was not what Jay Pritzker had intended.

Significance

Jay A. Pritzker and his wife, Cindy, established the Pritzker Architecture Prize in order to draw public attention to the importance of buildings and the architectural profession. The couple were lifelong residents of Chicago and were keenly aware of this city's historic importance in the field of architecture. Chicago was the birthplace of the skyscraper and home to many buildings designed by famous architects, such as Louis Sullivan and Frank Lloyd Wright. The Pritzkers were also aware of the impact of architecture upon human behavior and how buildings influence their environments.

In 1967, Jay Pritzker acquired a partially finished hotel in Atlanta featuring a soaring atrium that let in natural light and gave the building an open-air feel. This design had a very positive effect on both guests and hotel employees, and it became an architectural model for other hotels. His experience at this hotel gave Pritzker a new appreciation for architecture. In 1978, he and his wife were presented with the idea of creating an annual award, including a monetary prize, in order to honor living architects and to promote creativity in architectural design. The Pritzkers enthusiastically accepted this challenge and made preparations for the presentation of the first award in 1979. Criteria for selection of an honoree would follow guidelines similar to those established by the Nobel Prize committee.

Since 1979, the award has been made on an annual basis. In 2009, winners received a $100,000 grant, a formal citation certificate, and a bronze medallion. The award ceremony is held each year at an architecturally significant site. The award has become known as the architectural Nobel and is regarded as architecture's highest honor.

Jay A. Pritzker was innovative in business, loyal to his family, and generous to the community at large. He contributed to a variety of charities in support of the arts and sciences and to medical, religious, and civic organizations. There is no way of accurately measuring the effects of his generosity, but his gifts have supported many causes and have affected millions of lives.

Bibliography

Adrià, Ferran

Abend, Lisa. "Adrià's Next Course." *Time International* 175, no. 8 (March 1, 2010).

Abend, Lisa. *The Sorcerer's Apprentices: A Season in the Kitchen at Ferran Adrià's elBulli.* New York: Free Press, 2011.

Abend, Lisa. "Tastemaker." *Time International* 170, no. 2 (July 16, 2007).

Andrews, Colman. *Ferran; The Inside Story of El Bulli and the Man Who Reinvented Food.* New York: Gotham Books, 2010.

Jouary, Jean-Paul, and Ferran Adrià. *Ferran Adrià and El Bulli: The Art, the Philosophy, the Gastronomy.* London: Andre Deutsche, 2013.

Kummer, Corby. "Tyranny—It's What's for Dinner." *Vanity Fair* 55, no. 2 (February 2013).

Lander, Nicholas. *The Art of the Restaurateur* (London: Phaidon, 2012).

Lubow, Arthur. "A Laboratory of Taste." *New York Times Magazine,* August 10, 2003.

Matthews, Thomas. "Tasting the Future." *Wine Spectator* 28, no. 5 (June 30, 2003).

McInerney, Jay. "It Was Delicious While It Lasted." *Vanity Fair* 52, no.10 (October 2010).

Moslé Friedman, Amanda. "Culinary World Awaits the Post-Kitchen Future of Innovative Chef Ferran Adrià." *Nation's Restaurant News* 40, no. 3 (March 27, 2006).

Myhrvold, Nathan, Chris Young, and Maxime Bilet. *Modernist Cuisine: The Art and Science of Cooking. 6 vols. Bellevue, WA: Cooking Lab, 2011.*

Paterniti, Michael. "Ferran." Esquire 136, no. 1 (July 2001).

Richman, Phyllis. "The Chef of the Future." *Gourmet* 49, no. 10 (October 1999).

Sciolino, Elaine. "Adrià Turns the Charms of El Bulli into Fast Food," *New York Times,* July 28, 2004.

Smith, Rebecca. **"A Culinary Dalí, Delving into Palettes; 'Ferran Adrià' Opens at the Drawing Center."** *New York Times,* February 13, 2014.

Barnes, Brenda

Alexander, Delroy. "Barnes at Home in CEO Position." Chicago Tribune, February 11, 2005.

Alioto, Maryann. "Brenda Barnes (former president and CEO of Pepsi-Cola North America." Directors & Boards, June 22, 1998.

Blaylock, Debbie. "Former CEO Brenda Barnes Works the Plan." Augustana, May 30, 2012.

Burns, Greg. "Nobody's Business But Her Own." Chicago Tribune, October 14, 2007.

Coolidge, Shelley Donald. "Trading 30,000 Staff For 3 Kids." *Christian Science Monitor*, October 8, 1997.

Bastianich, Joseph

Bruni, Frank. "New Rituals in the Adoration of Italy." *New York Times,* March 1, 2006.

Duecy, Erica. "Babbo." *Nation's Restaurant News,* May 22, 2006.

Gay, Jason. "Italian for Dinner, a Triathlon for Dessert." *Wall Street Journal,* December 9, 2011.

Lander, Nicholas. *The Art of the Restaurateur* (London: Phaidon, 2012).

Lewine, Edward. "Domains: Italian Villa." *New York Times,* September 23, 2010.

Saxena, Jaya. "Eataly Aims to Give New Yorkers an Italian Lesson." *Gothamist,* August 25, 2010.

Sifton, Sam. "A Modern Italian Master." *New York Times,* September 29, 2010.

Beard, James

Barr, Luke. *Provence, 1970.* New York: Clarkson Potter, 2013.

Clark, Robert. *The Solace of Food: A Life of James Beard.* South Royalton, VT: Steerforth Press, 1993.

Jones, Evan. *Epicurean Delight: The Life and Times of James Beard.* New York: Knopf, 1990.

Claiborne, Craig

Avins, Jenni. "The Legacy of Craig Claiborne." *Saveur,* June 17, 2009.

Barr, Luke. *Provence, 1970.* New York, Clarkson Potter, 2013.

Clark, Robert. *The Solace of Food: A Life of James Beard.* South Royalton, VT: Steerforth Press, 1993.

McNamee, Thomas. *The Man Who Changed the Way We Eat: Craig Claiborne and the American Food Renaissance.* New York: Free Press, 2012.

Miller, Bryan. "Craig Claiborne, Times Food Editor and Critic, Is Dead." *New York Times,* Janaury 24, 2000.

Cointreau, André J.

Hesser, Amanda, "The Cooking School Report: France or U.S.? Now It's a Hard Choice." *New York Times,* June 24, 1998.

Iggers, Jeremy. "Cointreau's Visit Is Piece de Resistance for Brown Students." [Minneapolis, MN] *Star Tribune,* March 9, 2000.

Julian, Sheryl, "Going Back to London's Cordon Bleu: The London School Has Changed and So Have Its Students," *Boston Globe,* May 17, 2000.

Kraft, Scott. "French Liquor Scion Prospers by Striking Out on His Own." *Los Angeles Times,* July 25, 1995.

Schilling, Mark, "Le Cordon Bleu Takes Its Kitchens East," *Wall Street Journal,* September 12, 1991.

Turnbull, Tony. "Le Cordon Bleu Five Classic Recipes: The Revered French Cookery School Teaches Techniques Rather Than Recipes." [London] *Times,* February 4, 2012.

Whittle, Natalie. "Kitchen Stories: Cordon Bleu Cuts the Ribbon. *Financial Times,* March 3, 2012.

Cora, Cat

Adato, Allison. *Smart Chefs Stay Slim: Lessons in Eating and Living from America's Best Chefs.* New York: New American Library, 2012.

Bryan, Meredith. "The Family That Eats Together. ..." *O, the Oprah Magazine* 12, no. 7 (July 2011).

Riss, Suzanne. "Cat Cora." *Working Mother* 33, no. 6 (August-September 2010).

Salkin, Allen. *From Scratch: Inside the Food Network.* New York: G. P. Putnam, 2013.

Williams, Ashley. "Five Key Ingredients." *People Weekly* 68, no. 21 (November 19, 2007).

Disney, Walt

Barrier, Michael. *Hollywood Cartoons: American Animation in Its Golden Age.* Oxford, UK: Oxford University Press, 1999.

Gabler, Neal. *Walt Disney: The Triumph of American Imagination.* New York: Random House, 2006.

Mosley, Leonard. *Disney's World: A Biography.* Chelsea, MI.: Scarborough House, 2002.

Peri, Don. *Working with Walt: Interviews with Disney Artists.* Jackson: University Press of Mississippi, 2008.

Schickel, Richard. *The Disney Version: The Life, Times, Art, and Commerce of Walt Disney.* New York: Simon & Schuster, 1968.

Sherman, Robert B., and Richard M. Sherman. Walt's Time: From Before to Beyond. Santa Clarita, Calif.: Camphor Tree, 1998.

Watts, Steven. *The Magic Kingdom: Walt Disney and the American Way of Life.* Columbia: University of Missouri Press, 2001.

Donald, Arnold W.

Brown, Lisa. "Arnold Donald Takes Helm of Carnival Corp." *St. Louis Post-Dispatch,* June 26, 2013.

Childs, Ronald E. "It's Sweet at the Top: Arnold Donald is the Chairman CEO of Merisant Co." *Black Enterprise* 33, no. 10 (May 2003).

King, Chris. "Arnold Donald New CEO of Carnival." *St. Louis American,* June 27, 2013.

Olsen, Patricia R. "When Focus Leads the Way." *New York Times* (June 24, 2007).

Palmeri, Christopher, and Carol Massar. "Accidental CEO Charts New Course for Cruise Company." *Bloomberg News,* November 25, 2013.

Draper, Dorothy

Abercrombie, Stanley. "The Greenbrier: Dorothy Draper and Co. Continues a Longstanding Relationship with the Legendary Resort." *Interior Design* 60, no. 3 (February 1989).

Albrecht, Donald. *The High Style of Dorothy Draper: An Exhibition at the Museum of the City of New York.* New York: Museum of the City of New York/Pointed Leaf Press, 2006.

Collins, Nancy, "Draper's High Style." *Architectural Digest* 63, no. 5 (May 2006).

Hampton, Mark. *Legendary Decorators of the Twentieth Century.* New York: Doubleday, 1992.

Lewis, Adam. *The Great Lady Decorators: The Women Who Defined Interior Design, 1870–1955.* New York: Rizzoli, 2010.

Owens, Mitchell, "Living Large: The Brash, Bodacious Hotels of Dorothy Draper." *Journal of Decorative and Propaganda Arts* 25 (Spring 2005).

Owens, Mitchell. "The Surreal Deal." *New York Times Magazine,* April 2, 2006.

Sheehan, Susan. "The Greenbrier." *Architectural Digest* 62, no. 11 (November 2005).

Simpson, Jeffrey. "A Penchant for Bold Gestures and Audacious Scale." *Architectural Digest* 57, no. 1 (January 2000).

Turpin, John. "Dorothy Draper and the American Housewife: A Study of Class Values and Success," in *The Handbook of Interior Design,* ed. by Jo Ann Asher Thompson and Nancy H. Blossom. Hoboken, NJ: John Wiley, 2014.

Vaill, Amanda. "Flying Down to Rio: Dorothy Draper Brought High-Octane Glamor to a 1940s Casino Resort." *Architectural Digest* 59, no. 4, (April 2002).

Varney, Carlton. *The Draper Touch: The High Life and High Style of Dorothy Draper.* New York: Prentice-Hall Press, 1988.

Varney, Carlton. *In the Pink; Dorothy Draper, America's Most Fabulous Decorator.* New York: Pointed Leaf Press, 2006.

Flagler, Henry M.

Akin, Edward N. *Flagler: Rockefeller Partner and Florida Baron.* Gainesville: University Press of Florida, 1991.

Braden, Susan R. *The Architecture of Leisure: The Florida Resort Hotels of Henry Flagler and Henry Plant.* Gainesville: University Press of Florida, 2002.

Chandler, David Leon. *Henry Flagler: The Astonishing Life and Times of the Visionary Robber Baron Who Founded Florida.* New York: Macmillan, 1986.

Graham, Thomas. *Flagler's St. Augustine Hotels: The Ponce de Leon, the Alcazar, and the Casa Monica.* Sarasota, FL: Pineapple Press, 2002.

Standiford, Les. *Last Train to Paradise: Henry Flagler and the Spectacular Rise and Fall of the Railroad That Crossed an Ocean.* New York: Crown, 2002.

Gallo, Ernest

Fierman, Jaclyn. "How Gallo Crushes the Competition." *Fortune* 114 (September 1, 1986).

Hawkes, Ellen. *Blood and Wine: The Unauthorized Story of the Gallo Wine Empire.* New York: Simon & Schuster, 1993.

Henderson, Bruce, with Ernest Gallo and Julio Gallo. *Ernest & Julio: Our Story.* New York: Times Books, 1994.

Laube, James. "Crossfire with the Chairman." *Wine Spectator* 32, no. 2 (May 15, 2007.

Pinney, Thomas. *The Makers of American Wines: A Record of Two Hundred Years.* Berkeley: University of California Press, 2012.

Sansom, Ian, "Great Dynasties of the World: The Gallos; An American Wine-Making Family in Ferment." *Guardian,* August 27, 2010.

Shanken, Marvin R. "Ernest Gallo at 90." *Wine Spectator* 24, no. 5 (June 30, 1999).

Shanken, Marvin R. "An Interview with Ernest Gallo." *Wine Spectator* 24, no. 5 (June 30, 1999).

Time Magazine. "American Wine: There's Gold in Them Thar Grapes." November 27, 1972. [Cover story.]

Times [London]. "Ernest Gallo; Obituary." March 8, 2007.

Tucille, James. *Gallo Be Thy Name: The Inside Story of How One Family Rose to Dominate the U.S. Wine Market.* Beverly Hills, CA: Phoenix Books, 2009.

Ghermezian, Eskander

German, Jeff and Steve Kanigher. "Power of Triple Five." *Las Vegas Sun,* May 15, 2006.

Pristin, Terry. "Judge Rules Against Simon in Mall Suit." *New York Times,* September 12, 2003.

Salter, Michael. "The Ghermezians' Secrets." *Maclean's,* April 15, 1985.

Ho, Stanley

Berzon, Alexandra, and Jonathan Cheng. "Macau's Ho Denies Report of Crime Ties." *Wall Street Journal,* March 19, 2010.

Cohen, Muhammad. "Macau's Ho Bubbles ahead with Oceanus. *Asia Times,* May 14, 2010.

Cohen, Muhammad. "Stanley Ho Handover Unsettles Macau." *Asia Times,* January 28, 2011.

Flannery, Russell. "Like Father, Like Son." *Forbes,* November 30, 2011.

Gough, Neil. "SJM's Net Profit Soars on High-Stakes Gambling." *South China Morning Post,* May 18, 2011.

Master, Farah. "Stanley Ho's SJM Makes Fresh Start with New Macau Casino." Reuters, February 13, 2014.

Oster, Shay, and Kate O'Keeffe. "Stanley Ho Confirms Share Transfer to Wives, Daughter Angela Shocked." *Wall Street Journal, January 27, 2011.*

Studwell, Joe. *Asian Godfathers.* New York: Grove Press, 2008.

Wassener, Bettina. "Macao Casino Tycoon Says Family Dispute Is Over." *New York Times,* March 11, 2011.

Wassener, Bettina. "Macau Rides High on New Round of Casino Construction." *New York Times,* March 26, 2014.

Keller, Thomas

Bittman, Mark, "Thomas Keller Takes on the Recipes of a French Master." *New York Times,* April 19, 2012.

Burros, Marian. "On the Road to Acclaim, a Chef Learns Lessons in Humility." *New York Times,* October 16, 1996.

Fabricant, Florence. "Flights of Fancy." *New York Times Magazine,* December 11, 1988.

Frumkin, Paul. "Thomas Keller; Celebrated American Chef Takes Country's Cuisine to New Heights." *Nation's Restaurant News* 45, no. 25 (December 5, 2011).

Gold, Amanda. "French Laundry Chef Thomas Keller's Recipe for Success." *San Francisco Chronicle* (SFGate), June 9, 2014.

Harper's Bazaar staff. "Fashionable Food: Legendary Chef Thomas Keller of the French Laundry and Per Se Talks Trends, Talent, and the Joys of In-N-Out Burger." *Harper's Bazaar* 3616 (September 2013).

Hesser, Amanda. "The Way We Eat: Labor Party." *New York Times,* December 12, 2004.

Kramer, Jane. "The Quest." *New Yorker,* September 5, 2005.

Kummer, Corby. "Tyranny—It's What's for Dinner." *Vanity Fair* 55, no. 2 (February 2013).

Lucas, Roslyn. "Fashion Plate: Thomas Keller at Manhattan's Per Se." *Veranda* 22, no. 4 (May–June 2008).

Lucchesi, Paolo. "Deconstructing One Signature French Laundry Dish." *San Francisco Chronicle* (SFGate), June 10, 2014.

Moskin, Julia. "For Them, a Great Meal Tops Good Intentions." *New York Times* (May 15, 2012).

Ruhlman, Michael. "Natural-Born Keller: One Chef's Journey from Hamburgers to Haute Cuisine." *Gourmet* 59, no. 10 (October 1999).

Ruhlman, Michael. *The Reach of a Chef: Beyond the Kitchen.* New York: Viking, 2006.

Ruhlman, Michael. *The Soul of a Chef: The Journey toward Perfection.* 2000; reprint, Penguin, 2001.

Severson, Kim. "A Rat with a Whisk and a Dream." *New York Times,* June 13, 2007.

Severson, Kim. "What the Last Meal Taught Him." *New York Times,* October 27, 2009.

Steiman, Harvey. "The Phoenix and the French Laundry." *Wine Spectator* 35, no. 1 (April 30, 2010).

Stein, Joel. "Chef: Captain Cook." *Time,* September 17, 2001.

Steingarten, Jeffrey. "A Chef in Full." *Vogue* 202, no. 9 (September 2012).

Temple, James. "French Laundry's Keller Takes Plunge with Frozen Foods, Burgers." Bloomberg News, September 24, 2007.

Wilkey, Robin, and Aaron Sankin. "Thomas Keller on 'Vanity Fair,' Criticism, Iconic Restaurants, and What's Next for French Laundry." Huffington Post, March 19, 2013.

Kroc, Ray

Aaseng, Nathan. *Business Builders in Fast Food.* Minneapolis: Oliver Press, 2001.

Love, John F. *McDonald's: Behind the Arches.* New York: Bantam Books, 1995.

Marriott, J. Willard

Collins, Jim, and Jerry I. Porras. *Built to Last: Successful Habits of Visionary Companies,* 3d ed. New York: HarperBusiness, 2004.

Marriott, John Willard, Jr., and Kathi Ann Brown. *The Spirit to Serve: Marriott's Way.* New York: HarperBusiness, 1997.

Nagle, James J. "Marriott Embarks on New Hotel Expansion Program." *New York Times,* May 11, 1969.

O'Brien, Robert. *Marriott: The J. Willard Marriott Story.* Salt Lake City: Deseret, 1977.

Zuckerman, David. "J. Willard Marriott, a Retrospective, 1900–1985." *Nation's Restaurant News* 19 (October 7, 1985).

Matsuhisa, Nobu

Beard, Alison. "Life's Work: Nobu Matsuhisa; An Interview with Nobu Matsuhisa." *Harvard Business Review,* October 2013.

Benner, Kate. "Cutting Out Clutter." *Fortune* 155, no. 11 (June 11, 2007).

Fabricant, Florence. "De Niro Shares Bill with a Sushi Chef." *New York Times,* August 10, 1994.

Garratt, Sheryl. "Know Who? Nobu." [London] *Observer,* April 20, 2001.

Garvey, Hugh. "Tokyo Drifter." *Bon Appétit* 57, no. 5 (May 2012).

Higgins, Ria. "'De Niro and I? We're Partners in Sushi.'" [London] *Sunday Times,* February 6, 2011.

Issenberg, Sasha. *The Sushi Economy: Globalization and the Making of a Modern Delicacy.* 2007; reprint, New York: Gotham Books, 2008.

Lander, Nicholas. "Nobu's Empire Advances." *Financial Times,* November 25, 2000.

Lander, Nicholas. "Same Difference: Nicholas Lander Welcomes the Expansion of Nobu in London and New York." *Financial Times,* November 26, 2005.

Martin, Richard. "Matsuhisa: A Culinary Odyssey." *Nation's Restaurant News* 27, no. 21 (May 24, 1993).

Overfelt, Maggie. "How Chef Nobu Built His Sushi Empire." *Fortune,* Mar. 26, 2009.

Roux, Caroline. "Nobu's World." [London] *Guardian,* August 17, 2001.

Seal, Rebecca. "Nobu Matsuhisa's Los Angeles." *Financial Times,* August 7, 2010.

Spector, Amy. "Written Nobu or Ubon, Matsuhisa's New Restaurant Locations Spell Expansion." *Nation's Restaurant News* 33, no. 20 (May 17, 1999).

Michelin, André

Darmon, Olivier. *Michelin Man: One Hundred Years of Bibendum.* Minneapolis: Motorbooks International, 1998.

Harp, Stephen L. *Marketing Michelin: Advertising and Cultural Identity in Twentieth Century France.* Baltimore: Johns Hopkins University Press, 2001.

Lecoadic, Rudy. *The Michelin Man: An Unauthorized Advertising Showcase.* West Chester, PA: Schiffer, 2005.

Lottman, Herbert. *Michelin Men: Driving an Empire.* New York: I. B. Tauris, 2003.

Norbye, Jan P. *The Michelin Magic.* Blue Ridge Summit, PA: Tab Books, 1982.

Ribeill, Georges. From Pneumatics to Highway Logistics: André Michelin, Instigator of the "Automobile Revolution," Part I. *Flux* 7, no. 3 (January–March 1991). [In English. Available online at the Persée portal.]

Ribeill, Georges. From Pneumatics to Highway Logistics: André Michelin, Instigator of the "Automobile Revolution," Part II. *Flux* 7, no. 5 (July–September 1991). [In English. Available online at the Persée portal.]

Muñoz Zurita, Ricardo

Ulla, Gabe. "Ricardo Muñoz Zurita on His New Dictionary and the Richness of Mexican Gastronomy." Eater, January 11, 2013.

Webster, Kerry. "Fresh Today." *Seattle Times,* May 3, 1995.

Nelson, Marilyn Carlson

Flaherty, Julie. "Five Questions for Marilyn Carlson Nelson; Now Make the Traveler Want to Travel." *New York Times,* September 30, 2001.

Houston, Patrick. "A Patriarch Retires—Cautiously." *New York Times,* April 2, 1989.

Koli. Anuradha, and John Reed Forsman. "Marilyn Carlson Nelson." *Working Mother* 30, no. 8 (November 2007).

Levere, Jane L. "Poetry, Ping-Pong, All in a Day's Work." *New York Times,* August 9, 2008.

Levere, Jane L. "The Road to Vegas: $55 and 70 years." *New York Times,* October 10, 2004.

Levere, Jane L., and Marilyn Carlson Nelson. "A Line in the Snow." *New York Times,* October 10, 2004.

Mohn, Tanya. "The Travel Industry Takes on Human Trafficking." *New York Times,* November 8, 2012.

Papa, Mary Bader. "A Son Named Marilyn." *Corporate Report—Minnesota* 21, no. 3 (March 1990).

Pellet, Jennifer. "An Upside-Down Career Path to the Top." *Chief Executive* 236 (September–October 2008).

Shillinglaw, James. "From Father to Daughter." *Travel Agent* 281, no. 1 (May 27, 1996).

Weimer, De'Ann. "'I Want to Lead with Love, Not Fear': How Marilyn Nelson Is Putting Her Stamp on Carlson Companies." *BusinessWeek* 3591 (August 17, 1998).

Nooyi, Indra

Burnison, Gary. "How Pepsi's Indra Nooyi Learned to be a CEO." *Fast Company,* April 29, 2011.

Seabrook, John. "Snacks for a Fat Planet." *New Yorker,* May 16, 2011.

Strom, Stephanie. "Pepsi Chief Shuffles Management to Soothe Investors." *New York Times,* March 12, 2012.

Useem. Michael. "America's Best Leaders: Indra Nooyi, PepsiCo CEO." *U.S. News & World Report,* November 19, 2008.

Oliver, Garrett

Asimov, Eric. "White House Beer: A Brewer Weighs In: Garrett Oliver of Brooklyn Brewery Assesses the Beer Recipe the Obama Administration Released over the Weekend." *New York Times,* September 3, 2012.

Brennan, Emily. "The Brooklyn Brewmaster Garrett Oliver on Beer Drinking in Sweden." *New York Times,* November 17, 2013.

Byron, Dennis Malcolm. "Garrett Oliver: The Brewmaster." *Jet* 118, no.14–15, 2010).

Engelhart, Katie. "Garrett Oliver." *Financial Times,* September 24, 2011.

Townsend, Bob. "Q&A / Garrett Oliver: 'I consider chefs to be ... nonbrewing peers.'" *Atlanta Journal-Constitution* (July 19, 2007).

Wilson, Bee. "Drink Beer, It Makes You Drunk." *Times Literary Supplement* 5678 (January 27, 2012).

Otis, Clarence

Bryant, Adam. "Ensemble Acting, in Business." *New York Times,* June 6, 2009.

Chediak, Mark. "Leader Clarence Otis Sticks to Pursuit of Success for Orlando-Based Darden Restaurants." *Orlando Sentinel,* November 2, 2008.

Chediak, Mark. "Otis Talks about His Rise at Darden." *Orlando Sentinel,* September 29, 2006.

Davidoff, Steven M. "Battle over Darden Leaves Little Room for Compromise." New York Times, May 20, 2014.

Jones, Del. "Good Service Vital during Downturn." USA Today, August 17, 2009.

Martin, Andrew. "Drawing Up a Menu for America." New York Times, February 10, 2007.

Turner, Elisa, "Clarence Otis and Jacqueline Bradley: 'These Works Talk to Each Other." ARTnews 96, no. 5 (May 1997).

Winslow, Laurie. "Restaurant CEO Sees Curiosity as Key Trait." *Tulsa World,* February 21, 2008.

Oudolf, Piet

Barrett, Sara. "Q&A: Piet Oudolf on Designing a Winter Garden." *New York Times,* February 9, 2011.

Cunningham, Yvonne. "Piet Oudolf: Dutch Garden Designer Turns Traditional Perennial Planting on Its Ear." *Gardening Life* 4, no. 4 (Fall 2000).

David, Joshua, and Robert Hammond. *High Line: The Inside Story of New York City's Park in the Sky.* New York: Farrar, Straus and Giroux, 2011.

Dickey, Page. *Breaking Ground: Portraits of Ten Garden Designers.* 1997; reprint, New York: Artisan, 2003.

Donald, Caroline. "Dutch Courage." [London] *Sunday Times,* June 26, 2011.

Holland, Tristram. "Oh, To Be in England. (Piet Oudolf)." *House & Garden* 176, no. 9 (September 2007).

Kingsbury, Noël. *Garden Designers at Home: The Private Spaces of the World's Leading Designers.* London : Pavilion, 2011.

Kingsbury, Noël, "A Wilder Way." *New York Times,* April 10, 2013.

La Farge, Annik, *On the High Line.* New York: Thames & Hudson, 2012.

Pereire, Anita. *Gardens for the 21st Century.* 1999; reprint, London: Aurum, 2001.

McGrane, Sally. "A Landscape in Winter, Dying Heroically." *New York Times,* January 28, 2008.

Raver, Anne. "Replanting Nieuw Amsterdam." *New York Times,* January 16, 2003.

Richardson, Tim. *Futurescapes: Designers for Tomorrow's Outdoor Spaces.* New York: Thames and Hudson, 2011.

Saralegui, Alejandro. "Manhattan's Battery Gardens Is Restored and Rejuvenated." *New York Cottages and Gardens* (March 2013).

Stuart, David. *Classic Garden Plans.* London: Frances Lincoln, 2004.

Petrini, Carlo

Bittman, Mark. "Slow Food Quickens the Pace." *New York Times,* March 26, 2013.

Bruni, Frank. "Pollenzo Journal; A New Italian Campus, Where the Thought Is for Food." *New York Times,* April 2, 2004.

Ducasse, Alain. "The Slow Revolutionary: Carlo Petrini; Italy." *Time International* (Europe Edition), 2004 Oct 11.

Fabricant, Florence. "A Faintly Amused Answer to Fast Food." *New York Times,* November 15, 1989.

Hesser, Amanda. "Q&A; Endangered Species: Slow Food." *New York Times,* July 26, 2003.

Kummer, Corby. *The Pleasures of Slow Food: Celebrating Authentic Traditions, Flavors, and Recipes* (San Francisco: Chronicle Books, 2002).

McBride, Stewart. Diversity at the Table; A Fight against Blandness; The Brillat-Savarins of Slow Food: They're Eating Well and Doing Right." *New York Times,* November 18, 2003.

Severson, Kim. "Slow Food Savors Its Big Moment." *New York Times,* July 23, 2008.

Singleton, Kate. "The Slow Food Movement Is Gearing Down to a Snail's Pace." *New York Times,* April 17, 1998.

Zeppelin, Andra, "Slow Food's Carlo Petrini on Biodiversity, Food Politics and Home-Cooking" *Denver Post,* May 2, 2013.

Poon Tip, Bruce

Davidson, Hilary. *Profit,* May 2000.

Gignac, Tamara. *Calgary Herald,* July 25, 2004.

Kennedy, Sarah. *Calgary Sun,* November 18, 2004.

Lilley, Wayne. *National Post Business Magazine,* December 1, 2002.

Luke, Paul. Vancouver Province, October 27, 2002.

Pratt, Laura. *National Post,* August 8, 2001.

Pritzker, Jay A.

Andrews, Suzanna. "Shattered Dynasty." *Vanity Fair*, May 2003.

Bernstein, Peter W., and Annalyn Swan, eds. *All the Money in the World.* New York: Alfred A. Knopf, 2007.

Chandler, Susan, and Kathy Bergen. "Inside the Pritzker Family Feud." *Chicago Tribune*, June 12, 2005.

Martel, Judy, and James E. Hughes, Jr. *The Dilemmas of Family Wealth: Insights on Succession, Cohesion, and Legacy.* New York: Bloomberg Press, 2006.

Polner, Murray. *American Jewish Biographies.* New York: Facts On File, 1982.

Worthy, Ford S. "The Pritzkers: Unveiling a Private Family." *Fortune*, April 23, 1988.

Robinson, Jancis

Asimov, Eric, "Decanting Robert Parker." *New York Times,* March 22, 2008.

Asimov, Eric. "A Master of Wine Takes a Fresh Look." *New York Times,* November 1, 2006.

Moir, Jan. "Grape Expectations." *Guardian,* November 9, 1994.

Summers, Sue. "Wine Wars." [London] *Daily Telegraph,* November 27, 2004.

Sutherland, N. S., "Jancis Robinson on the Demon Drink" *Times Literary Supplement* 4454, August 12, 1988.

Nicholas Wroe. "Taste and Plenty of Bottle." *Guardian,* 23 December 2005

Robuchon, Joël

Art Culinaire. "An interview with Joel Robuchon; Chef and Restaurateur, Paris, Tokyo, Macao, New York and Las Vegas." *Art Culinaire* 85 (Summer 2007).

Boyer, Xavier. "Letting the Ingredient Speak for Itself." *Art Culinaire* 95 (Winter 2009).

Fabricant, Florence. "Joël Robuchon to Close at the Four Seasons." *New York Times,* May 30, 2012.

Fabricant, Florence. "New York: Joël Robuchon Strides In." *New York Times,* August 9, 2006.

Fiedler, Jennifer. "Top Chefs in Two Worlds." *Wine Spectator* 36, no. 7 (September 30, 2011).

Kraft, Scott. "Joël Robuchon: France's Finest Chef Reflects on the 'French Paradox.'" *Los Angeles Times,* June 9, 1996.

Platus, Libby. "Going for Broke: Legendary French Chef Joël Robuchon Opens a Pair of Restaurants at the MGM Grand in Las Vegas." *Restaurant Hospitality* 89, no. 12 (December 2005).

Sigal, Jane. "The Chef: Joël Robuchon; Three Fish Walk into a Bar." *New York Times,* March 28, 2007.

Steiman, Harvey. "Three-Star Cooking with Joël Robuchon." *Wine Spectator* 18, no. 12 (October 15, 1993).

Virbila, S. Irene. "Las Vegas, Lighted by Stars: Joël Robuchon Was at the Pinnacle When He Retired 10 Years Ago, Now He's Back." *Los Angeles Times,* December 28, 2005.

Wells, Patricia. *L'Atelier of Joël Robuchon: The Artistry of a Master Chef and His Protégés.* New York: Van Nostrand Reinhold, 1998.

Willett, Megan. "Here's What Top Chef Joël Robuchon Eats for Breakfast." *Business Insider,* March 28, 2014.

Rosenfeld, Irene B.

Carpenter, Dave. Associated Press, June 26, 2006.

Carter, Adrienne. BusinessWeek, June 26, 2006.

Chandler, Susan. Chicago Tribune, June 27, 2006.

Manor, Robert. Chicago Tribune, September 12, 2006.

Reyes, Sonia. Brandweek, September 18, 2006.

Schmeltzer, John. Chicago Tribune, October 24, 2006.

Sellers, Patricia . Fortune, October 16, 2006.

Thompson, Stephanie. Advertising Age, July 3, 2006.

VanderMey, Anne, and Nicolas Rapp. Fortune, October 2, 2012.

Yue, Lorene. Crain's Chicago Business, June 29, 2006.

Rusesabagina, Paul

Chang, Justin. *Variety,* January 3-9, 2005.

CollegeNews.org. February 10, 2005.

Nesti, Bob. *Boston-Bay State Banner*, January 13, 2005.

O'Connor, Anne-Marie. *Los Angeles Times*, December 28, 2004.

Smith, Kyle, Dietland Lerner, and Michael Fleeman. *People*, January 24, 2005.

Steves, Rick

Blain, Joanne. Canwest News Service, May 10, 2008.

Contra Costa (California) *Times*, April 10, 2008.

Corbett, Sara. *New York Times*, July 4, 2004.

Emmons, Becky. *South Bend* (Indiana) *Tribune*, December 11, 2005.

Greteman, Blaine. *Time*, June 6, 2003.

Jackson, Kristin. *Seattle Times*, February 11, 1996.

Karras, Christy. *Salt Lake Tribune*, October 31, 2004.

Libman, Norma. *Chicago Tribune*, April 23, 1995.

Shattuck, Harry. *Houston Chronicle*, March 21, 2004.

Wheeler, Tony

Anderson, Linda. *Financial Times*, September 8, 2003.

Brennan, Emily. *New York Times*, June 7, 2013.

Friend, Tad. *The New Yorker*, April 18, 2005.

Potts, Rolf. *Vagabonding* Web site, August 2003.

Riley, Alasdair. *London Times*, January 6, 2001.

Shenon, Philip. *New York Times*, June 30, 1996.

Wollaston, Sam. *London Guardian,* July 7, 1998.

Young Pioneers Web site, Spring 2004.

Waters, Alice

Burros, Marian. "Alice Waters: Food Revolutionary." *New York Times,* August 14, 1996.

Geraci, Victor W., and Elizabeth S. Demers, eds. *Icons of American Cooking.* Santa Barbara, CA: Greenwood, 2011.

Heron, Katrina, ed. *Slow Food Nation's Come to the Table: The Slow Food Way of Living.* Emmaus, PA: Rodale, 2008.

Kamp, David. *The United States of Arugula; How We Became a Gourmet Nation.* New York: Broadway Books, 2006.

Lander, Nicholas. "The Wonder of Alice" *Financial Times,* March 20, 2010.

Martin, Andrew, "Is the Food Revolution Now in Season?" *New York Times,* March 22, 2009.

McNamee, Thomas. *Alice Waters and Chez Panisse: The Romantic, Impractical, Often Eccentric, Ultimately Brilliant Making of a Food Revolution.* New York: Penguin Press, 2007.

Parker-Pope, Tara. "Alice Waters and Obama's 'Kitchen' Cabinet." *New York Times,* December 11, 2008.

Pickert, Kate. "Q&A with Alice Waters." *Time,* March 25, 2009.

Reardon, Joan. *M. F. K. Fisher, Julia Child, and Alice Waters: Celebrating the Pleasures of the Table.* New York: Harmony Books, 1994.

Rosenthal, Elizabeth. "In Rome, the Academy Learns to Cook." *New York Times,* March 13, 2009.

Severson, Kim. "Lunch with Alice Waters, Food Revolutionary: Don't Worry, She'll Bring the Capers." *New York Times,* September 19, 2007.

Wynn, Steve

Creswell, Julie. "The Chips Are Down in Vegas, but Steve Wynn Is Betting Big." *New York Times*, August 3, 2008.

Paumgarten, Nick. "The $40-Million Elbow." *The New Yorker*, October 23, 2006.

Ruddock, Steve. "Steve Wynn Changes Position on Online Gambling Again; What it Means for New Jersey." *NJ.com*, February 10, 2014.

Zagat, Tim
Zagat, Nina

De la Merced, Michael, Ron Lieber, and Claire Cain Miller. "In a Twist, Google Reviews Zagat, and Decides to Bite. *New York Times,* September 8, 2011.

Deutschman, Alan. "Travel Guides." *Fortune* 123, no. 1 (January 14, 1991).

Enfield, Susan. "The Zagat Edge." *M Inc.* 8, no.7 (April 1991).

Geraci, Victor W., and Elizabeth S. Demers, eds. *Icons of American Cooking.* Santa Barbara, CA: Greenwood, 2011.

Hall, Trish. "Zagat Guides: Whose Voice Is Being Heard?" *New York Times,* February 8, 1989.

Hoffman, Jan. "The Gustatory Life of Dining-Scene Royals." *New York Times,* March 1, 2000.

Parseghian, Pamela. "Tim and Nina Zagat." *Nation's Restaurant News* 38, no. 40 October 4, 2004.

Rigg, Cynthia. "Fine Dining's Arbiter Has a Lot on His Plate*." Crain's New York Business* 13, no. 13 (March 31, 1997).

Ryan, Nancy Ross. "The Zagats." *Restaurants & Institutions* 103, no. 21 (September 1, 1993).

Soeder, John. "Tim Zagat." *Restaurant Hospitality* 76, no. 7, (July 1992).

Solomon, Deborah. "Of Fats and Food." *New York Times Magazine,* December 17, 2006.

Weinstein, Bob. "Rave Reviews: The Creators of America's Bestselling Restaurant Guides Are Masters of All They Survey." *Entrepreneur* 24, no. 8 (August 1996).

Wise, Stuart M. "The Way to a Lawyer's Heart?" *National Law Journal* 5 (December 27, 1982).

Yee, Laura. "Tim Zagat." *Restaurants & Institutions* 110, no. 12 (May 1, 2000).

Zhang Xin

Bartiromo, Maria. "On the Ground in China." *BusinessWeek,* August 21, 2006.

BusinessWeek. "Zhang Xin; Co-Chief Executive, SOHO China." *BusinessWeek,* July 12, 2004.

Leow, Jason. "Power Pair Builds Beijing-and a Life; Zhang and Husband Find 'Middle Ground' to Develop Chinese Real-Estate Empire." *Wall Street Journal Eastern Edition,* September 17, 2007.

Luce, Edward, and Anjli Raval. "View from the Top: Zhang Xin, Chief Executive, Soho China." *Financial Times,* March 26, 2012.

Webb, Michael. "Raising the Bar; Enlightened Patrons and Developers Are Key in China's Struggle to Forge a New Architectural Identity." *Architectural Review* 224, no. 1337 (July 2008).

Zha, Jianying. "The Turtles." *New Yorker* 81, no. 20 (July 11, 2005).

Selected Works

Adrià, Ferran

Adrià, Ferran. *Los secretos de El Bulli.* Barcelona: Altaya, 1997.

Adrià, Ferran, Albert Adrià, and Juli Soler. *elBulli 2005–2011,* 7 vols. New York: Phaidon, 2014.

Adrià, Ferran, and Eugeni de Diego. *The Family Meal.* New York: Phaidon Press, 2011.

Adrià, Ferran, and the Alícia Foundation elBullitaller. *Modern Gastronomy A to Z.* Boca Raton, FL: CRC Press, 2010.

Adrià, Ferran, Juli Soler, and Albert Adrià. *A Day at elBulli: An Insight into the Ideas, Methods, and Creativity of Ferran Adrià.* 2008; reprint, London: Phaidon Press, 2010.

Bastianich, Joseph

Bastianich, Joe. *Restaurant Man.* New York: Viking, 2012.

Beard, James

Beard, James. *Beard on Bread.* New York: Knopf, 1974.

Beard, James. *Beard on Pasta.* New York: Knopf, 1983.

Beard, James. *James Beard's Simple Foods.* New York: Macmillan, 1993.

Beard, James. *The Essential James Beard Cookbook.* New York: St. Martin's Press, 2012.

Cora, Cat

Cora, Cat, and Ann Krueger Spivack. *Cat Cora's Kitchen: Favorite Meals for Family and Friends.* San Francisco: Chronicle Books, 2004.

Cora, Cat, and Ann Krueger Spivack. *Cooking from the Hip: Fast, Easy, Phenomenal Meals.* New York: Houghton Mifflin, 2007.

Cora, Cat. *Fresh Takes on Favorite Dishes: Cat Cora's Classics with a Twist.* Boston: Houghton Mifflin Harcourt, 2010.

Cora, Cat. *A Suitcase Surprise for Mommy.* New York: Dial Books for Young Readers, 2011.

Disney, Walt

Kathy Merlock Jackson, ed. *Walt Disney: Conversations.* Jackson: University Press of Mississippi, 2006.

Draper, Dorothy

Draper, Dorothy. *Learn to Live; The Story of Dorothy Draper's Fascinating New Correspondence Course.* New York: Nordlinger, Riegelman & Cooper, 1937.

Draper, Dorothy. *Decorating Is Fun! How to Be Your Own Decorator.* New York: Pointed Leaf Press, 2006. [Original edition 1939.]

Draper, Dorothy. *Entertaining Is Fun! How to Be a Popular Hostess.* New York: Rizzoli, 2004. [Original edition 1941.]

Draper, Dorothy. *365 Shortcuts to Home Decorating.* New York, Dodd, Mead, 1965.

Keller, Thomas

Keller, Thomas, and Sebastien Rouxel, et al., *Bouchon Bakery Cookbook.* New York: Artisan, 2012.

Keller, Thomas, et al. *Bouchon.* New York: Artisan, 2004.

Keller, Thomas, et al. *Under Pressure: Cooking Sous Vide.* New York: Artisan, 2008.

Keller, Thomas, with David Cruz, et al. *Ad Hoc at Home.* New York: Artisan Books, 2009.

Keller, Thomas, with Susie Heller and Michael Ruhlman. *The French Laundry Cookbook,* 2d ed. New York: Artisan, 1999.

Matsuhisa, Nobu

Matsuhisa, Nobuyuki. *Nobu: The Cookbook,* tr. by Laura Holland. Tokyo: Kodansha, 2001.

Matsuhisa, Nobuyuki. *Nobu Now.* New York: Clarkson Potter, 2004.

Matsuhisa, Nobuyuki, and Mark Edwards. *Nobu West.* Kansas City, MO: Andrews McMeel 2007.

Matsuhisa, Nobuyuki, and Thomas Buckley. *Nobu Miami: The Party Cookbook.* Tokyo: Kodansha, 2008

Oliver, Garrett

Harper, Timothy, and Garrett Oliver. *The Good Beer Book: Brewing and Drinking Quality Ales and Lagers.* New York: Berkley Books, 1997.

Oliver, Garrett, *The Brewmaster's Table: Discovering the Pleasures of Real Beer with Real Food.* New York: Ecco, 2003.

Oliver, Garrett, ed., *Oxford Companion to Beer.* New York: Oxford University Press, 2012.

Oudolf, Piet

King, Michael, and Oudolf, Piet. *Gardening with Grasses.* Portland, OR: Timber Press, 1998.

Oudolf, Piet, and Henk Gerritsen. *Dream Plants for the Natural Garden.* Portland, OR: Timber Press, 2000.

Oudolf, Piet, and Henk Gerritsen. *Planting the Natural Garden.* Portland, OR: Timber Press, 2003.

Oudolf, Piet, and Noël Kingsbury. *Designing with Plants.* Portland, OR: Timber Press, 1999.

Oudolf, Piet, and Noël Kingsbury. *Landscapes in Landscapes.* New York: Monacelli Press, 2010.

Oudolf, Piet, and Noël Kingsbury. *Planting: A New Perspective.* Portland, OR: Timber Press, 2013.

Oudolf, Piet, and Noël Kingsbury. *Planting Design: Gardens in Time and Space.*

Portland, OR: Timber Press, 2005.

Petrini, Carlo

Petrini, Carlo. *Slow Food: The Case for Taste,* tr. by William McCuaig. New York: Columbia University Press, 2003.

Petrini, Carlo. *Slow Food Nation: The Creation of a New Gastronomy.* New York: Rizzoli Ex Libris, 2007.

Petrini, Carlo. *Slow Food Nation: Why Our Food Should Be Good, Clean, and Fair.* 2007; reprint, New York: Rizzoli Ex Libris, 2013.

Petrini, Carlo. *Terra Madre: Forging a New Global Network of Sustainable Food Communities.* White River Junction, VT: Chelsea Green, 2009.

Petrini, Carlo, with Ben Watson and Slow Food Editore, eds. *Slow Food: Collected Thoughts on Taste, Tradition, and the Honest Pleasures of Food.* White River Junction, VT: Chelsea Green, 2001.

Petrini, Carlo, with Gigi Padovani. *Slow Food Revolution: A New Culture for Eating and Living,* tr. by Francesca Santovetti. New York: Rizzoli, 2006.

Robinson, Jancis

Johnson, Hugh, and Jancis Robinson. *The World Atlas of Wine,* 7th ed. London: Mitchell Beazley, 2013.

Robinson, Jancis. *The Demon Drink.* London: Mitchell Beazley, 1988.

Robinson, Jancis. *The Great Wine Book.* New York: Morrow, 1982.

Robinson, Jancis. *How to Taste: A Guide to Enjoying Wine.* New York: Simon & Schuster, 2000. [Revised edition of *Masterglass,* 2d ed., 1987]

Robinson, Jancis. *Jancis Robinson's Concise Wine Companion.* Oxford; New York: Oxford University Press, 2001.

Robinson, Jancis. *Jancis Robinson's Guide to Wine Grapes.* New York: Oxford University Press, 1996.

Robinson, Jancis. *Jancis Robinson's Wine Course,* 2d ed. New York: Abbeville Press, 2003.

Robinson, Jancis. *Tasting Pleasure: Confessions of a Wine Lover.* New York: Viking, 1997.

Robinson, Jancis. *Vines, Grapes & Wines.* New York: Knopf, 1986.

Robinson, Jancis. *Vintage Timecharts: The Pedigree and Performance of Fine Wines to the Year 2000.* London: Mitchell Beazley, c1989.

Robinson, Jancis, ed. *The Oxford Companion to Wine,* 3d ed. New York: Oxford University Press, 2006.

Robinson, Jancis, and Linda Murphy. *American Wine: The Ultimate Companion to the Wines and Wineries of the United States.* Berkeley: University of California Press, 2013.

Robinson, Jancis, with Julia Harding and José Vouillamoz. *Wine Grapes; A Complete Guide to 1,368 Wine Varieties.* New York: Ecco, 2012.

Robuchon, Joël

Robuchon, Joël. *The Complete Robuchon,* tr. by Robin H. R. Bellinger. New York: Alfred A. Knopf, 2008.

Robuchon, Joël, with Nicholas de Rabaudy. *Joël Robuchon: Cooking through the Seasons.* New York: Rizzoli, 1995.

Wells, Patricia. *Simply French: Patricia Wells Presents the Cuisine of Joël Robuchon.* New York: W. Morrow, 1991.

Waters, Alice

Bertolli, Paul, and Alice Waters. *Chez Panisse Cooking.* 1988; reprint, New York: Random House, 1996.

Waters, Alice. *Forty Years of Chez Panisse: The Power of Gathering.* New York: Clarkson Potter, 2011.

Waters, Alice. *In the Green Kitchen: Techniques to Learn by Heart.* New York: Clarkson Potter, 2010.

Waters, Alice, et al. *The Art of Simple Food: Notes, Lessons, and Recipes from a Delicious Revolution.* New York: Clarkson Potter, 2007.

Waters, Alice, et al. *The Art of Simple Food II.* New York: Clarkson Potter, 2013.

Waters, Alice, et al. *Chez Panisse Café Cookbook.* New York: HarperCollins, 1999.

Waters, Alice, et al. *Chez Panisse Fruit.* New York: HarperCollins, 2002.

Waters, Alice, et al. *Chez Panisse Pasta, Pizza, and Calzone.* New York: Random House, 1984.

Waters, Alice, et al. *Chez Panisse Vegetables.* New York: HarperCollins, 1996.

Waters, Alice, et al. *Fanny at Chez Panisse.* New York: HarperCollins, 1992.

Waters, Alice, with Daniel Duane. *Edible Schoolyard: A Universal Idea.* San Francisco: Chronicle Books, 2008.

Waters, Alice, with Linda Guenzel. *Chez Panisse Menu Cookbook.* New York: Random House, 1982.

Profession Index

Activist
Petrini, Carlo

Waters, Alice

Actor
Matsuhia, Nobu

Animator
Disney, Walt

Author
Keller, Thomas

Muñoz Zurita, Ricardo

Oliver, Garrett

Robinson, Jancis

Rubuchon, Joël

Steves, Rick

Waters, Alice

Wheeler, Tony

Beer Expert
Oliver, Garrett

Business Executive
Barnes, Brenda

Cointreau, André

Donald, Arnold

Gallo, Ernest

Ho, Stanley

Marriott, John Willard

Michelin, André

Nelson, Marilyn Carson

Otis, Clarence, Jr.

Zagat, Nina

Zagat, Tim

Zhang, Xin

Casino Magnate
Wynn, Stephen

Chef
Adrià, Ferran

Beard, James

Cora, Cat

Keller, Thomas

Matsuhisa, Nobu

Muñoz Zurita, Ricardo

Rubuchon, Joël

Waters, Alice

Chief Executive Officer
Nooyi, Indra

Rosenfeld, Irene B.

Conglomorate Owner
Pritzker, Jay A.

Culinary Entrepreneur
Cointreau, André